AF443200

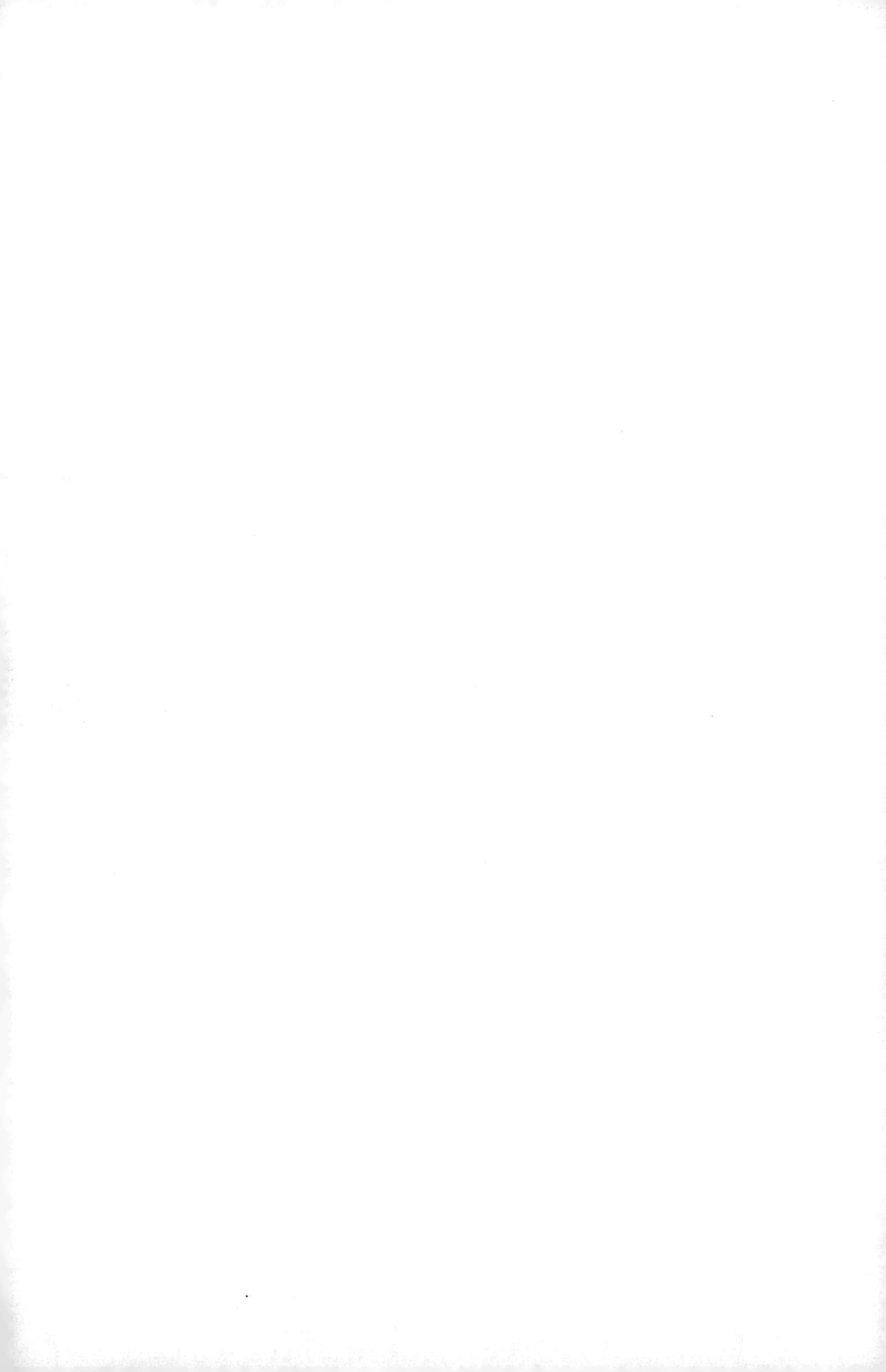

Dancer – Researcher – Performer: A Learning Process

INTERDISCIPLINARY STUDIES IN PERFORMANCE

HISTORICAL NARRATIVES. THEATER. PUBLIC LIFE

Edited by Mirosław Kocur

VOL. 6

Zu Qualitätssicherung und Peer Review der vorliegenden Publikation

Die Qualität der in dieser Reihe erscheinenden Arbeiten wird vor der Publikation durch einen externen, von der Herausgeberschaft benannten Gutachter geprüft.

Notes on the quality assurance and peer review of this publication

Prior to publication, the quality of the work published in this series is reviewed by an external referee appointed by the editorship.

Graziela Rodrigues

Dancer – Researcher – Performer: A Learning Process

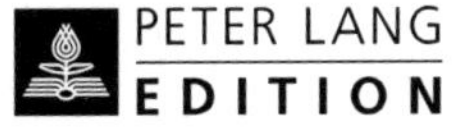

Bibliographic Information published by the Deutsche Nationalbibliothek
The Deutsche Nationalbibliothek lists this publication in the Deutsche
Nationalbibliografie; detailed bibliographic data is available in the internet at
http://dnb.d-nb.de.

Library of Congress Cataloging-in-Publication Data
Names: Rodrigues, Graziela, 1954- author.
Title: Dancer, researcher, performer : a learning process / Graziela Rodrigues.
Other titles: Bailarino, pesquisador, intérprete. English
Description: Peter Lang : Frankfurt am Main, 2016. | Series: Interdisciplinary studies in
performance ; Bd. 6 | Translation of: Bailarino, pesquisador, intérprete. | Includes bibli-
ographical references.
Identifiers: LCCN 2016039066| ISBN 9783631676707 | ISBN 9783653070996 (E-PDF) |
ISBN 9783631699553 (EPUB) | ISBN 9783631699560 (MOBI)
Subjects: LCSH: Dance–Brazil. | Folk dancing, Brazilian. | Dance–Anthropological as-
pects–Brazil. | Dance–Philosophy.
Classification: LCC GV1637 .R6313 2016 | DDC 792.80981–dc23 LC record available at
https://lccn.loc.gov/2016039066

This publication was financially supported by the grant #2015/12074-4,
São Paulo Research Foundation (FAPESP).

English translation by Andrea Paula Justino dos Santos; English revision by Renato C.
Gonzalez and Larissa Sato Turtelli; Graphical Design by Enéas Guerra and Valéria
Pergentino; Pictures Processing by Elaine Quirelli; Illustrations by Enéas Guerra

ISSN 2364-3919
ISBN 978-3-631-67670-7 (Print)
E-ISBN 978-3-653-07099-6 (E-PDF)
E-ISBN 978-3-631-69955-3 (EPUB)
E-ISBN 978-3-631-69956-0 (MOBI)
DOI 10.3726/b10614

© Peter Lang GmbH
Internationaler Verlag der Wissenschaften
Frankfurt am Main 2016
All rights reserved.
Peter Lang Edition is an Imprint of Peter Lang GmbH.

Peter Lang – Frankfurt am Main · Bern · Bruxelles · New York ·
Oxford · Warszawa · Wien

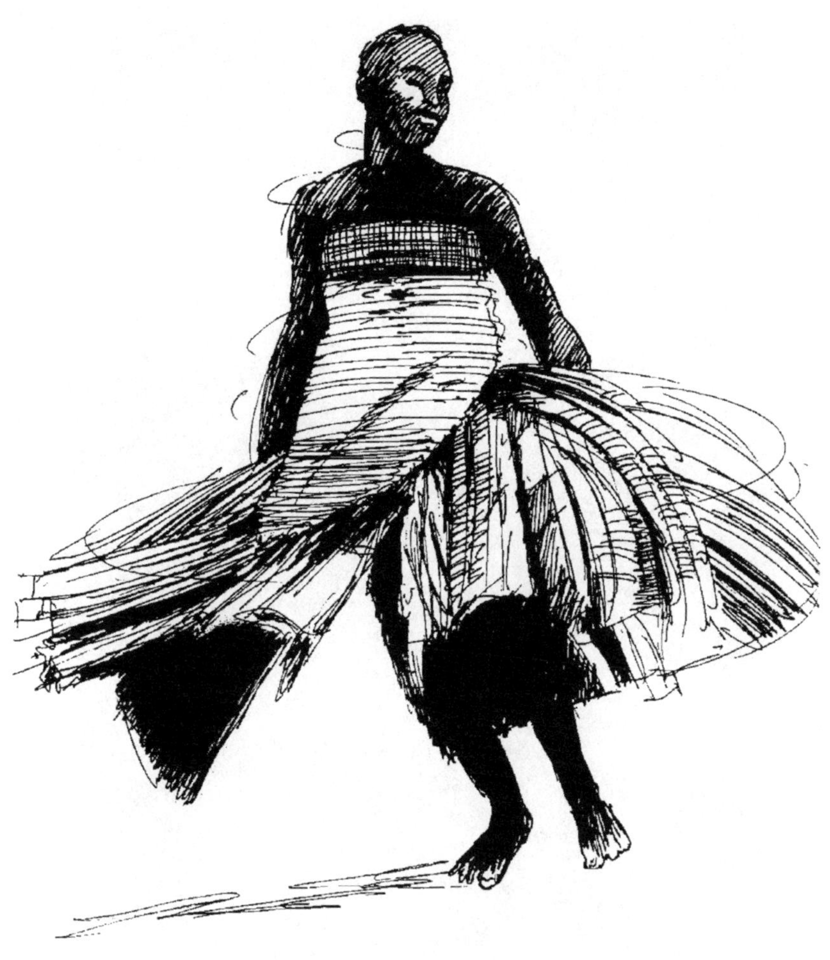

O paradoxo nessa história de descobertas, e também de ocultamentos, diz respeito a alguém teimosamente não descoberto: o brasileiro que nem eu[1]...

Marlyse Meyer

---

1   *The paradox of this story made of discoveries and concealment is related to someone who, stubbornly, we have not discovered yet: the Brazilian person who remains in me...* (Marlyse Meyer refers to the fact that Brazilian people, especially the highbrows, often deny the Brazilian aspects related to themselves, by covering what comes from popular culture, thus identifying with the culture from their former colonizers.)

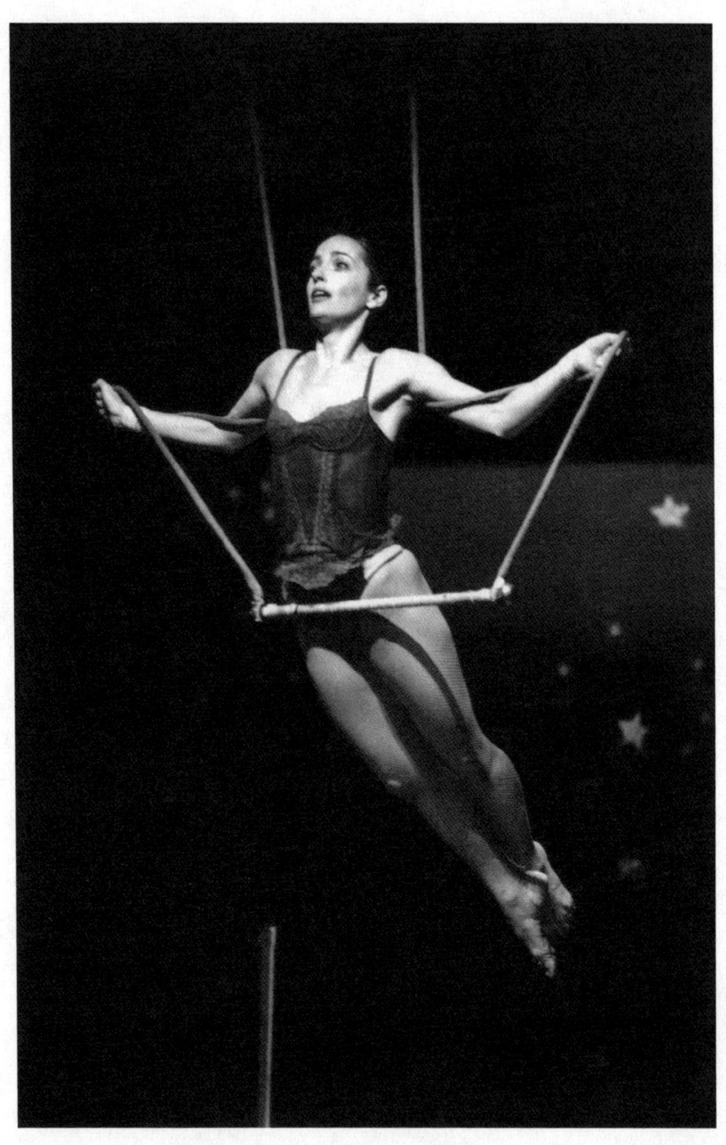

Graziela Rodrigues *in Coração*
Vermelho (Red Heart), 1985.
Archive: IDART
Photo: João Caldas

*I dedicate this work to the new dancers
who adventure themselves in the art of
self-searching.*

Acknowledgments

To the field research nuclei: Communities, Terreiros, Villages
To Carlos Alberto da Costa
To Arturos' Comunity

To all who directly or indirectly contributed to this work

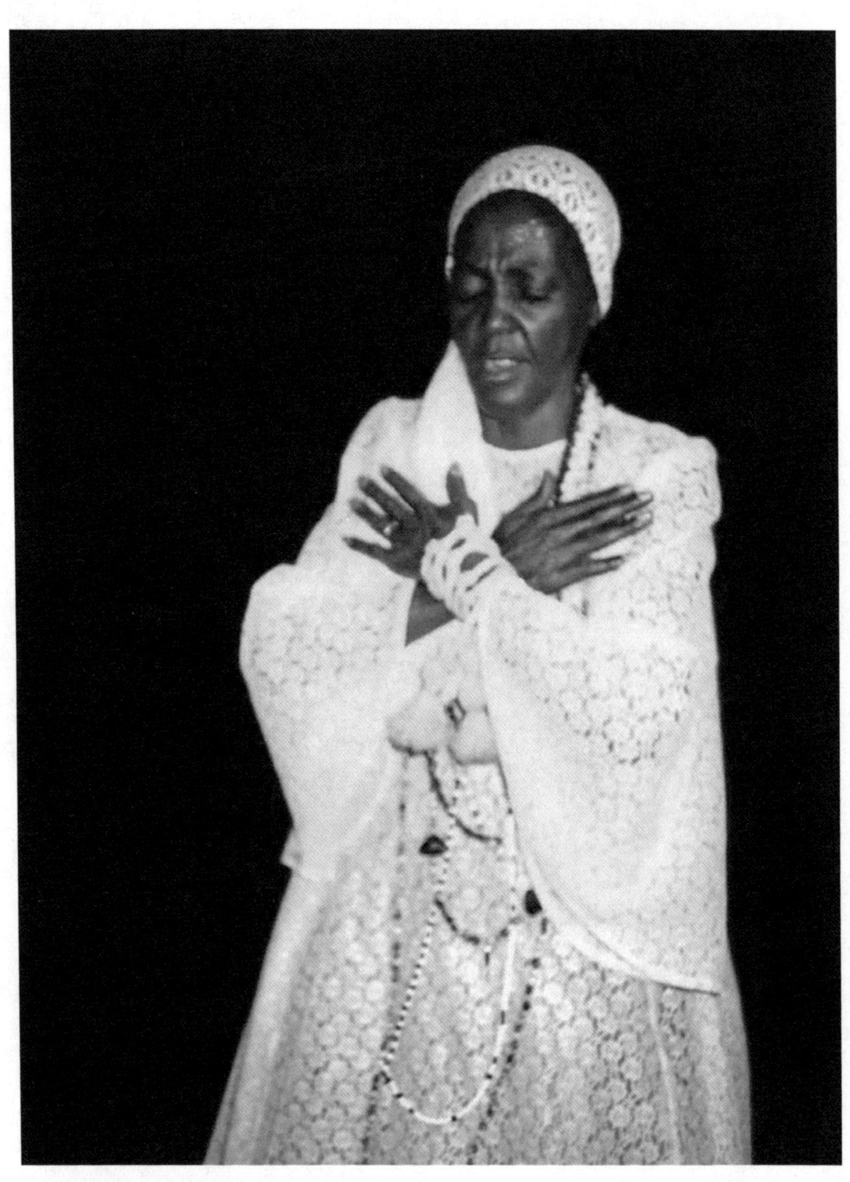

Sebastiana
Umbandista and Captain of Mozambique
Bom Despacho, MG – 1987
Author's arc

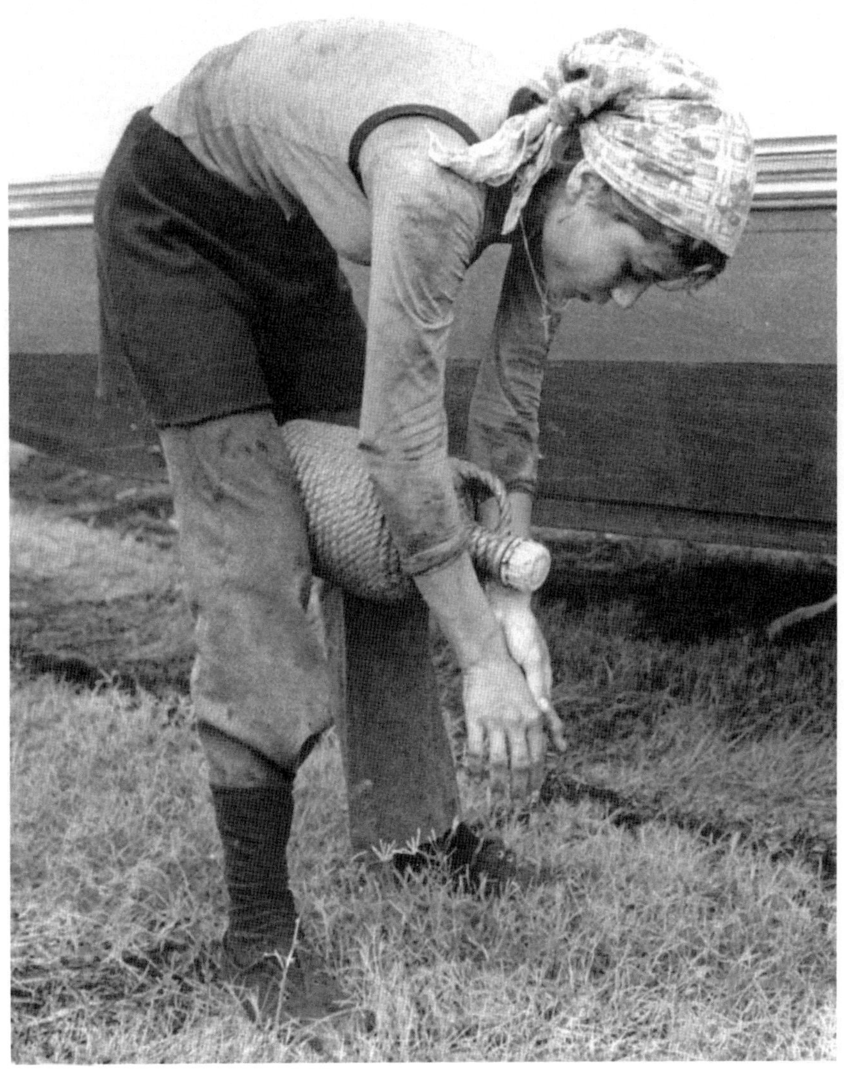

Bóia Fria
Ribeirão Preto, SP - 1979
Photo: Vicente Sampaio

Preface

I was one of Graziela's students in the eighties. This was our first meeting. I had no gift for dancing, but a great appreciation for such a complete art. In the rehearsal room, along with more skillful colleagues, I was carried away by the exercises and the guidance of that young teacher. That indigenous world of the forest, which I had just started to research in the Amazon, was born, to me, as something real, starting from my inner universe in relation to the movement and the learning process of the body – in silence, in sound, in music. I had never had such a strong feeling while being in the city – as I had the chance to live in huts, by the fire, in the hammocks, and lulled by music along with my Suruí Paiter friends. As a Demiurge, she created, inside us, the whole humanity, with different images that took shape through our dancing steps and gestures, something close to a trance experience.

Only now, as I reread Graziela's book, whose first edition was 1997, I realize how well thought out was her teaching, being a result of a story marked by reflection, research and interpretation, in which body, soul, emotional and intellectual self-knowledge, and the search for traditions – especially Brazilian and Afro-Brazilian traditions – were combined to show, through performance, a visceral expression.

Graziela likes that adjective – "visceral school of rituals," as she says about the Maracatu, one of the many aspects of popular religiosity which she observed and studied, and by which she was inspired. Early on, our affinity lied in our passion for the Brazilian people, in the history that was, and still is, visible in the art, made with stubbornness by great characters, humble men and women, able to turn poverty into beauty, or into the gates to afterlife, generally closed to us. It was not by chance that the first (modest) financial resources received by IAMÁ (Institute of Anthropology and Environment – a non-governmental institute in which I worked for ten years) were devoted to the production of a chant/dance video about the Candombe of the Community of Arturos in Minas Gerais. On this occasion, Graziela collaborated with Núbia Pereira de Magalhães Gomes and Edimilson Pereira, who wrote the book *Negras raízes mineiras, Os Arturos*, published for the centenary of Abolition. The focus of IAMÁ was indigenous and environmental, but the choice of Afro-dance tradition was symbolic.

The chapters of Graziela's book bring to each page a surprise, releasing the orishas, slavery memories, Caboclos, standard-bearers, flags, masts joining earth and sky, pomba-giras, skirts flying and spinning like dervishes, ceremonies, saint,

altars, congás, terreiros, afoxés, capoeiras, Umbanda chanting and even a demon…
Among many subjects, Graziela learned and lived with bóias-frias women (seasonal field workers) suffering hard living and working conditions which crumbled their physical endurance, but which – surprise! – was combined with festivity and the mastery of the body, as they were moved by an unbreakable will.

I remember seeing Graziela walking majestically in a tightrope, or creating the character of Maria Padilha – both the performer and the character became a model for women with no strings attached, totally dedicated to freedom. Graziela repeatedly mentions Marlyse Meyer, a friend of my family, whose masterful book, *Maria Padilha e toda sua quadrilha*, is, at the same time, a historical research, a literary novel, an anthropological work and an imaginary flight.

I am neither a dance researcher, nor a person who knows the many wonders, schools and experiences in this field, which is why I cannot dare to comment. However, Graziela's path seems rare to me, concretizing the amalgam of movements, a study of each part and limb of the human body in different dances, sounds, and musical traditions, in forms, contents, and social history, in the field research and cautious, laboratory production of performances, in discipline, exercise, expression and emotion, in interpretation and creation. In this approach, no sphere is out of what the dancers have to experience. She uses the expression "listening to the body and seeing the sound," "playing and singing" in dance, "body pronunciations," and so on. The body, spirit and immaterial origin merge, and so do music, voice and dance; reflection, thought and expression mingle, and so do art and trance.

Beautiful testimonies, recorded in the researches, photos and quotes, permeate the text, making us imagine what she underwent.

If we could have seen all the performances produced or directed by Graziela, listed in the last pages, or if they had all been filmed… We have this textbook – made of insights, rather than logical sequences: essential to all arts, including writing, which could be danceable.

Sao Paulo, December 3rd, 2015

Betty Mindlin, Anthropologist

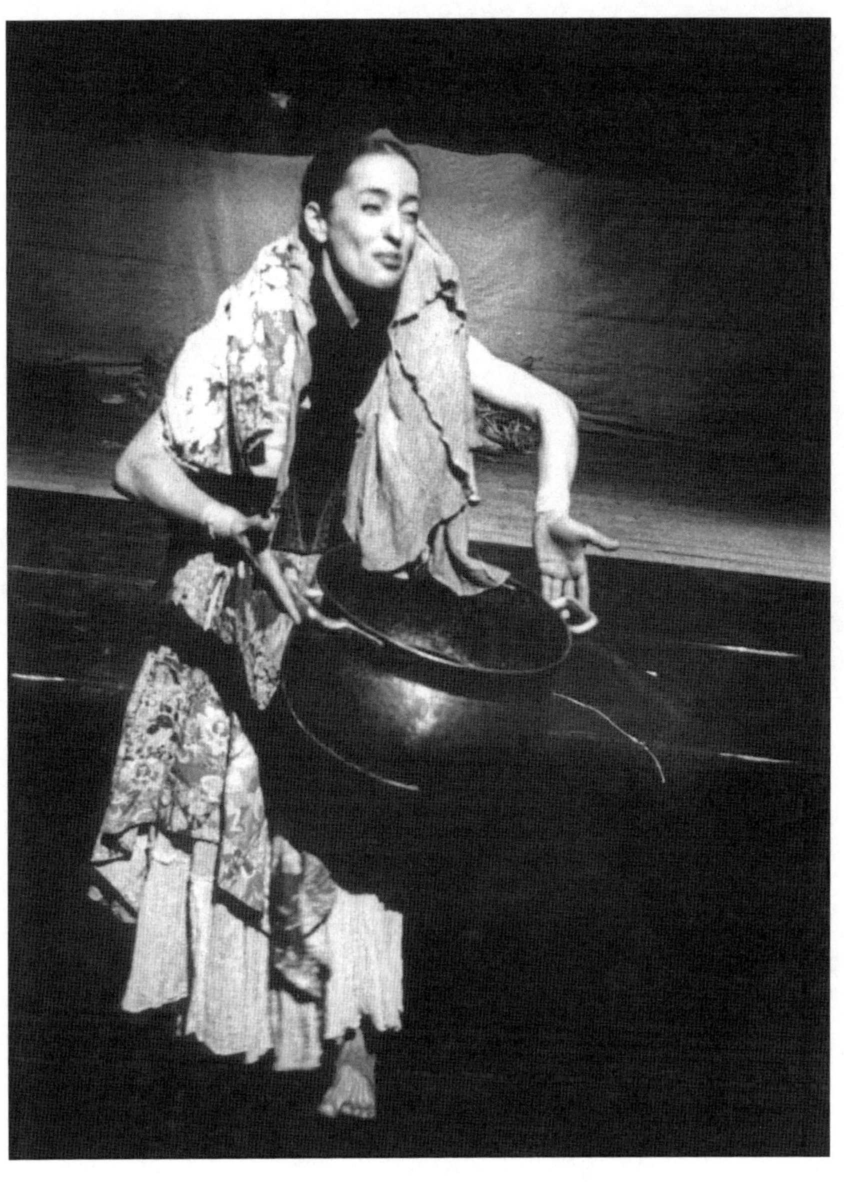

Graziela Rodrigues in *Coração
Vermelho (Red Heart)*
IDART, 1985
Photo: João Caldas

Crystals in the Mirror

Graziela Rodrigues proposes a search for a gestural reality as an aesthetic proposal within the poetics of a flexible body that is written, musicalized, and understood as a human body.

But not only.

She also proposes the search for a gestural reality in daily life poetry of cracked feet in wild fields, with claws instead of fingers, feet dug in the ground, roots, and solid rocks resembling the souls of women able to go through lost battles without experiencing any defeats. Women who do not have dreams, as they just ignore them, who grab the land, sculpturing boys and girls bathed in the saliva of love. Redeemer's bellies and feet, recreating the pulse of the people born from starving wolves, floating boas, and who knows what else.

Graziela's challenge does not lie in the precepts of an unfulfilled (and not promised) recipe. Not even a single image, nor a reflex to imitate – that is a forbidden word. Mirrors were broken and crystal pieces were spread to the wind – find yourself your own crystal! There were neither signals nor informations concerning the paths to be followed in these backlands. Generally costly and painful, the redemption lies in personal – but unavoidable – discoveries.

It is simple and easy (as well as stupid) to become a slave of rules imposed by foreign empires in order to wait, at the end of each year, for examiners coming out of the blue; and, during secret meetings, check every inch of these impossible bodies, gestures and pirouettes created by skillful dancers that have never thought about the people from their countries – nothing to disturb the serenity of the nights in the castle. Graziela accepts the weight of ballet shoes as a means of disciplinary exercises, but never as the aesthetic of the predictable – a circus in its primary exhibition of resistance and balance, that is, the perfect aesthetics for both robotic dancers and trained seals.

In Graziela's work, the paths are opened. She does not offer models or solutions. This is not a recipe book to be auctioned in the balcony of franchises, against the procession of stillbirths. Through her hard, methodical work, and in the belief that only an accurate technique may lead to a penetrating and modulated expression, Graziela offers her example only as a possibility.

The belief of the humble, the family life amidst a poverty we keep ignoring; the unknown Brazilian features, the heart of any and all woman; the ashamed treasures of our popular culture.

The search for and investigation of the people's truth, from the human dance to everyone's return that few people can see. The translation of this truth into authentic gestures, rhythms, colors and drawings of a new space created by sweating, expressive bodies.

The ascetic refuse of seductions. The scientific profile research as a vital behavior for the artist. Uneasiness and permanent renovation of its sources and means.

The best of our best. Dance, theatre, folklore, cultural anthropology, sociology of art. Dance as life in itself and in relation to raw state poetry, and dance as her writing and writ.

Graziela is even more than an excellent teacher. She is a pioneering teacher and encourager of creative artists interested in the life we suffer today, in this piece of land, where it seems that only the true artists volunteer to fight the dragons of evil.

Fausto Fuser

Table of Contents

1 Introduction

The process of conceiving the dancer-researcher-performer was organized from two interrelated stages. In the first stage, I experienced a crisis in relation to my knowledge about dance, including my experience with the classical, modern, and contemporary dance as well as techniques related to the dynamics of the body and the theatrical performance.

This crisis did not mean a rejection of my previous knowledge; it meant a re-interpretation, drawing on the interaction between my personal findings and the knowledge acquired in the field research about Brazilian cultural manifestations. Beginning with the field research with the *candanga* women[1] from Brasília – after the interaction between my personal findings and the universe of the investigated reality – I initiated the formulation of the body form of the dancer-researcher-performer. The final outcome of this stage was the creation of several dance performances, such as *Graça Bailarina de Jesus* (*Grace, Ballerina of Jesus*) and *Coração Vermelho I* and *II* (*Red Heart I* and *II*).

During the second stage of the *Dancer-researcher-performer training process* I developed the following script (for more, refer to chapter 9):

- self-questioning of the dancer concerning his/her relationship with his/her body and the dance itself;
- the implementation of initial experiences gained in the laboratory with Brazilian cultural manifestations;
- direct contact of the dancer with the sources in the field research;
- the dancer returns to the laboratory to articulate his/her creative work.

It is important to note that the stages mentioned above may be inconsistent with other stages resulting from the demands of each dancer. The Process is subject to the addition of other stages after the elaboration of the creative work to the extent that it leads to the constitution of a living, flexible, individualized body opened to different dance creations. The references to my personal history are due to the fact that the Process of the dancer-researcher-performer was developed in my own body.

---

1   "Candangos" are the people that broke in new lands, without heroism; and until today, they fight in this concrete landscape surrounded by a futuristic beauty. Within this mass of underemployed people, housekeepers ("candanga" women) are one of the most problematic groups.

My dance training was marked by rigorous discipline. During the time when I have followed every step of the formality of ballet (starting from 1967), there have been an ongoing tempest inside my body; the questions that have been arising were far beyond what the body could express, jump, or twist. Through this time there have been a number of sensations and feelings impossible to fit in the body I have been constructing. After all, what was my body? What was the other's body established to be my model?

This search had no borders: in dance, theater or my work as a dancer and choreographer. I wanted to believe that the answers could be found in the different techniques and forms. The questions I could not answer were grouped in a single one: Am I a performer?[2] The route indicated that I had to look for an inner answer.

The professional experiences in Europe (1977/1978) indicated an important question about the relation of the culture of a country with its artistic creation. In Israel, dance had an important role of unifying identities. In Spain, during a period when artists from different nationalities converged, cultural differences were evident among a unifying desire within the arts. My adherence to these movements and the invitation to continue working in these countries made me even more uneasy in relation to the questioning of my own cultural identity.

Due to the inner feelings that have been increasingly driving my body towards the construction of my own story, I decided to come back to Brazil, specifically to Brasília, in order to develop a project with other professionals.[3] After having finished this collective project, whose importance lied in the exchange of experiences based on equality of relationships, I was in need of new personal resolutions.

My senses realized that a new process was under development. I felt under huge pressure caused by what I had experienced until then. A vital necessity urged me to put my effective answer as a performer through my pace. After several twists and turns, endowed with technical and expressive skills, what would this body (my body) organically establish in the artistic creation? At that moment, I had quit everything I had built until then in order to find the answer. Searching for a character was an alternative, but the search through the texts was in vain; everything seemed to be so distant from my own reality and the desire to find myself. This conjuncture convinced me that the character was alive on the streets, pushing me into researching the *candanga* women.

---

2   I reaffirm the importance of the works developed by the theatrical director Ademar Guerra in Ballet Stagium (1975), in which I participated as a student as such works awoke deep questions on the role of the performer in Dance.

The power of that moment and my intuitive conviction pointed to an immediate implementation of the research; there was no reason to systematize a project and no time to seek funding. That moment required a full commitment to live that experience with freedom of action. The following procedure was found to be coherent: The "constructed" dancer would be "deconstructed", as she interacted with the universe of the research. Therefore, the observation of the facts required accuracy, without any type of interpretation. Field experience and writing diaries were the only activities performed without previous establishment of duration. The geographical proximity determined the choice for the *candanga* women, as I needed to find a "flesh and blood" character.

The field research: during the urban bus journeys from Plano Piloto station (Brasília) to the satellite cities I found a huge number of women. I kept observing them, without any comments or interpretation, opening my senses with absolute concentration and neutrality. During the several bus trips, I identified that most of these women were housemaids. In Plano Piloto I followed one of them and I found out that she was heading to an employment agency for housemaids. I started to attend that agency, trying to remain as anonymous as possible.

Nobody ever asked me who I was and I have never asked anything as well, thereby generating a complicity. The intimacy led me to learn these women's bodies, as I slowly began to apprehend them in my own body. A clear attempt to hide their dirty feet was observed. When they realized that someone noticed their attempt, they got clearly ashamed, rebelling against that poverty. Therefore, *in view of the life of afflicted people we do not speak, we just remain in silence; we forget the civilized people's ideas, get humble, and start to think...*[3]

A world of pain, struggle, and disillusion, along with a life force and a great mystical belief, was revealed to me during the field research. It was a history of great disillusion as completed with this type of phrases: *But I have the power of Pomba-Gira*, or *at night my shining siren passes into the holes of my shed, full of light, bringing me a message.*

A "new space" was opened: the *terreiros of Umbanda* and several other spaces attended by these women. I began to co-inhabit with the source, as Carlos Mesters made us wonder in *A parábola da porta* (*The Door Parable*):

> *Entering the front door I looked at the richness and beauty of the house from a new perspective... The house unveiled beautiful things which were not told in books and [whom]*

---

3 Ensaio Teatro Dança – Escola Núcleo de Pesquisa e Produções Artísticas.

After three months of intense daily contact, a rich lady, acting as if she were choosing a piece of clothing to buy, analyzed the row of women upside down, and pointed at me: "I'll pick up this one." The main part of the field research ended.

When I later came back to the space of my dance room that used to be so familiar, it started to cause a feeling of emptiness inside me. The laboratories conducted by the director[6] used the field notes as reference. We talked very little, and with few words he suggested the actions and situations to be performed.

In the beginning, my body was not answering, but the emotional records gradually began to emerge in contact with my own affective memory, as a result of the universe experienced during the field research. The body assumed various sensations and configurations resulting from the images of places visited during the field research and the "unknown" images from my inner self. These images together exhibited a new landscape configuration – a space where life experiences established in the body were developed.

This stage lasted until the day I was asked to reveal the name of the character. In other words, this character began to rise as a synthesis of all the women that participated in the research. Information on the character that came from the laboratory showed a considerable coherence in relation to the universe in question. *Graça* (Grace) was the name chosen for the character. This fact marked the beginning of her existence in the space of the body that should dance the reality of the *candanga* women. This woman, Graça, amongst so many dreams, dreamed of dancing.

The result was presented in the form of a performance called: "Graça Bailarina de Jesus ou Sete Linhas de Umbanda, Salvem o Brasil"[7] (*Grace, Ballerina of Jesus or Seven Lines of Umbanda, Save Brazil*). Its main meaning lies in the difference established, when the dancer-performer performs: there is a gift of the individual. He/she is totally involved in each fragment of the scene and the content becomes a part of him/her. In the subject-character interweaving, the dancer does not

---

4   *Carlos Mesters - "A Parábola da Porta" (The Door Parable)* - Por trás das Palavras, 1984.

5   *Carlos Mesters - "A Parábola da Porta" (The Door Parable)* - Por trás das Palavras, 1984.

6   *The theatre director João Antonio de Lima Esteves followed all the process and is the director of* Graça Bailarina de Jesus.

7   Stage performances: Teatro Santo Antônio - Salvador, 1980. Tenda Xangô Ayra do Caboclo Itajaci (Casa de Candomblé) - Brasília, 1980. Teatro Dulcina - Rio de janeiro, 1980 Teatro Dulcina - Brasília, 1980 Teatro Goiânia - Goiânia, 1980 Teatro Ruth Escobar - SãoPaulo, 1980.

interpret; he/she lives in his/her body – without restrictions – the life shaped by the performance.

From the whole experience of "Graça Bailarina de Jesus", with several complementary researches, technical works, and other stages until its final synthesis, the *Character Incorporation* is highlighted as the main stage. The character is a result coming from the field research, from the co-inhabiting with the source and what this experience awakened in the performer. In the laboratory work, the dancer-performer's body assumes an imaginary body, "as if it did not belong to him/her", producing the freedom of expression and permissiveness in the dance to experience voices and chanting without worrying about meeting any standards.

The dance is organized from the history of the character. The body works for the idea that the dancer-performer is free to be what he/she is at that moment. The needs of the dancer become crystal clear and acquire a reference of work continuity in relation to expanding the technical resources in a more sensitive manner.

The departure from space and time (mainly delimited by the dance universe) to step into a surrounding reality – now with an internal view of a culture at the margin of the Brazilian society – meant a contact axis interacting in my body. This experience provided the basis for the development of a line of work of the performer in the dance.

At the beginning, I saw this work in Brasília as a single experience. The subsequent professional experiences included the questioning of my own work. I also checked, in a practical manner, certain ways to reach the process of the performer. These experiences did not last long. The process was organically established, whether I wanted it or not. Soon I came back to the continuous field researches. The ritual dances demanded a deeper investigation of movement, leading me to study Chinese Eastern Arts in order to experientially understand the use of the internal movement of energy circuits in my body.

The strictness of the technique became intentional, as it was closely related to an increasingly demanding performance elaboration and the overcoming of limits of the dancer-performer. The daily technical training became more challenging because the focus had been changed. The technique became a research, enabling a self-reflection and, at diverse moments, insights about the development of the Process.

My personal growth as a performer led me to a continuous deepening of the process, not only in relation to body techniques but also in relation to the voice and interpretation connected to researches on different scenic expressions.

The creation of dance performances, along with my work as a performer, has always meant an integration of experiences. I experienced by myself many "obscure women", as it was well put by Cora Coralina (a Brazilian writer and poet), coming from urban, suburban, and rural universes of Brazil. They taught me to *rebojar* (to eddy). *The "rebojo" (the eddy) is the part of the river where the water moves in circles due to the presence of a deeper part narrowed by stones. The danger is detected by the water effervescence, whose agitation reaches the surface. When an object or individual falls in the eddy, this object or individual emerges, swirling, and then disappears. "Rebojar" is exactly to leave the bottom of the "rebojo" (the eddy) towards the vein of water* (Núbia Gomes).[8]

Around 1986, I realized the importance of this work in the field of dance. I decided to quit my career as a performer to pursuit and develop this idea of a Process in which the dancer is not an object, but a subject. I made an extensive examination of my experience as a dancer-researcher-performer and elaborated the main synthesis. I structured the fundamentals from the Brazilian popular manifestations researched until then and created a technical body of knowledge in dance to be worked on in the rehearsal room, based on the decoding of the essential elements structuring this body. Different symbolic aspects of the Brazilian ritualistic dances were also considered, as well as the importance of making a personal history inventory. Diversified dynamics were created for practical purposes, including breaking with the conventional spaces of dance and conducting the field research and laboratories.

The projects after this stage aimed at expanding the field researches on the Brazilian popular manifestations in order to decode this universe from the performer's perspective.[9]

The experience that I have been living since 1987 as a professor at Unicamp (University of Campinas, São Paulo) in the Body Arts Department brought me the inestimable satisfaction of having the contact with "new" dancers. Fundamentally, opening the Process enabled these students to see their dance from a new dimension as the performers-subjects. Through them, the Process is developed and sedimented every day. The outcomes have been performed in various syntheses of researches in the form of performances like: *Bailarinas de Terreiro* (*Terreiro Ballerinas*), *Interiores* (*Interiors*) *Diante dos olhos* (*Before the eyes*), among others. The satisfaction lies not only in good results of these dance performances but also in what they have been enabling (as practical exercises) their performers to do when undergoing the personal processes of growth.

---

8   Edmilson Pereira - Rebojo, 1995.

9   The project "Trilhas e Veredas da Dança Brasileira" – (Trails and Paths of Brazilian Dance), (1987), initiated this stage counting on the support of IAMÁ (Instituto de Antropologia e Meio Ambiente, SP - Institute of Anthropology and Environment).

The question of the dancer-performer remains as the main axis of my work. To be freed from styles and techniques without throwing them away represents an attribute of the dancer-performer. The instrumentalization of the body must create conditions for the dancer to be a "living organism", ready to answer to the contents arising from his/her personal reality as well as the surrounding reality.

I see the Brazilian popular manifestations (with a sense of cultural resistance) as the frame of the development of the dancer-performer who is about to become a researcher. As Harvey Cox affirms: *We cannot really see one thing when it completely fills our visual horizon. We need an anti-horizon against which to project its profile. The background or visual field is an essential element in the perception. We need a new frame*[10]. It was necessary to penetrate this frame, that is, to co-inhabit with these sources of our culture, breaking prejudices, internally opening myself to relate with a world where the expressed devotion experienced through the body is an ability to survive as a human being.

In my path as a performer there was a rupture due to this new idea that arose as a consequence of my experiences. Now, I must assume that I open myself to new ruptures, as this is what I have learned in my path as a performer. This is not a research with a beginning, middle, and end structure, as it was neither premeditated nor planned in this sense. It consists in a history of life in which Dance is included.

In the existential context of the dancer, there is a passage that leads to his/her development as a performer. The progress of the Dance depends on his/her Process.

---

10 Harvey Cox - A Festa dos Foliões - um ensaio teológico sobre festividade e fantasia, 1974. (The Party of the Foliões - a teological essay on festivity and fantasy).

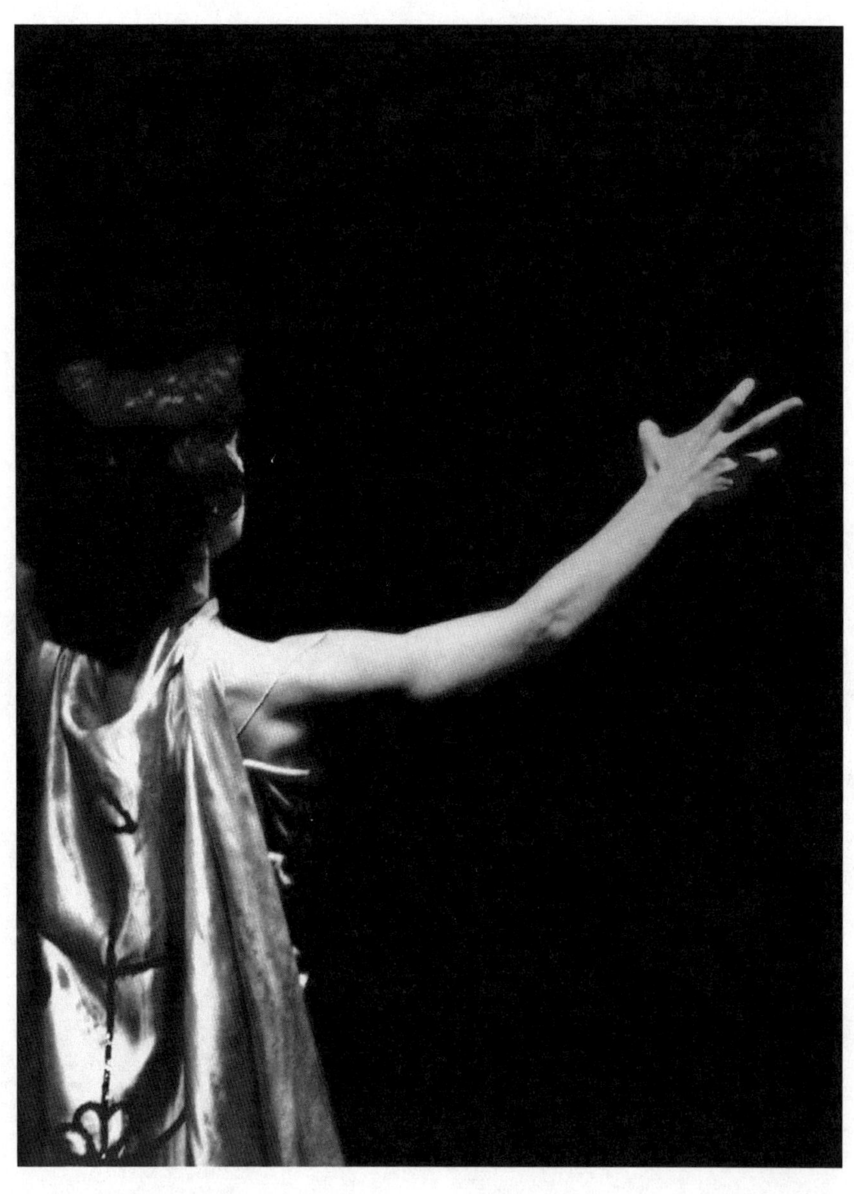

Graziela Rodrigues
Grace Ballerina of Jesus spectacle
Publicity photo

2 Some Important Questions

The fragmentation of the body is often shown in the dancer as a consequence of his/her own training. The acquisition of physical skills is centered on the desire to give an answer to the proposed model. The dancer constructs his/her self-image from the physical modeling – external to the dancer – and, each day, without any questions, the dancer assumes this image. The dancer rejects his/her own body in order to pursuit an idealized image. The dissatisfaction and emptiness generated by this process are compensated by the safety offered by this path, because, as the dancer follows the command instructions guided by the model, he/she reaches the estimated and socially accepted answer.

In this context, the dancer calls him/herself an Instrument and places the Dance in a oneiric space distant from him/herself. Upon tuning this Body-Instrument, in which the Dance will be performed, the history and the deepest senses of the dancer must be absent as they interfere in the balance of the perfect shapes. This proposal of body fragmentation dates back to Plato:

> *Throughout the time that we have the body and our soul is mixed with such bad thing, we will never fully possess the object of our desires! ... The body floods us with love, passions, fears, imagination of all sorts, in short, an infinitude of trifles that through it (yes, true is what is said), actually we do not receive any sensible thought, no, not even once!*[1]

The dualistic tradition of Plato, body and soul, echoes in the Dance.

The question is not to reject the official techniques and forms, but reevaluate their imperative usage to the detriment of other aspects of the body. The non-fragmentation of the dancer's body represents the main plot of the present work.

We place dance as an activity in which various bodies are integrated to produce knowledge in the realm of the sensible, the perceptible, and the human relations from a direct contact with the surrounding reality. The detachment and running away performed by the dancer are replaced by a conflict – the dancer embodying him/herself:

> *Once the physical, the vital, and the psychic subject are distinguished only as different levels of integration as the body no longer allows the operation of systems of isolated behaviors, body and soul are no longer distinguishable.*[2]

---

1 *Plato - Os pensadores, 1972.*

2 *Maurice Merleau Ponty -* Fenomenologia da percepção (Phenomenology of perception), *1994.*

The freedom of action "without a project", without "academicism" represented an important aspect for the construction of the learning Process of the dancer-researcher-performer. As if it had become a life of its own, the maturation of its synthesis was expected as the imposition of guidelines. The interpretations of this process would result in a different work. In "quitting" the path offered by the acquired training, there was an inversion in the behavior of the dancer-researcher-performer, as such knowledge suffered changes due to what the sources have taught me. Therefore, a broadening of scope occurred, instead of losses.

The field researches were the sources in which the body depicted its history interweaving festivity and daily life in a personal integrity of being. When co-inhabiting without masks, the relationships of the body-identity became inevitable.

Speaking of a symbolic anatomy, we use the "*mastro votivo*" (votive mast), as it summarizes the unity of this body that is present in the daily life and constantly reaffirmed in celebrations. The body becomes a mast when it materializes its relations of human and divine being, understanding that it occupies a space and is beyond what its shape reproduces.

The references of the collective unconscious fly through the festive spaces of the Brazilian popular manifestations; *Umbanda* is a well-grounded example. Hence its importance to the research. Among the archetypes enunciated by its entities, we chose two in order to cover and find several important aspects: *Eshu* for his excellence of the movement, and *Pomba-Gira*, as our dancer-researcher-performer is identified in her archetype.

The approach to the Brazilian body based on the research sources results in a technique integrated to the senses. This is the basis of development of the Process; it prepares the dancer's body, or even better, the dancer's bodies, favoring his/her "gaze" in interaction with the field research. Then we have a stage called co-inhabiting with the source, followed by a creative process in laboratory in which the Brazilian Popular Manifestations are the focus, while the dancer is oriented on his/her inner self.

Continuing the training of the dancer-researcher-performer, the stage called Character Incorporation represents its main key. The character provides the aspects found in its reality. Its gestures are elaborated, resulting in a poetic answer in motion. When performing for an audience, both the potential and the limits of the dancer-researcher-performer become evident. Regarding the audience, each individual experiences the work from the level they can reach.

The results related to the dancers experiencing the Process are mainly linked to the discovery of their potential and of the autonomy of their performance. The awareness of prejudices, the questioning of values, the acceptance of their conflicts, and the identification of the fact that the model was inside them, produced a certain feeling described by the dancers as a "body being alive". The "gaze" and the organicity of the movement became an incorporated reference, irrespectively of the chosen path.

The research sources presented new circumstances until the closing of the syntheses, either reinforcing or expanding what I had already learned as a dancer-researcher-performer. The researches about the *Congado*, *Umbanda*, and other manifestations were extended to several groups and places. The main researched places include the *Comunidade dos Arturos* (MG) (Arturos' Community), since 1987, and the *Terreiro de Umbanda "Pai Joaquim de Aruanda and Boiadeiro de Minas"* (DF), since 1980. In my last visits to these places, a tuning was established in the relationships with the interviewees, as if we were writing some pages of this book together.

We did not foster an illusion in relation to the full possession of these sources or the line of research. This would mean to become crystallized, losing the flow that enabled us to go ahead. We glimpsed ruptures – protecting the essence – and transformations that were timely stimulated by life. Why? Because "the world is not what I think"; it is what I live. I communicate with it, but it does not belong to me. The world is endless. *There is a world*, or rather, *there is the world*.[3]

We acknowledge our limitations in relation to a non-fragmented report of the work, as the use of words may dismiss several things. Also, some things cannot be expressed in words, as they belong to the silence of the senses.

---

3   *Maurice Merleau Ponty* - Fenomenologia da percepção (Phenomenology of perception), *1994.*

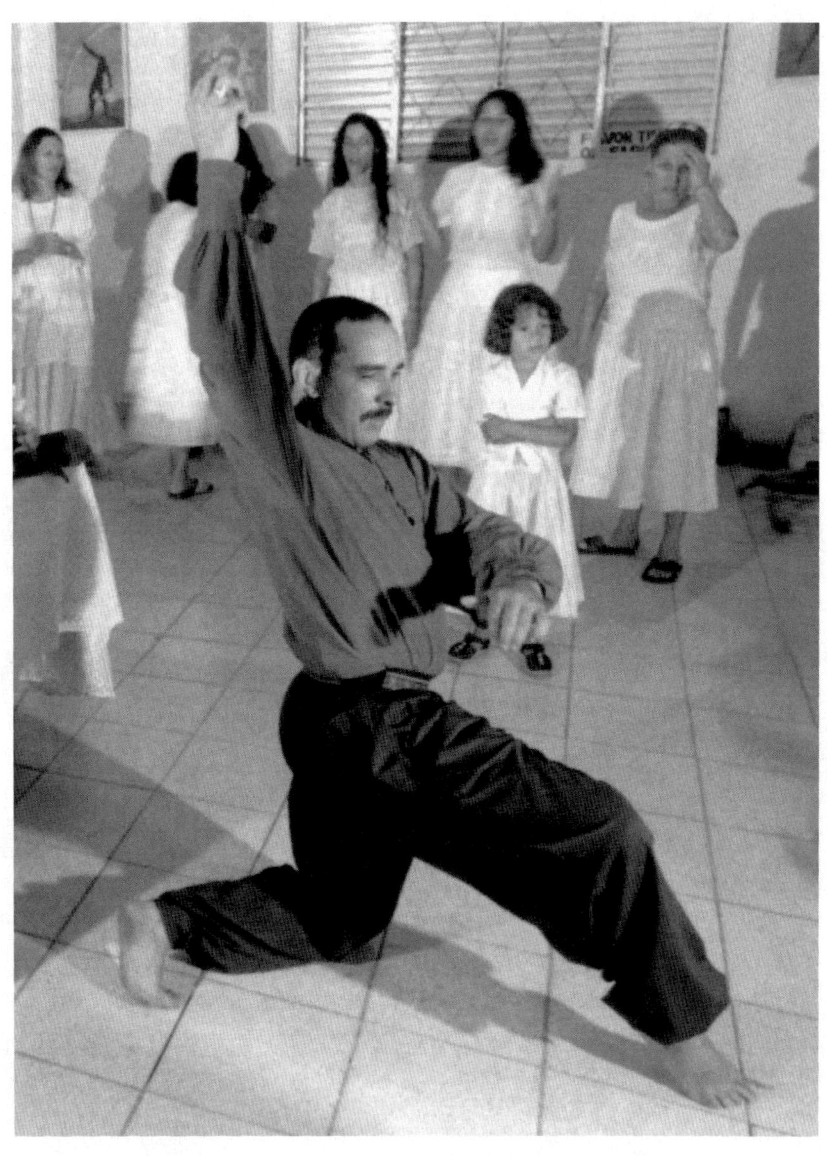

Terreiro de Umbanda *Pai Joaquim de Aruanda.*
Front: Gypsy Alejandro incorporated in
Carlos Aberto da Costa, Brasília DF
Photo: Juan Pratginesto's

3 Which Brazilian Body is Talked About: The Source, the School, the Reference

We talk about a body that lies on the margin of the Brazilian society. However, this body contains the collective unconsciousness. Among various expressions, this body captures the sacred among the contingencies of the profane. Its manifestation, resulting from the integrations, deepens the meaning of the Dance.

In search of a dance characterized by its identity we traveled through Brazil, where *the astonishing similarities of its cultural manifestations create a network throughout the country. It is something that could be mixed up with the folklore and that I will identify as popular culture.*[1] Breaking the official cultural barriers, we found a school that taught rare stuff.

In the search of this Brazilian body, it was impossible not to consider this body when it produces sings, talks, manipulates objects (incorporating their meanings), goes through, remakes, and retells its own history in an intimate relationship with both personal and collective identity. The integration of all these aspects leads to a unity of the whole body and, as a consequence, the movement exhibits a highly expressive quality. The sources of this study consist of individuals and communities where these senses were located as a result of a cultural resistance. In some groups, there were only traces of a given manifestation and cultural resistance was just a memory. The movement was diffuse and poorly designed, demanding a higher and more detailed effort in its observation. These sources helped to corroborate data from other locations where integrity of the manifestation was observed.

We approach this body from the learning experienced in the field research. It is important to mention that each manifestation has its specificities. It is singular in each region, and each group is unique in its expression. Therefore, we present a synthesis pointing out common and outstanding aspects. Each reference has ramifications that would be impossible to express in this first work.

The conducted researches included *Umbanda, Candomblé, Capoeira, Congado, Maracatu, Folia de Reis, Folia do Divino* and other *Folias, Batuque,* and several regional dances. The *Divino* cycles were also investigated, including its *Cavalhadas* and agricultural rites, such as the *Festa do João do Mato* or *Festa de Capina.* Regarding the researched communities, we had little contact with the indigenous

---

1   *Marlyse Meyer* - Caminhos do Imaginário no Brasil, *1993. (Imaginagy Paths in Brazil).*

community *Xavante* and a long time cohabiting with the Afro-Brazilian community of the *Arturos*. In relation to the female universe, we had contact with the rural workers (*bóias-frias*) and the healers (*benzedeiras*). The researches were mainly conducted in the Brazilian Federal District and in the states of São Paulo, Minas Gerais, Goiás and Mato Grosso. Relevant contacts also occurred in Bahia, Pernambuco and Rio Grande do Sul. Also, there were manifestations of other regions of the country that were told by the Mestres Populares (Popular Masters) out of their locations.

The researches present several contents (Afro-Brazilian, European, and Indigenous cultures) joined by discrimination. A cultural mix took place in the slave quarters, *terreiros*, and various covered and uncovered fields. Affinities and necessities allowed distinct bodies to find a common manifestation. Therefore, it can be noticed the existing cultural diversity in Brazil results from the oppressive conditions produced in the infinite network of human relationships. The work points out the importance of our African inheritance as a resistance power and as a source and receptor of several forms of expression.

The *Congado* is present in several regions of the country, but it is mainly found in the state of Minas Gerais. It was developed based on the reverences to Our Lady of the Rosary and several black saints, such as Saint Benedict and Saint Ephigenia. The main dynamics of the *Congado* is related to the presence of different groups called *guardas*, along with kings and queens representing the reincarnation of divine forces. The *candombe* (word meaning "sacred dance") precedes all the *guardas* in the hierarchy; it is considered the oldest group of *Congado*. The *guardas* of *Congo* and *Mozambique* stand out during the manifestations of the *Congado* in Minas Gerais based on the following myth:

Our Lady came from the sea through the waves, coming and going. The powerful white people made a rich altar and prepared the litter to carry the Mother of God to the house of men. But the image moved away into the sea, refusing the offering made by those powerful people. The white people tried to bring the Saint to the land, but it was in vain: the more they tried, the more she moved away. The slaves requested permission to chant, and, next to the sea, they beat their drums to honor Our Lady. The simplicity of the request made the farmers annoyed and they mocked them: bring the saint if you believe you are able to move it. Otherwise, you will be punished for not recognizing your insignificance.

The first group that approached the sea was the Congo, with its strong and fast chanting. Upon hearing them, the image slightly headed to their direction in a movement of approximation. The Congo made Our Lady move, but after a moment she stopped. Then there was the Mozambique's grief, slowly calling Our Lady and asking her to come closer through the voice of the instruments and the pleading rhythm of the chanting. And then, with the movement of black mozambiqueiros, the Virgin was coming, little by little, to reach the sand of the beach. But when the image reached the sand, it was taken by the white men to their church, where it was worshiped until the night.

But this went on only until the night. In the morning, the chapel denounced the Saint's discontentment. And once again the chant of the Mozambique took it back to turn it into the Saint Mother of Black People. The image remained and remains in the altar where it was placed, expecting the religiosity of her pure and first children: those who know how to love her through their dancing bodies and crying souls.[2]

Other brothers, called the *guardas* of *Marujos, Caboclinhos, Cavaleiros, Catopés* and *Vilão* have joined the *Congo* and the *Mozambique.*

In relation to the Black Community of *Arturos,*[3] the *Congado* is the unifying force of its members. Their *Congado*'s roots were left by Father Arthur. For the *Arturos,* the *Congado* means a sacred commitment to their ancestors, along with "old tree trunk" that came from Africa through the slaves. Through the chants, the *Mozambique* and the *Congo of the Arturos,* they call Our Lady, *São Jorge Guerreiro* (Saint George), *Shango, Sereia do Mar* (Mermaid of the Sea), *Marinheiro* (Sailor) and many other entities and saints.

Coming from different regions of Minas Gerais, several *guardas* are received in the territory of the *Arturos* during the celebrations of the *Congado. Brotherhood is a beautiful combination because of the festivity,* tells José Arthur. The festivity brings together all the differences, without distinctions. In the open space, at the same time, dozens of groups express their devotion, intercrossing the most diverse sounds, chants and instruments. Through their dancing bodies, the *Marujos* talk about the instability at high seas; through the free flow of their dancers, the *Congos* open and boost the space; through the movement the concentration and strength of their bodies, the *caboclos* draw their insignia in the space; through the movement, the density and outcry of their bodies, the *mozambiqueiros* harmonically convey the chanting into lament. In a single context, different forms are developed and each movement stems from a role. The festivity of the *Congado* is characterized by the meeting of all groups.

---

2   *Núbia Gomes e Edimilson Pereira - Negras raízes mineiras*: Os Arturos, 1988. (Black roots from Minas: the Arturos).

3   Communities of the Arturos - Contagem (MG). The research in this community were conducted in the years of 1987, 1988, 1995, and 1996. They were part of the Projeto Trilhas e Veredas da Dança Brasileira (Trails and Paths of Brazilian Dance Project), presenting extensive documentation, study and analysis. This community represented one of the most important learning centers as it concentrates several manifestations and has a cultural resistance nature.

We found some *terreiros of Umbanda* that see the period of the *Congado* as the festivity of the *Pretos-Velhos* (entities related to old slaves). In addition to the media that incorporate the entities of *Pretos-Velhos*, groups of *Candombe, Congo* and *Mozambique* were also present in the *Terreiro of Dona Ifigênia,* in Belo Horizonte during that period. Other groups were also observed in one of its festivities, including the representation of an indigenous community (*Guarani*) through a shaman and a group of *capoeiristas.* Around the same votive masts of Saint Ephigenia, St. Benedict, and the slave Anastácia, different voices and movements were developed in a single act – the reverence. The African memories in Brazil are evident in several manifestations, where different cultural roots are interrelated.

The *Umbanda*, positively Brazilian, presents a complexity and symbolic wealth that are in constant development. In each village of the Brazilian territory the *terreiro of Umbanda* occupies a space according to its own identity. The research led us to consider them as an important reference to understand the expressive body of Brazilian Popular manifestations. It is commonly characterized as an *Umbanda* movement, whose origin dates back to the religious processes of the four ethnic groups (red, black, yellow and white).

The *Umbanda* reveals a large number of entities which originated in African pantheon (*orishas*), Europe, Eastern hemisphere, and even in Brazilian lands, such as the *Boiadeiros, Caboclos, Marinheiros* and *Baianos.* Grouped in the right or left side, they significantly show the two sides of the same face. As a characteristic of the *Umbanda*, the medium receives entities from both "sides". Such polarities are part of a single body that will denote plasticity in the performance of bodily actions.

Through a single entity it is possible to observe the intercrossed cultural mixtures that are then transformed to acquire a new form in the body.

We followed the path of the *Pomba Gira Maceió* in a *terreiro* in the Midwest.[4] Her performances and stories are consistent with the following reference:

---

4   Terreiro of Umbanda Pai Joaquim de Aruanda e Boiadeiro de Minas - Brasilia (DF). Researches in this terreiro started in 1980, with Carlos Alberto da Costa as the main pai-de-santo (the maximum authority in the Afro-Brazilian religions. It could be translated as the "father of saint". In the hierarchy, there also is a filho-de-santo, which could be translated as "son of saint"). Among the various entities incorporated by him, Pomba-Gira Maceió wasstrictly studied, then becoming, along with other researches, the basis for the creation of the performance Graça Bailarina de Jesus (Grace, Ballerina of Jesus). In the years that followed, the presence of the Umbanda in the researches was incisive and striking. The various terreiros researched presented numerous aspects that referred to the terreiro of Carlos, showing its clarity and diversity of entities and bodily forms.

The evolution of the *Pomba Gira Maceió* culminated in her passage to another line, the *Caboclos*. Let us observe a given moment of its identity as *Pomba Gira*: dressing seven skirts varying from chintz to silk, wearing high-heeled shoes and many ornaments in the body, *Maceió* performs the movements of *Ijesha* (from the *Candomblé*) strumming their castanets to the sound of the conga drums. She also undresses the skirts and adornments, takes the shoes off, and performs stripped movements. The representation of the *Pomba Gira* consists exactly in this construction and deconstruction with no aesthetic censorship, where all elements are possible in the different forms developed from her movement.

Breaking the spatial limits of the *terreiro of Umbanda*, the archetypes invoked by the *Umbanda* entities inhabit other territories of manifestations. In the *Rural Maracatu* of Pernambuco the *Caboclos de Lança* tell us about a feminine protection, an entity that, according to their descriptions, is very similar to the *Pomba-Gira*. Several aspects of the *Umbanda* were observed, including the representation of some of its archetypes or some content mainly enounced through its *pontos* (chantings) in the *Congados*, in the *Bois*, in the *Folias,* and other *folguedos*. The opposite also occurs, that is, some specific representations related to the dances and chantings of various manifestations are present in the *Umbanda*.

The spaces of the manifestations have flexible boundaries. Like the *Bois* in different regions, the *Candomblés* and other Afro-Brazilian rites receive in their homes the various *folguedos* before they go to the streets. Another aspect refers to the individual: the need to be part of a festivity cycle leads the individual or group to participate in different manifestations in the course of the year. Thus there is

---

These aspects were present in a number of other religious communities (terreiros), but in a fragmented manner. Another characteristic relates to the dynamism of transformation witnessed in this terreiro, with the continuous occurrence of new entities and consequently new rites. The rituals and entities evolved together for an increasingly elaborated "performance". The continuation of the research in this terreiro occurred in 1982, 1985, 1988, and 1995. In 1988, there was the rite of passage (or farewell) of the entity Pomba-Gira Maceió. In the same ritual, after the disincorporation of Maceió, the medium received a new entity Pomba-Gira, a certain Maria Padilha. New developments followed, whose syntheses occurred in 1995.

5   *Marlyse Meyer* - Maria Padilha e toda a sua quadrilha: de amante de um rei de Castela à Pomba-Gira de Umbanda (Maria Padilha and her group: from lover of a king of Castela to *Pomba-Gira of Umbanda*), 1993.

the occurrence of a composition of bodily forms enriched by the integration of different elements. However, there is a predominance of one of the forms that will be strongly imprinted in the body of the individual, irrespective of the manifestation this body is participating. The particularization of this evidence in the body is much more related to a choice of the soul than to an aesthetic choice for the body:

On the day that I die, I talked to my family, for God's sake, I want the Congado. The drums beating and taking me to the cemetery. Leave the matter there, but my soul will be inside the Congado.

This testimony of Joaquim (*Captain of Mozambique*, from the *Congado of the Arturos*) is consistent with what his body expressed. Amid the diversity of forms that his body mastered, the *Mozambique* was his greatest expression. In the agrarian ritual *festivity of João do Mato*, Captain Joaquim replaced the stick with the hoe; however, a *mozambiqueiro* body played behind the *João do Mato*.

The maintenance of this culture, the basis of the manifestations, requires a commitment. The keepers of this culture are personified as father, mother, grandfather, grandmother, godfather, godmother, master, or captain. They transmit the secrets and the history contained in the manifestation to the chosen ones. The transmission requires the sacred commitment to continuity.

Near the cruise, the *Captain of Mozambique* recalls the old Captain that is gone. Through the *berimbau* (a percussion instrument), the *capoeirista* (*Capoeira player*) brings out the memory of the old masters. The *Boi Janeiro de Rubim* (from the Valley of the Jequitinhonha, MG) enters the cemetery saluting the masters of the *Boi*, these fellow *foliões* (merrymakers). The bodies move through a strong ancestral memory. At every moment of the present, the past is rescued and connected to the future, enduring the difficulties when the body, along with the "other" – the affective memory – performs the movement that is doubled by the force of maintenance.

Dance plays the role of reviving the memory; it is build up from the senses of the festivities. This is because *the festivity is a reserved period for the full expression of feelings, including the acknowledgment of the tragic element. The affirmation of life and joy in spite of the failures and deaths. The recognition and overcoming of negative realities.*[6]

To understand this Festive Body, it is necessary to consider the periods of preparations before the festivities as well as the daily lives of people involved in the celebrations. In the period surrounding the special days, the body is in a state

---

6   Harvey Cox - A Festa dos Foliões - um ensaio teológico sobre festividade e fantasia, 1974. (The Party of the Foliões - a teological essay on festivity and fantasy).

of readiness, remaining sharp and alert. Small, subtle movements occur which are linked to the roles and forms of the festivity or ritual to which the individual belongs. José Artur carries a cattle and the flag of *Congo*. The devotion expressed by his body is built in the two time-spaces: the daily life and the festivity:

The day I do not feel the smell of a cattle I get sick. I dance carrying the flag of Congo.

Within this context and this place, the ritual is conducted with the sense that the body becomes able to receive forces that lie within and beyond the individual himself.

The emotional extension expressed by the body is wide. From a profound seclusion, it goes through various emotional gradations until it reaches catharsis. This emotional gradation of varied hues has its overwhelming periods in which the body joins other bodies: *When I dance, the other in me dances.* There is a single moment when this meeting occurs, enunciated by the momentum of strong, precise, energetic movement. The individual is under intense emotional record. Another reference is the momentary loss of his/her own body to incorporate another body, belonging to the entity. In the lose-win passage, the body presents a commotion followed by self-reorganization and rebalance to turn into a new configuration – the incorporated entity.

A single manifestation contains several categories of dances, and each one of these dances has a specific movement form, common to all dancers. However, the force presented by the collective movement does not lie in the uniformity, but in the individuality through which each dancer receives the movement in his or her body. It is possible to say that the collective form is a matrix that remains alive due to the peculiarities and meanings that each person imprints to the movement.

In relation to these matrices that compose the dances, it is not possible to define their origins based on transplanted cultural references. The *Batuque* is an example: field researches conducted in several regions revealed a wide variety of dances that were considered *Batuque* by their "performers". In some places the *Batuque* had a profane nature, called *Bizarrias*; in others, Sacred *Batuque*. Some *Batuques* exhibit certain similarities with the Flamenco dance in a series of aspects, particularly in relation to some steps/movements. Common characteristics found in the *Batuques de Bizarria* include: the prevalence of the circle and pairs, the use of stomping and clapping, and the mention of the *umbigada* (belly bucking). Old *Batuqueiras* revealed that *the* umbigada *had been lost in time.* Covertly, the sensuality and sexuality senses were present all the time. The presence of love games, conquests and challenges induced several characteristics in the dance movements composition. The sacred *Batuques* were performed before the altar or *Conga*, already interconnected with other rites.

All the *batuqueira* presented a fragment of the *Batuque* in their bodies and had many stories from their memories. However, not all data led to a single track; seemingly, at some point the *Batuque* was constituted of an entire manifestation in a broad context. There are chances that the *Batuque* has originated from the fertility rites, thereby bringing us to the genesis of dance.[7]

Various references to the ancient times were present throughout the course of the field research. When asked about the origin of his *folia*, a *folião* from *Bandeira do Divino Espírito Santo*, in Turmalina (MG), said: *Ah ma'am, it comes from the dawn of the world.*

The Brazilian countryside still rediscovers in their festivities the ancient and medieval scenery where man dives into the mysteries of his essential roots. In the *Cavalhadas* of Pirenópolis (Goiás) the Knight archetype was identified, as the *"engrazamento"*[8] of the Moor, with the Christian knight. When a gift was conquered in the game of ringlets a Moorish knight opened and extended his arms horizontally over the horse, with the gaze and projection of the whole body opened to the sky. At the same time, after his conquest the Christian knight dismounted, genuflected, crossed himself and, upon restraining his body, headed the gaze and the whole body towards the ground. It was observed that every manifestation teaches a specificity of dynamics. The example of the *cavalhadas* – whose outcome leads to the reconciliation between Moors and Christians – shows the union of polarities through two bodies.

The concreteness of this body as matter and soul teaches that dancing is a result of diverse interactions whose key is the memory of affection. Hence, to penetrate the symbolism of the *Boi* is to die and reborn, restoring vitality to the body. The *capoeiragem*, through which the body passes, means that the movement will have a strategic action force.

The development of the movements requires a constant opposition to the resistances. The shifts in values (mainly reflected in young people) increasingly intercept the transmission of knowledge from the old masters. As Antonio, Captain of *Candombe*, says: *To lead a Candombe, one gotta have intuition, and this intuition is disappearing.* But Salustiano, the old Master of *Maracatu*, although tired of his isolation in the command, resists: *Sometimes you want to stop, but something makes you want to insist.* Therefore, this culture is characterized by the tension of oppositions, configuring its own sense of existence.

---

7   *Núbia Gomes eEdimilson Pereira* - Negras raízes mineiras: Os Arturos, 1988. (Black roots from Minas: the Arturos).

8   In the Cavalhadas of Pirenópolis. The word "engrazamento" is often used to refer to the various choreographic times when the sequence of lines formed by horsemen occurs.

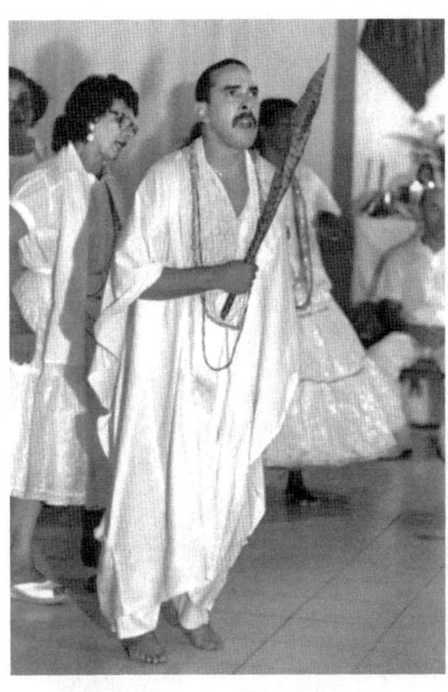

*Ogum incorporated in
Carlos Alberto da Costa
1995
Photo: Juan Pratginesto*

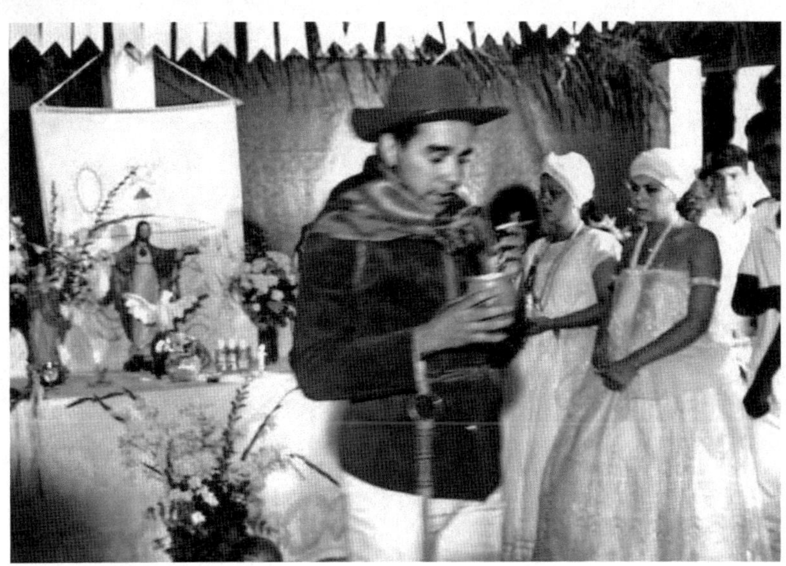

*Boiadeiro de Minas incorporated in
Carlos Alberto da Costa, 1988
Author's archive*

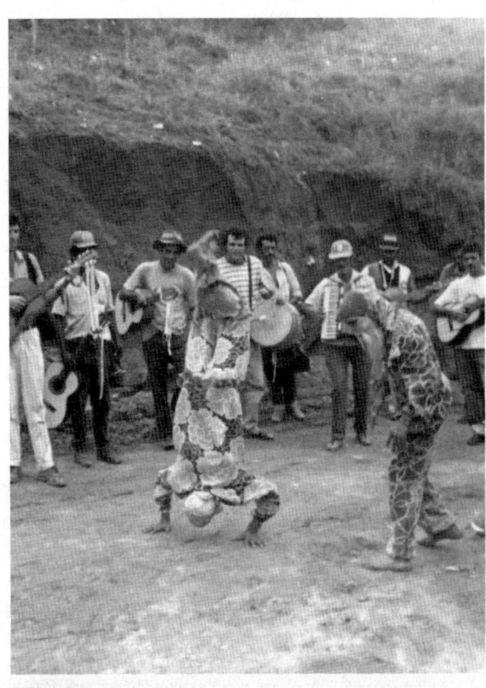

Folias de Reis
Heliodora MG, 1994
Author's archive

Maracatu Rural *Piaba de Ouro de*
Mestre Salustino Tabajara,
Pernambuco, 1992
Author's archive

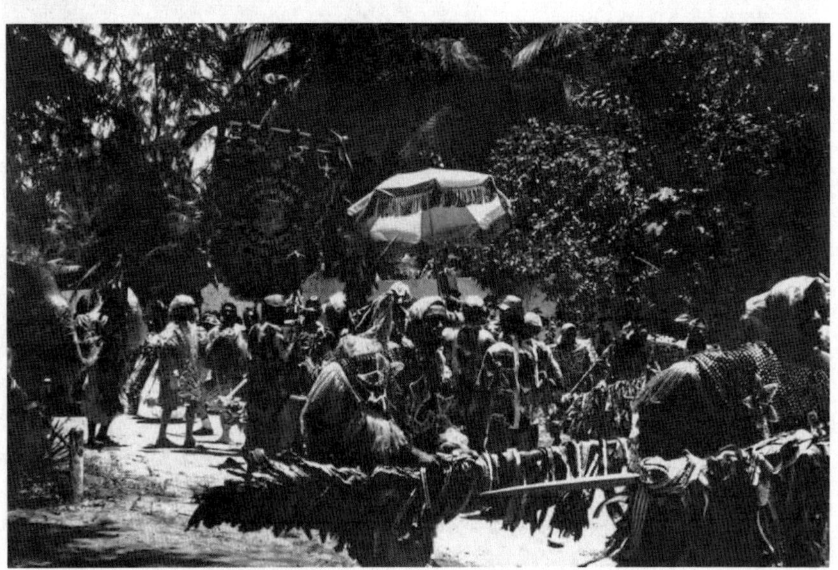

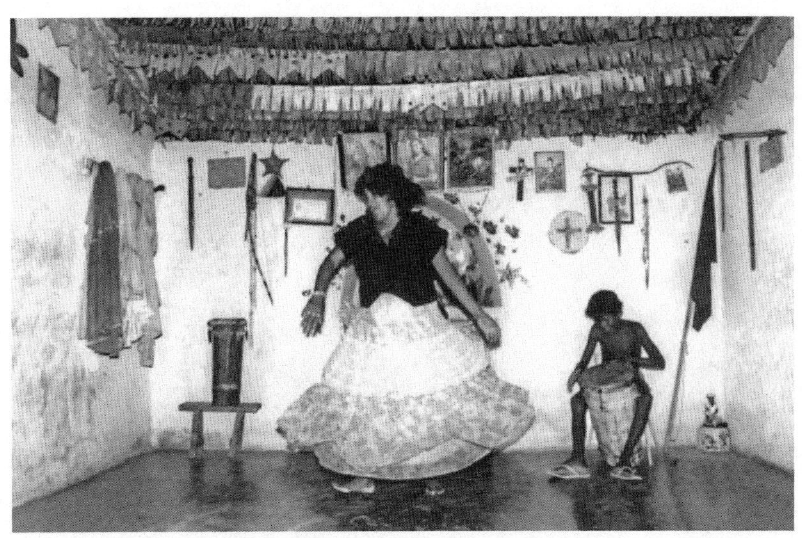

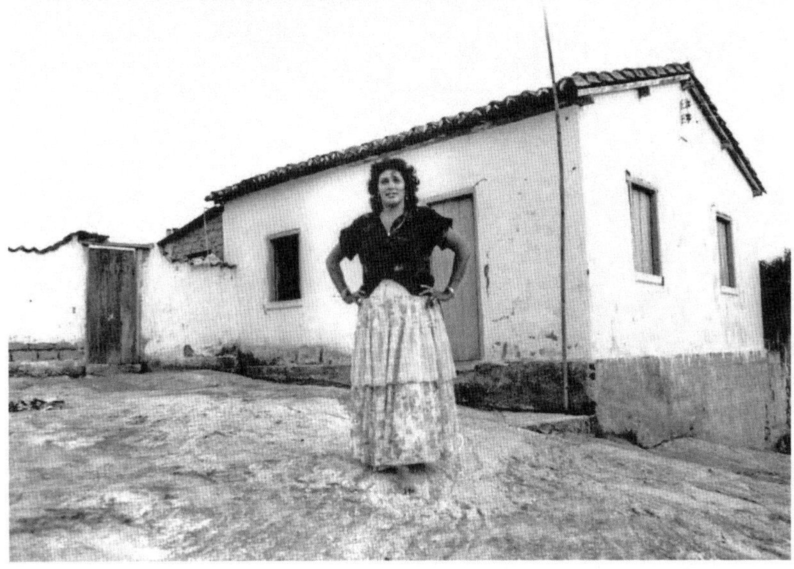

Leni, Umbandista from
Vale do Jequitinhonha, MG - 1987
Photos: Ricardo Oliveira
Author's archive

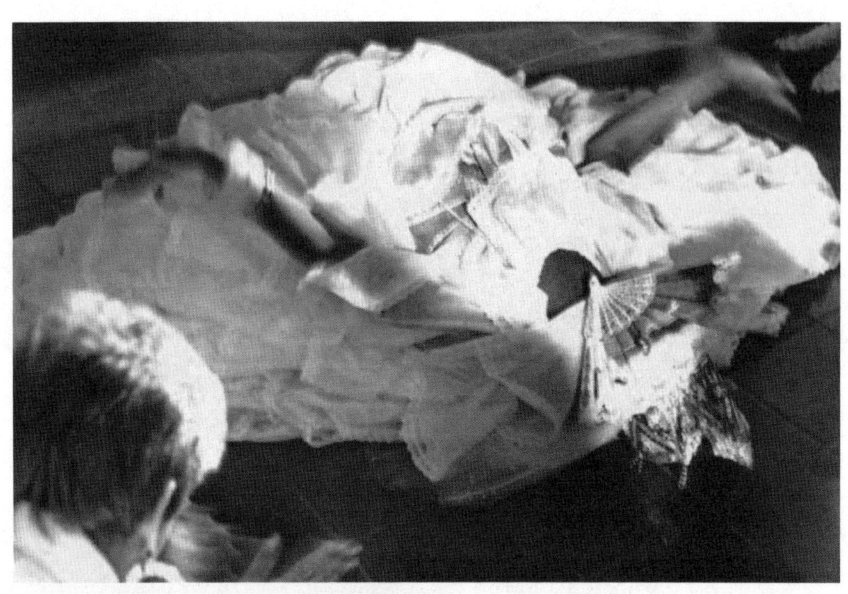

Entidade Maceió *incorporated*
in Carlos Alberto da Costa
Brasília, DF - 1988
Author's archive

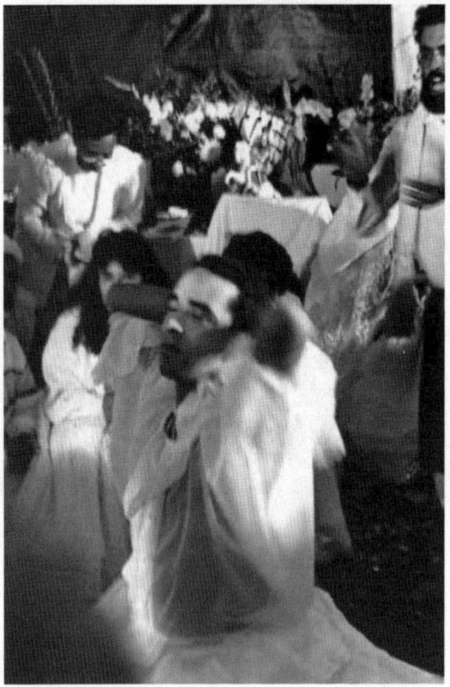

First incorporation of ***Maria Padilha*** *in*
Carlos Alberto da Costa
Brasília, DF - 1988
Author's archive

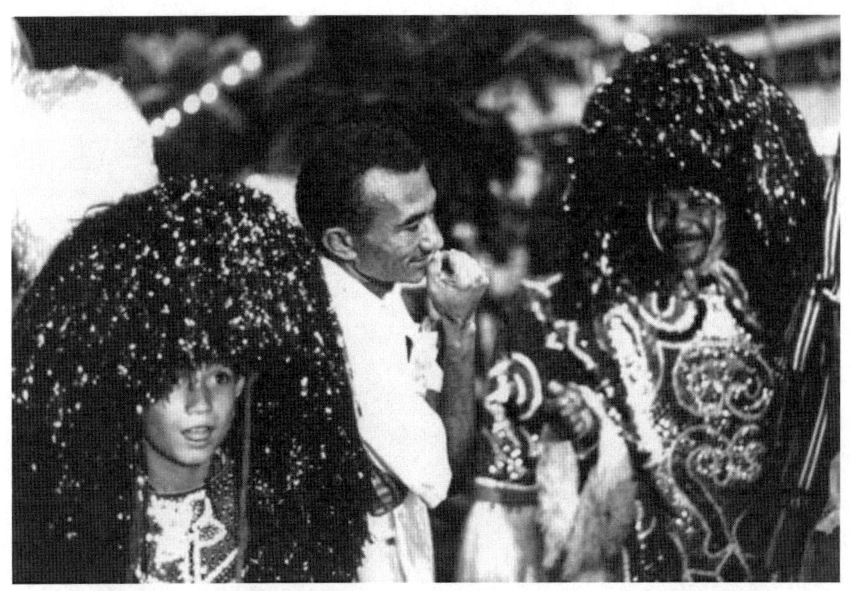

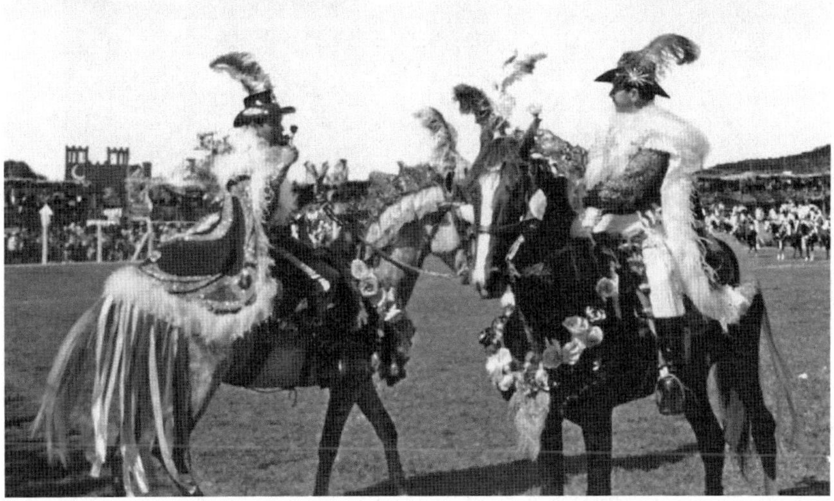

Above:
Mestre Salustiano, *in the center, among the*
Caboclos de Lança do Maracatu Rural
Piaba de Ouro, PE - 1992
Author's archive

Cavaleiro Mouro e Cristão
Cavalhadas de Pirenópolis, GO
1994
Author's archive

45

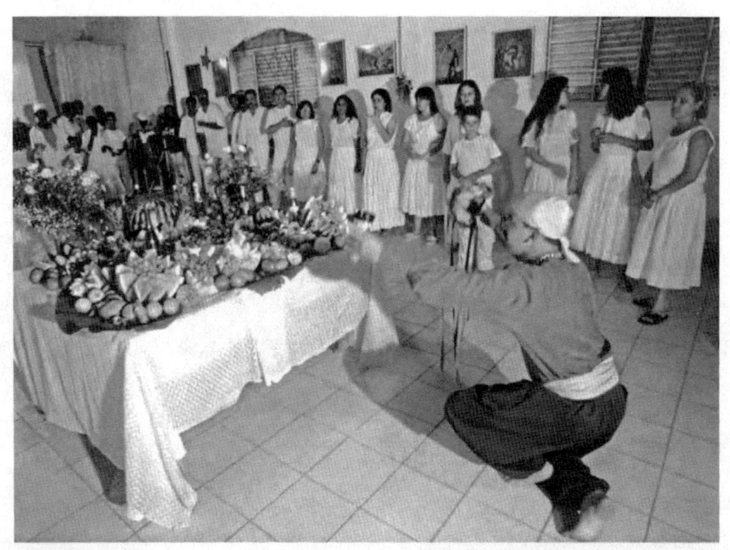

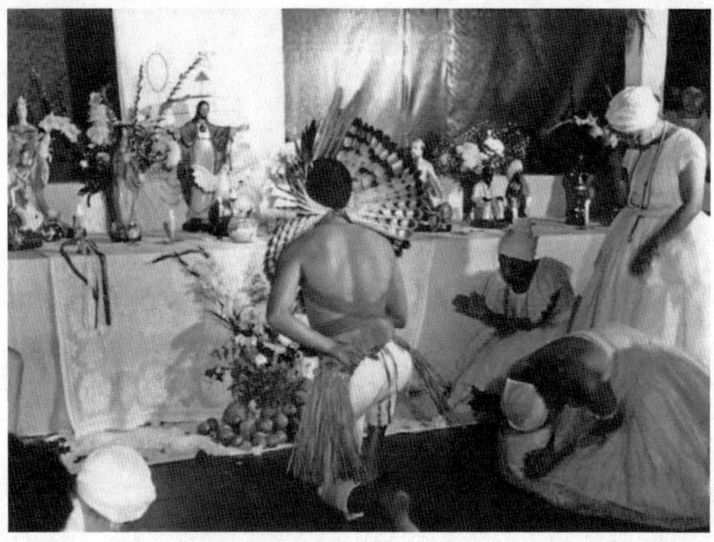

<table>
<tr>
<td>

Above:
Cigano Alexandro *incorporated in*
Carlos Alberto da Costa -1995
Photos Juan Pratginesto's

</td>
<td>

Caboclo Serra Negra incorporated in
Carlos Alberto da Costa
Terreiro Pai Joaquim de Aruanda and
Boiadeiro de Minas - Brasília, DF
1988
Author's archive

</td>
</tr>
</table>

46

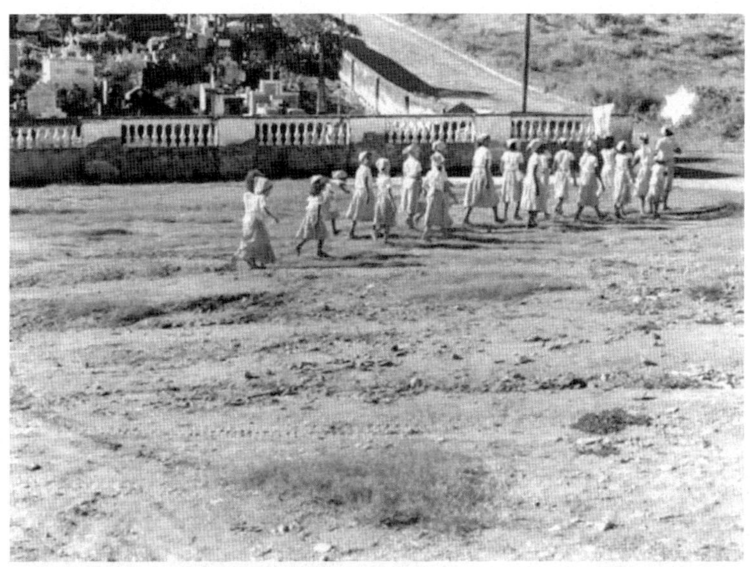

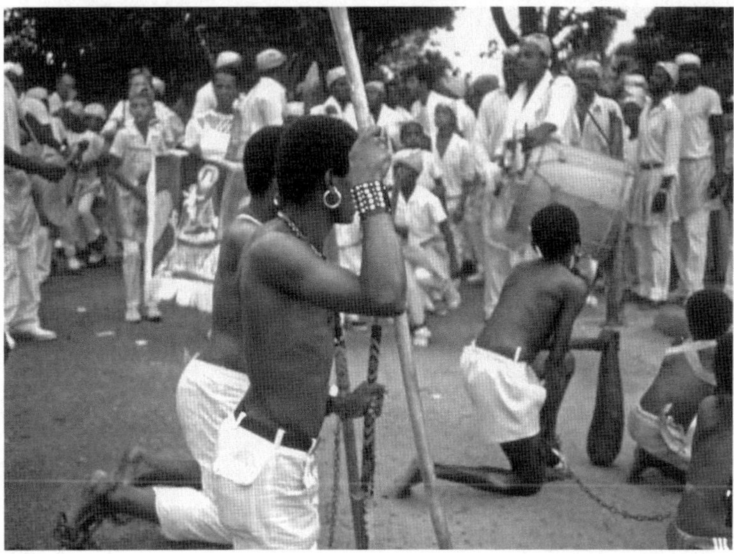

<table>
<tr><td>

Above:
As Pastorinhas do Natal
Araçuaí, MG - 1978
Photo: Vicente Sampaio

</td><td>

Festa de Libertação dos Escravos - *Arturos*
Contagem, MG - 1987
Author's archive

</td></tr>
</table>

47

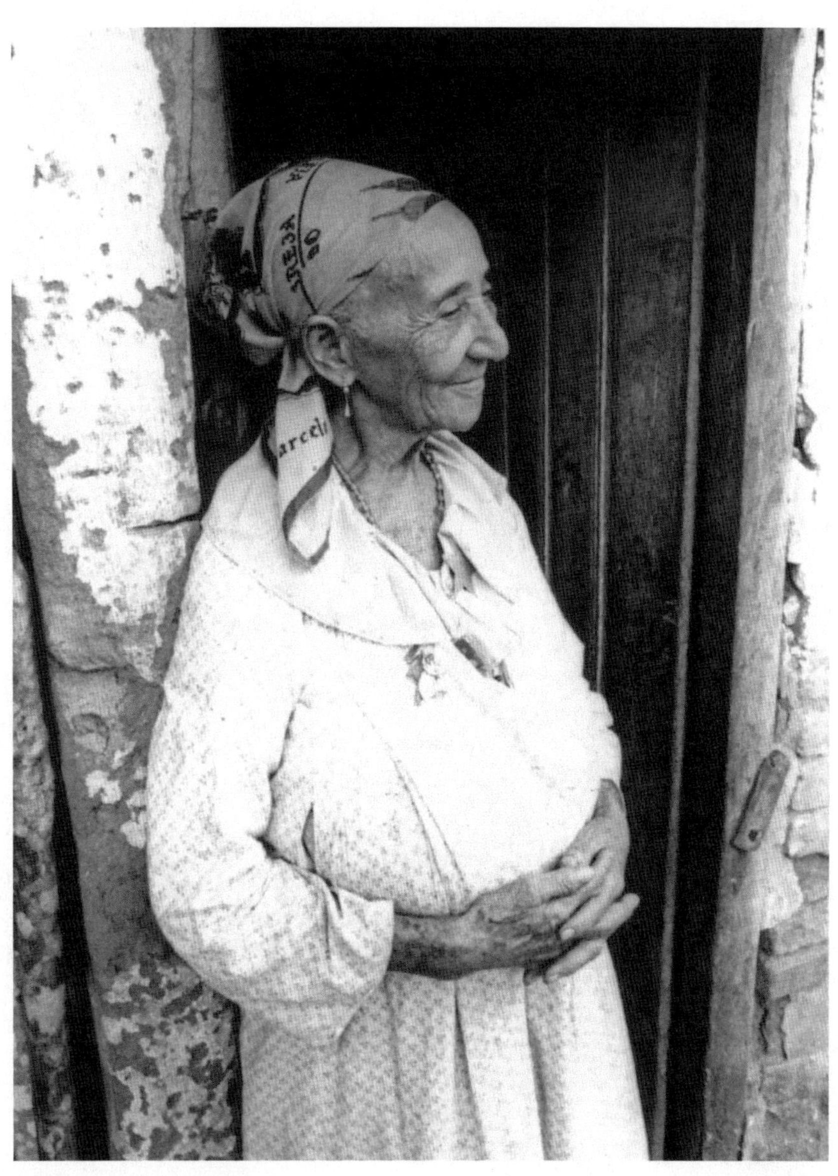

Sá Luiza, *benzedeira of*
Araçuai, MG, 1988
Photo: Ricardo Oliveira

48

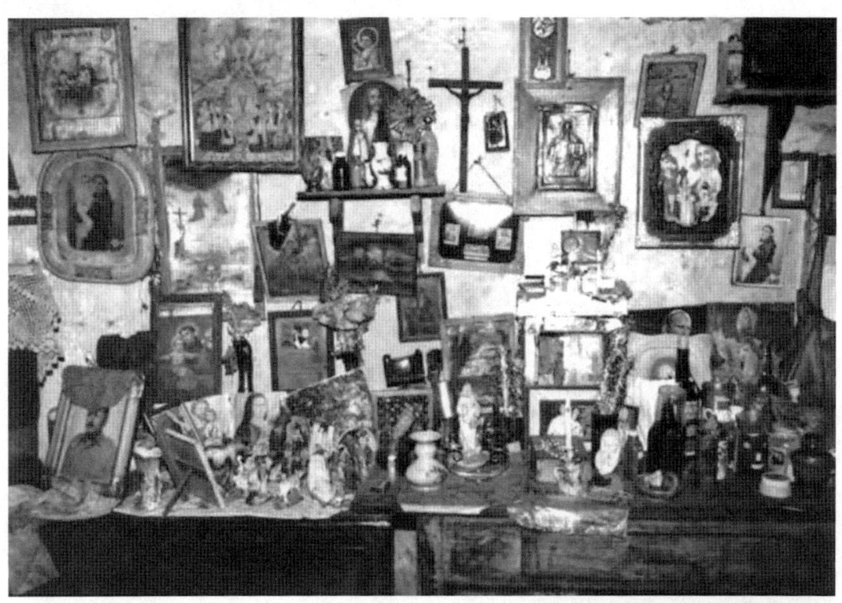

*Details of the space in the
house of **Sá Luiza***
Photo Ricardo Oliveira

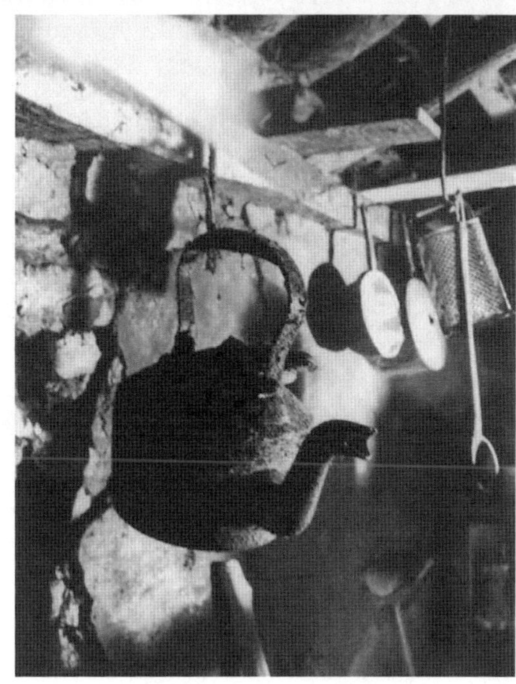

***I am crazy about dancing -
Every kind of dance
I like dancing***

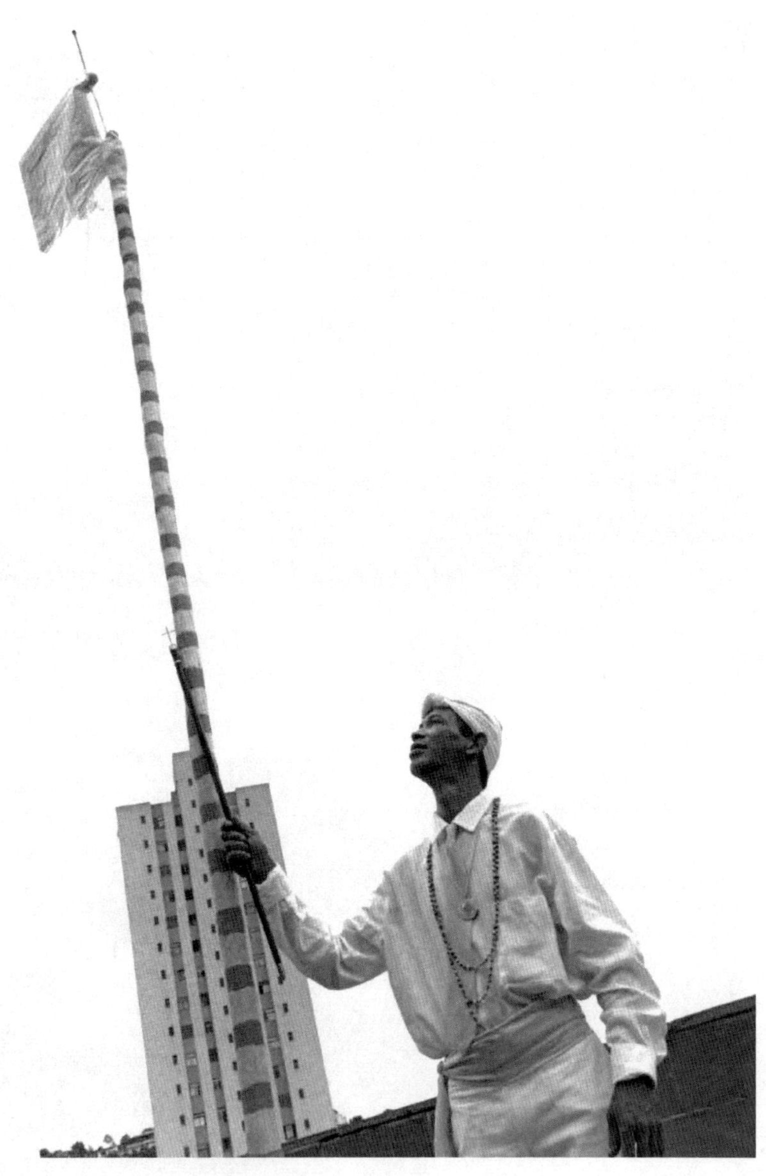

Mastro hasteado in Terreiro de Dona Efigênia, 1996
Photo: Eustáquio Neves

4 Physical Structure

Physical structure is how the body is organized to perform various categories of movement expressions.

The analysis and decoding process of the physical structure and movements of the body parts were conducted within some Brazilian popular manifestations. In addition to the fragments of the dynamics in question, commonly referred to as "the dance moments", the actions permeating the rituals were also taken into account.

Study procedures included:

(1) observation and learning the movements with popular masters during the field research;
(2) analysis from the video recordings performed in the field;
(3) learning from the actions of characters stemmed from research.

The association between observing and doing (experienced in the body) was constant. The ramifications of every movement were performed taking into account the body parts involved, the amount of efforts applied, the quality of the generated flow and other analysis of the body in action and inaction. The aim was to understand the configurations and meanings of the body. By virtue of relating with one another the movement forms of various manifestations, it was possible to identify a single physical structure.

The criterion of observation in each study was established as a "new way of looking". After analyzing and decoding our previous research, we were able to avoid the crystallization of the references. Thus, the reading of the body was performed at each point of the study. The conclusions presented herein come from the data found throughout the research and evidenced in the movement practice.

We emphasize the idea that this structure is more explicit if the individual is integrated to the ritualistic manifestations. The senses through which a person connects to the sacred drive him/her to react in a symbolic way. It was observed that the quality of the physical structure enables one to be a part of the symbolic field and that a sensitivity in the apprehension of symbols causes the body to be able to gain this structure.

Dance in popular culture is embedded in a broader context that goes beyond what we consider as the choreographic framework. The forms vary, but the way how the body is moved and structured within the Brazilian popular manifestations is quite homogenous.

4.1 Symbolic anatomy

The body is organized for dancing through its intense relationship with the earth. The feet's ability to be deeply placed on the ground allows the entire physical structure to be built up from its base. The image we have of the alignment is that the structure has its roots.

Through the parallel position of the feet, the entire bone structure is aligned and the muscles are activated by following its own constitution, in spiral. In the alignment, we intend to comply with the joint space and the broadened mobility of each of the joints.

The structure absorbs the symbolism of the votive mast that is enunciated by the flag representing the saints of devotion. The lower part of the mast is connected to the ground and the upper reaches up to the sky. An energetic circuit takes place around the festive mast represented by the body. With this symbolism, the body assumes the configuration of its psychical power.[1]

In the lower part of the body-mast, in addition to the intense contact of the feet with the ground, the sacral region exerts its force in favor of gravity through the coccyx. As a continuation of the spine pointing down to the feet, the coccyx establishes a third base. As a result of these images, the recurring action of placing the mast on the ground is represented by the consequent elevation of the iliac crests.

The coxofemoral joints present no tension, and the pelvis, "supported by the ischia", finds its place at the midpoint of the physical structure. Through the coccyx image, the pelvis takes part in the alignment of the mast-axis. While favoring the movement towards the ground with some level of flexion, the knees and ankles are sustained. Like a tree penetrating the earth – in the two directions of the mast connecting the high and the low – the body enables the sap to scroll through its trunk.

The upper part of the body is symbolized by the flag mobilizing the ethereal space around and beyond itself. From the spinal column, the breastbone centralizes the flag. As a fabric that opens and closes, the breastbone region mobilizes the emotional space. Arms and hands interact in the construction of the mast and the flag by invigorating the energies in the upper part. The belly centralizes the gathering of forces, working as a part of the maintenance. The bottom part of the spinal column places the mast on the ground; the upper part climbs toward the sky, moving to the top of the mast.

---

1   We refer to the emotional intensity, when the person integrates in him or herself the meanings of the mast as an energy center of the party.

The energies from the ground and from the top go through the body-mast. The energetic circuit directs the force to specific parts of the body when they become evident in the performance of the movement.

The crossing of energies (relationship between the upper right and the lower left sides and vice-versa) strengthens the center of the body, promoting a high level of balance and a sense of unity (overall participation of the body in the movement).

When maintaining an apparent inaction, the structure reveals the moment when the inner movement strongly happens. Pulsations and small significant changes are observed; and, in the next moment, the explosion of the movement is triggered.

The body-mast is firm and flexible; it is articulated in all directions and integrates the inner and outer parts, the upper and the lower, the front and the back. It receives and processes the symbols. From the parts to the whole, the unity of the body is established.

The physical structure is in harmony with the very nature of men, that is, the attempt to overcome the limits of one's physical body.

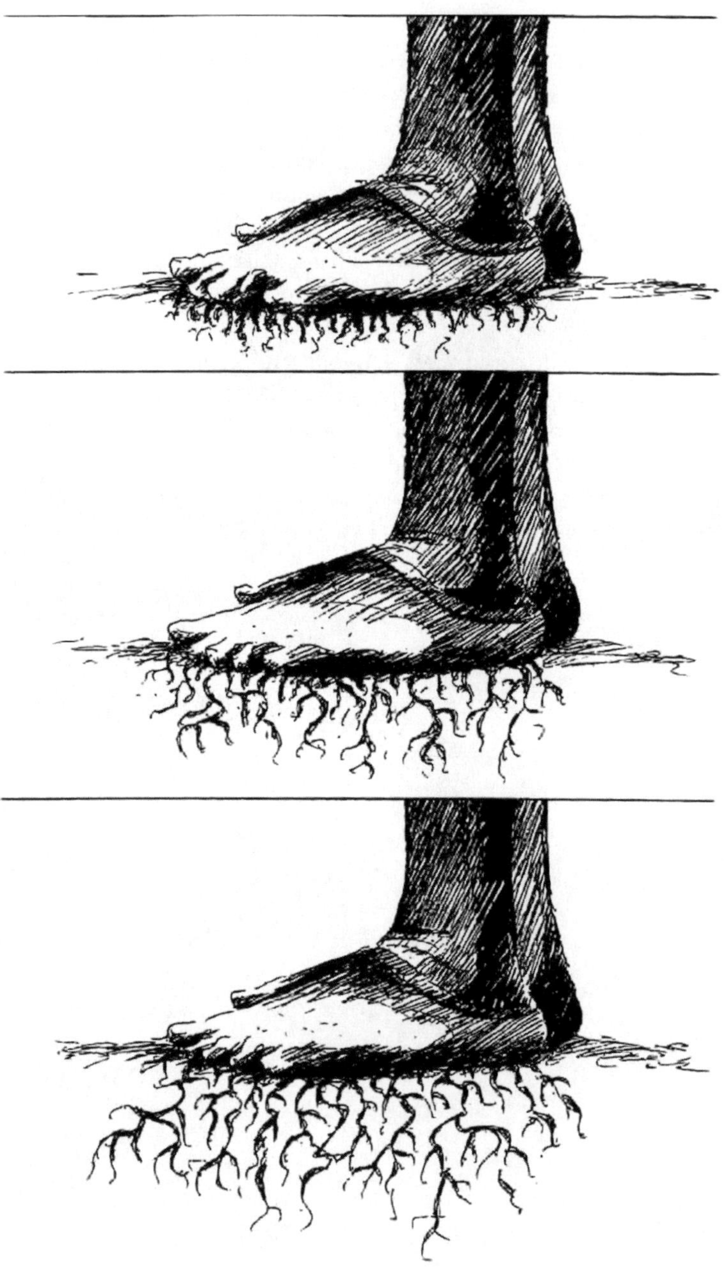

4.2 The movement of the parts

We presented a vision of the sources experienced in the way they have been practiced in our classes with the basis for the development of the dancer-researcher-performer. The data are full with subtleties and it is necessary to be careful about their interpretation and practice. We also observed that relevant kinesiological studies should be developed in order to contribute to the improvement and better understanding of this work. We will present the movement of the parts of the body as a starting point in this and other parts of this essay.

4.2.1 Lower parts – the roots of the mast

Feet

The feet have an intimate relationship with the ground. They penetrate the earth as if they had roots; they absorb it as if they collected sap; they work the clay; they raise dust; and they chew, restore, and revolve the earth through its multiple supports.

We call "supports" the parts of the feet that act in the movement, establishing different types of contact with the ground and printing a certain strength followed by different levels of flexion, extension, and rotations. The language of the feet developed through their support mainly involves tibiotarsal and coxofemoral joints.

Examples of such support include: fingers, metatarsus, heel, dorsal, lateral and medial parts of the feet. Through the intention during the movement, the arches of the feet also seek contact. The dynamics of the feet is characterized by different combinations of supports and their various efforts.

The efforts employed by the feet in relation to the ground are:

Minimum – superficial contact, subtleness of support.
Medium – contact beyond the surface, loose roots.
Maximum – penetration, rooting.

In addition to these efforts, there are other graduations that take part in the movement dynamics. The predominance of a given effort represents an important characteristic in the dance form. Therefore, the amount of effort applied in the movement of the feet is directly related to specific meanings that are different for each dance mode.

The quality of the use of feet presents resonance as they assume the conduction and trace paths to be fully followed by the body.

Among the various functions performed by the feet, we highlight some that are found in the *giras* of Umbanda and in the rites of Candomblé. At the beginning of a ritual and during its development, the feet play the role of tuning each individual with him or herself and establishing a relationship with the ritual space. We highlight the following movements performed in the circular mobility of the *gira*:

- By keeping the contact of the whole sole of the feet, the movement is developed through intensification (pressing the ground) and, at the same time, through the mobility of the support of metatarsals and heels. The feet alternate, heading out, maintaining relation with the center of the circle; in its return, they are defined in relation to the center of the body.
- Two actions occur simultaneously: while one foot collects energy from the ground, the other releases energy to the ground. In the action of retracting, the feet absorb the ground (similarly to a suction cup) stressing the contact of the metatarsus and the heel, and thereby increasing the foot arch. In the action of releasing, the feet expand in the ground, gradually increasing their area of contact. The movement is developed by alternating the feet in their actions.

In the two movements described above the energy accumulated in the body is unloaded and a new energy is absorbed by the body.

In the different dance forms of each entity and *Orisha*, their configurations, associated with the respective meanings, are enunciated through the feet. The ways in which the combination of supports is used and the amount of efforts applied are often associated with a particular action. Every movement dynamics presents a rhythmic composition that is supported by the beats of the drums.

We introduce some frequencies of feet characterizations, emphasizing the existence of several variables. There is a number of *Eshus*, Caboclos, Yemanjas… Apart from that, in the body of each horse[2], the *orisha* or entity assumes its own identity. Some syntheses of this ramification lead us to consider various configurations and meanings.

In the *Eshus*, there is a predominance of feet entrenched into the ground with maximum effort; in its movements, the dynamics relies on a constant use of the inner edges support. The feet often become claws revolving the earth. In the Caboclos, the feet present agility and determination as their main characteristics, with predominance of the middle effort. These feet are often characterized by the metatarsal support on the right foot and the entire sole of the left foot. Obaluaê's feet present density, rarely not touching the ground, as if the feet had wires that were continuously connected to the ground during the movement. The traction is maximum. In contrast, Oxuns's feet present a subtle contact: through the micro

---

2   Horse = medium.

supports around the foot, the movement is characterized by a suspension, as the feet work the ground in small portions as if they were caressing it. Their feet convey a great sensuality. The action of the feet of Yemanja seeks to expand the space and bring the sea. Being spread out, they go outwards and retract to the center of the body stressing the heels. With the middle effort, the feet alternate in and outwards. Command and security are characteristics of these feet. The impulsivity of Iansã's feet makes the supports, metatarsus, and toes to push the ground and the heels to work in counterpoint to the axis of the feet. They are projected at the sides of the body in a quick shift through the space involving the suspension of the heels. The Pomba-Giras, mainly researched in Umbanda, use and go through all the supports, including the lap of the feet and toes. They like to be placed under the metatarsus (half-point), an attribute of their vanity. They have great elasticity and their feet have no limits in terms of patterning and elaborating movements.

Among the manifestations of the Congado in Minas Gerais, we highlight the movement form of the *mozambiqueiros'* feet. In the body of these devotees, the feet assume other meanings and roles.

The old shackles used to imprison slaves are transformed into dance tools: the *gungas* (consisting of cans with lead in the inside, supported by leather straps hugging the ankles). The feet invested by the *gungas* help in the transportation to another world, where the past, present, and future are parts of the same journey. During the course of the *guardas*, the *mozambiqueiro* raises the dust, trembles the earth, and gets strength from its inner part. The feet penetrate the ground by employing maximum effort in an absolute commitment involving the whole body. The image is that the earth moves in response to this call, boosting the feet backwards. At times, when this contact reaches its peak, one feels as if the body is transported. Over time, the foot-ground dialogue starts to involve the whole body and causes a suspension of the torso; the feet almost float.

The chants announce the senses of the feet's movements:

Chora gunga de vovô, chora gunga, ô gente ...
Minha povo eu peço licença prá minha gunga reiná ...

(Grandpa's gunga cry, cry gunga, oh people ...
My people, I request your permission, so my gunga may reign)[3]

The right foot carries the largest number of *gungas* (bass sound); the energy is released through it. It represents the downbeat, the beat that "calls". The reply

---

3　Among the various researched groups of Mozambique, this aspect was highly clear among the Arturos.

comes through the *repique* – a variation of the third or triplet (as it is called by the *mozambiqueiros*). It is initiated by the left foot (which receives the energy of the earth). This process of calling and answering generates multiple variations with the use of the entire foot and its supports: the metatarsus, toes, tip, and heel are used with varied qualities of efforts.

The feet of *mozambiqueiros* advance, retreat, and are maintained in their place as if they were rooted in it; then, they are projected out of the ground. The distinct intentions result in the diversities of "steps" that influence the entire dance of the *mozambiqueiro.*

Differences and similarities

The similarities between some movements may be only apparent. In the *Batuques* and *Mozambiques*, the feet stomp, but these are completely different movements as they have different functions and intentions. In the *Mozambique*, the feet penetrate the ground, being subsequently moved upwards. In the *Batuque*, there is no impulse during the stomping; the feet leave the concentrated force on the ground. This fact was confirmed with the same group of people during their performances in the *Mozambique* and *Batuque.*

In the *Batuque*, sensuality and winning are well defined and expressed by the feet in their male and female polarities: while women's feet scratch around (performing *escovilha*, a movement in flamenco dance); they remain restrained, maintaining subtle contact with the ground, while men's feet either glide, or perform an insistent stomping in an expansive way directing the action onto the ground. Following the same descriptions, we found these same movements among the *Xavantes* (*Brazilian indigenous tribe*) in *Tisipá* dance (associated with marital rituals).

The previous examples show that the feet cross the boundaries and reveal their ability to articulate meanings and connect emotionally to the ground.

Knees

The predominance of their flexions in different dance forms, enables the feet to perform a range of highly articulated movements, while the support and expansion of the knees' space are related to the quality of work of the feet's support.

Besides, the knees have a significant impact on the positioning of the hips in the alignment of the entire physical structure.

Some body movements evidence a projection of the knees (requiring an increased use of the internal musculature of the legs) and change the position of the axis of the body.

When the knees are protagonists of the movement, they can reach all bending possibilities. Gradually, or through an impulse, they are demonstrated in every ritual through their expressive and differentiated actions, when saluting the flag, the altar, the *Conga*, etc.

The knees' "folding"[4] through impulse is quite significant in the language of the movement, when spirit possession occurs (*Umbanda, Candomblé*). The "knee-break" movement (fast bending through impulse) results from the displacement of the sacral region, but in these moments the knees announce the entry of new directions into the body.

In the *Caboclos de Lança* from the *Rural Maracatu* of Pernambuco, the knees are the most perceptible parts of the body in its all dance forms. They drive the action of the whole body within several dynamics, pushing themselves to return to the ground, to punctuate the space, or to establish contact between two people.

In *Capoeira*, during the *ginga*, the knees are a reference used to centralize the pelvis in relation to the toes, helping the weight to shift forward. Punctuation occurs in some strikes such as the "*joelhada*".

In several dances, the knees' extension occurs only in the moments of transition or stressing, in a sequence of movements, or before the execution of a deep flexion.

The "*molejo*"[5] of the knees – a part of various rituals – marks the beginning of the *Congado* rituals, favoring the release of the joints throughout the body.

Various manifestations are characterized by the presence of keepers of promises, and kneeling down expresses the act of contrition by the body.

Through this symbolic relationship, and through the concreteness of the physical action of the knees, men seek to redeem their imperfections and invoke the presence of perfection in contact with the sacred.

Pelvis

In the physical structure, pelvis has the role of establishing an opposition. Iliac crests go up when the coccyx is moved towards the ground. The traction in the sacral region is materialized imaginatively by the physical sense of owning a "tail." Therefore, the relationship between this coccyx-tail and the ground is a part of the hip's movement. The intention of this traction has several variations, and the higher levels of this intention lead to more evident verticality of the torso.

---

4   "Folding" is a word used in practical classes, referring to the bending of the knees.

5   "Molejo" are fast knee bendings, performed continuously.

The movement of the pelvis drawing the infinity

Through the coccycx, the pelvis horizontally draws the infinity. Producing a rounded shape on the sides and passing through the axis, the pelvis continuously assimilates the drawing. The internal space of the pelvis expands. By reducing and expanding the drawing, the pelvis remains suspended by the very dynamics of the movement. There is also an expansion of the hip joints and a stretching of pelvic floor. The movement of the "tail", or the hips, causes the torso to work, even though its expression is not so evident in relation to the movement's size.

When this matrix of movement is performed with the use of a great traction (proportion of weight in the tail), the movement denotes density and volume. By decreasing the traction, the movement gains speed and agility, but the intention of the "tail" is continuously directed to the ground.

Regardless of whether the dancers are men or women, when the female element appears, this configuration of the pelvis is the most significant movement of the whole body. Therefore, the infinity symbol movement of the hips is integrated into the dance forms with no gender distinction (for example, the *Boi do Maranhão* and the *Congo* of Minas Gerais). In the *Batuques*, characterized by well-accentuated male and female polarities, the infinity symbol movement is present only in the women's movement forms.

In the ritualistic dances, this matrix of movement (with its variants depending on the weight and magnitude degree – broad or narrow) is widely expressed.

Our research provided a very significant datum: in the same dance categories, especially the *orisha* dances were performed with the infinity symbol movement of the pelvis originating from the coccyx. However, in the case of dances performed by people that were far from the meanings, and out of the context, one could notice that the movement of the pelvis was coming from the iliac crests, losing the "tail", the distance of the axis, and the neatness of the movement drawing.

The swing and movements of the hips, so emphasized in various descriptions of Brazilian dances, probably originate from the matrix of the pelvis imbued with meanings. However, many movements have been utterly devoid of any content, losing their original physical structure. Other movements of the hips, like those that use sides (pendulum) and twists, follow the same principle of the coccyx-tail.

The saint penetrates through the sacrum

Some *pais-de-santo* revealed that the sacrum is the entry point of the *orishas* (pure, divine energy); being in contact with the energies of the person through the sacral holes, they favor body possessions. The master of Chinese martial arts, Liu Pai Lin, refers to the sacral region in the following terms: *Eight Saints dive into the sea (eight distinct energies related to the eight holes in the sacrum penetrate into the womb).* This description concerns the training of the inner movement, located in this area of the body.

There is an emphasis on the performance, the gaze focusing on the inside of the lower abdomen, promoting expansion and contraction: the inner pulse, the root of every tai-chi-chuan movement. The association of this training with the dances of the *orishas* enabled a true knowledge, as the important procedure of the pelvis in the penetrating field of inner movement was experienced and studied through the body: the generation, concentration and energy flow lie in it.

During the *giras*, the sacral region is activated by the pelvis bascule, moving forward and backwards. During the possession of the body, there is a strong impulse in the sacral region that affects the entire body. Then the body is "taken" and a change occurs in the entire physical structure, increasing the plasticity of the received content: the entity. The delicate field of the movement is expressed in the sacrum through various pulsations, including the little pelvis bascule and other actions that expose the active region, as it is felt.

These delicate movements permeate the moments of transformation of the body during the ritual, gaining more expressivity when the individual is controlled by the saint or *orisha*.

The pelvis represents a vase which receives and nourishes. In that sense, it is connected to the aspect of vitality, becoming an energy generator for the whole body. As we observed, intense sensuality and sexuality combined with the most genuine sense of sacredness were present in the pelvis.

4.2.2 Upper parts – the movement of the flag

The firm base structured in the roots of the mast enables the upper parts of the spinal column, torso, and limbs to generate an opposition in relation to the direction of its expansion and integrate these different parts of the body, forming the body-mast with the flag.

The spinal column is flexibly stretched throughout its length, assuming different postures.

Verticality is the main posture that takes over the energy circuit and enables the opening of the chakras (life-force energy centers). This posture – a drive shaft of the body language in the rituals – allows the force field of the individual to remain present and to interact with the meanings of each moment.

Verticality is worked through some movements that denote the action of raising the mast for a long time. Also, more delicate movements are performed, originating from the physical sensations felt throughout the length of the column. In both cases, energy is pumped from the spinal column to the head; energy following the inner path goes downwards through the front of the torso. Seeking what is behind, this energy eventually embraces the front. Therefore, the torso emerges from the back.[6] At the beginning of the rituals, verticality is the preparation posture, and during its development – with energy seeking space – the axis work is incisive to balance the plenty of destabilizing movement forms. When the *pai-de-santo* requests the *filho-de-santo* to stand his head up, he strengthens the vertical axis. The same occurs when the Captain of *Mozambique*, vested with his stick, greets each *mozambiqueiro*.

The perpendicular position and the mast-column bending forward are important to acquire and increase the agility of fast-paced movements; in this case, the inclination is small, favoring the dynamism of the body language. When the perpendicularity is accentuated, the torso enters a relationship with the ground – evidenced by the gaze – inducing a more direct dialogue with the earth. This posture reveals that the torso is nourished by the force of the earth and indicates the reverence for the sacred.

The convex posture, accentuated curvature of the column-axis, is assumed when the ancestrality is present. The movements in this posture are slow, the torso presents density; however, it does not denote the ruin of the physical body, it actually represents the archetype of the *Preto-Velho* bringing the wisdom acquired from his plenty of experiences.

The horizontal posture (torso positioned in parallel with the ground) is found in the *folguedos do Boi*: in the individual who carries the carcass representing the Ox and in other *folguedos* that present animal characters. In some *Umbanda terreiros*, certain entities, like the black Africans of Cabinda and Massapés, appear in horizontal posture. The body remains in this posture all the time during the dances, whose main function is to perform an energy cleaning of the space.

There will always be a predominant position emerging from the interactions between these factors and the movement (resulting in the dance). However, there is a postural dynamism involving the passages from one posture to another. Meaning and significance are strongly marked by a posture, and in the dynamics of the postural passages there is an articulation of other meanings that make up the whole of the dance form.

---

6   The trainings of the inner movement learned with master Liu Pai Lin and Lucia Lee (1981) were important tools for the perception of the energy circuit in relation to the quality of movement.

The *mozambiqueiro* assumes the vertical position resulting from a continuous interaction with the festive mast, passing through the perpendicular position in the dynamics of more accelerated movements; the convex position occurs when there is a strong presence of ancestors. The *Pretos-Velhos* are characterized by the convex posture, taking the perpendicular position in the dynamics of the dance form.

In the *Boi Janeiro* of the city of Rubim (MG) the Ox was characterized by a continuous movement of passage from horizontal to vertical position; in the latter, the individual was framed by the carcass, so that the Ox was humanized. The meaning of Ox-man was strong in this particular *folguedo*.

In the *Umbanda*, we find some references in which the postures are related to a tenuous connection promoted by the entities through the chakras: *the entities fully control the psychomotor part by stimulating these energy centers in the astral body of the medium, in order to allow a satisfactory possession. Certain characteristics assumed by entities are reflected in the body of the medium in the form of body postures. This is due to the use of the corresponding chakras that are more connected to the line[7] in question.*[8]

One of the explanations for the convex posture of the *Pretos-Velhos* is that certain entities *use the sacral or genetic chakra (also called the second chakra) more often, and that's why the medium bends when these entities act in their bodies. When they use this secondary chakra, all other chakras lose their function, becoming almost non-active and being used only for secondary functions, such as intermediations*[9].

This correspondence of chakras with postures is also found in the *Congado*: in the case of greeting, the movement of the hands is specifically directed to the parts of the body related to the heart, throat and third eye chakras, whereupon the vertical posture is well shaped.

We conclude that the individual embodies the posture from the attributes and functions of the entity or character that is manifested in his/her body. There is no tension in how the posture is shaped, and the entire body works within a proposed alignment.

---

7   Line: energy line where a certain entity is manifested.

8   Umbanda: Uma religião brasileira / Revista. São Paulo: Escala, ano I, n. 3. (Umbanda: A Brazilian religion / Magazine).

9   Umbanda: Uma religião brasileira / Revista. São Paulo: Escala, ano I, n. 3. (Umbanda: A Brazilian religion / Magazine).

Torso

This is a machinery of forces in which the pulses are left aside, so that seemingly chaotic movements may emerge. A careful look reveals a sophisticated elaboration that leads us to take into account the fact that there are several factors involved in each "moment" of the torso. The image we have of its mobility is sometimes a force that comes from the gut, but sometimes it shows a softness that sprouts from the skin's surface.

The *Capoeira* exhibits a torso that is agile and elastic in the execution of actions – a consequence of the instinctive heritage of surviving. Quick reflexes involve a gearing consisting of small punctuations, as if the torso were charged with electricity, becoming responsive to the lowest stimulation levels. The movements of the torso travel a range of amplitude, passing through movements of great contraction (such as vibrations and pulsations in certain parts corresponding to the vital centers) and expanding through the movements of greater projection (such as the "bridges" and "arches" in all directions of the torso in the space).

Listing the most distinct body actions present in the various Brazilian manifestations, we observed that the region of the shoulder blades often moves in alternation, favoring the release of the shoulders. This region also actively participates in the twists. With one of the shoulder blades as a reference, it is possible to verify that it is in opposition to its lower parts. In other words, they become related with their opposite sides; that is why their links with the feet or knees are very common. Frequent twists intensify the traction toward the center of the body, as this movement causes the torso to snake along the balance axis.

Shoulders gain contour and space characterized by the following movements: alternations between suspension and falling with slight continuous rotation, shakings, and vibrations.

In the region of the shoulder girdle, from the breastbone (the center of the flag), the arms are extended to the end of the fingers. This is an area of abundant joint mobility, where the movements of greater expression of the arms are related to the actions executed by the hands. In a number of occasions, the elbows work as the helm of the torso, angling and emphasizing the movements of punctuations in the various spatial directions. One of the meaningful movements of the arms results from the action of the elbows; when moved backwards, in flexion, they open the front of the torso; when returning forward, they enable the arms to move as if protecting the body. The torso does not close, it is contracted to keep the axis and to be subsequently projected.

Hands

Just like it occurs with the feet, the movements of the hands use the range of possibilities that this part of the body offers. Its essential function (apprehension) is present in a wide range of gestural forms, for example, in the *Shango* dances in which the hands, materializing the imaginary through the movement, remove granites from the body and release them into space.

The *Caboclo* snaps his fingers in the region of the mount of Venus: according to the *Umbanda*, this gesture is performed to adjust the entity to the medium's body:

> *Our hands have a huge amount of nerve terminals that communicate with each of the chakras of our body: 1. Thumb: sacral chakra; 2. Index: heart chakra; 3. Ring: base chakra; 4. Middle: crown chakra: 5. Baby Finger: throat chakra; 6. Approximately an inch below the middle finger in the center of the palm: solar-plexus chakra, 7. Below the solar-plexus chakra, just before the wrist, brow chakra.*[10]

We observed that these points of the hands – active in the moving forms of the individual incorporating the entity – are related to the plexus that provides the determining quality of the entity. In the *Caboclo*, the hands take the form of a bow and arrow, represented by the opening and stretching of the thumb and index finger associated with the sacral and heart chakras (that are related to this entity). During this movement, all other fingers remain closed.

As sensitive receptors, the hands acquire a movement shape that characterizes an archetype. This shape results from the unification of energetic points in the physical structure related to the incorporation of the *orishas*. Let us examine one of these archetypes.

Ogoun, whose hands and arms turn into swords "that cut demands and open ways", assumes – during this movement of cutting – the side of the right hand in contact with the palm of the left hand, moving directly toward the solar-plexus chakra, and thus referring to the performance of this *orisha*. Another corresponding point lies in the fact that in the war dance of *Ogoun* the movement of hands, resembling a sword before being thrown to space, is developed toward the other plexus located in the torso and related to *Ogoun's* posture.

The expressive movements of hands are determined by the actions that characterize the *orisha*. *Iansã*, aiming to expel the *eguns* (wandering souls), develops the action of continuous pushing. Its hands start moving to the front, where the act of

---

10 Umbanda: Uma religião brasileira / Revista. São Paulo: Escala, ano I, n. 3. (Umbanda: A Brazilian religion / Magazine).

pushing follows a rhythm and dynamics that become parts of its characteristics: wind and storm.

The plasticity of the manual form is also connected to an element of nature: the hands of *Yemanja* are under the sea, its habitat; its flat hands open the waters, enabling the body to pass through and drawing the magnitude of the sea. *Oshun*, the *orisha* of rivers and waterfalls, develops smooth hand movements working in fresh waters; fingers are closed and palms are curved inwards. The element of earth, commonly associated with *Eshu*, is modified by it, as its hands become claws and perform this movement of digging the soil.

The sense of the polarity between earth and sky – as well as the integration of these opposites – is substantially placed by the hands in the ritualistic circle. When one hand points to the earth and the other to the sky, they rotate in a dynamic manner; then, the movement initiated in the hands begins to interact with the arms, in spiral, until it reaches the whole body.

In the territories of *Umbanda* and *Candomblé*, the language of hands is more intense, but several hand expressions are present in other manifestations. They consist of categories of shapes that integrate the movement in the body unit and visibly interfere in the muscle tone.

Correlatively, the hands collect what lies in the space around them and express what is stored in the body.

In the magical manipulation of objects, the hands make use of symbols: the *Maracatu* spears, the *Congado* sticks, the *Folias* flag, among others. The hands seem to expand as a result of mastering the movement towards the targeted object.

In codified or spontaneous salutations, the hands present a sharp touch in the region of the heart followed by the projections upward, downward, and toward the points of symbolic power, giving and receiving different meanings. Delimitating the top of the mast, the hands touch head (forehead and neck simultaneously).

Head

Devotees and *filhos-de-santo* tell us that the Holy lives in the head. Belonging to an energy crown consisting of the brow, solar-plexus, and crown chakras, the head is often related to the superior connections. As the bearer of mental forces, this area of the body promotes a range of physical sensations that are reflected in the movements, whose proportions vary according to the intensity of the interchange between what is inside and what is outside.

The gesture of "banging the head" is more than a greeting; it signifies surrendering to divine forces and establishing the union of the inner and the outer side. At the beginning of the rituals, this gesture is represented by the contact of the head with symbolic objects and spaces, aggregating divine power. The movement is performed in a timid manner, but it can expand in a way that involves the impulsion of the whole body. The person is thrown to the ground and, before the symbol, first touches the ground with the head, and subsequently does the same thing with entire body.

The relationships established by the gaze are critical to the head posture:

The mozambiqueiro dances looking downwards, head down, because humbleness is the power of the mozambiqueiro.[11]

But when the *mozambiqueiros* and the other *foliões* of the Divine run through the paths, the gaze reaches the horizon and the head focuses on the top of the mast.

When the gaze is introjected, the head movements are the natural consequence of the impulses coming from various parts of the body. During or after the incorporations, the gaze is introjected; the head surrenders to the dynamics of the movement forms.

Both the meaning and the direction of the head-mast's movement integrate it with its own top, resulting in different combinations of movements: the head goes upwards in small circles, then leans to the side and diagonals, without tensioning the cervical vertebrae.

The head, in its position of pride when upwards or in a humble posture when downwards, moves between these polarities through rotations and punctuations.

From the head, where the sacred lies, we return to the unity of this body: the psychic energy expands through the torso, splits in the belly, and reaches the ground from the representations set by the feet.

---

11 Sebastiana, captain of Mozambique, Bom Despacho (MG), 1987.

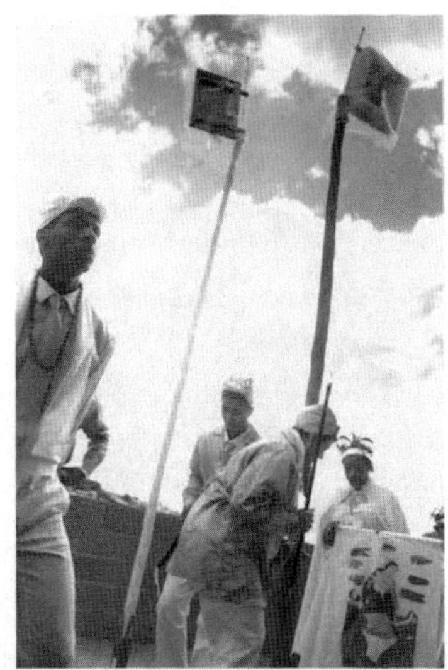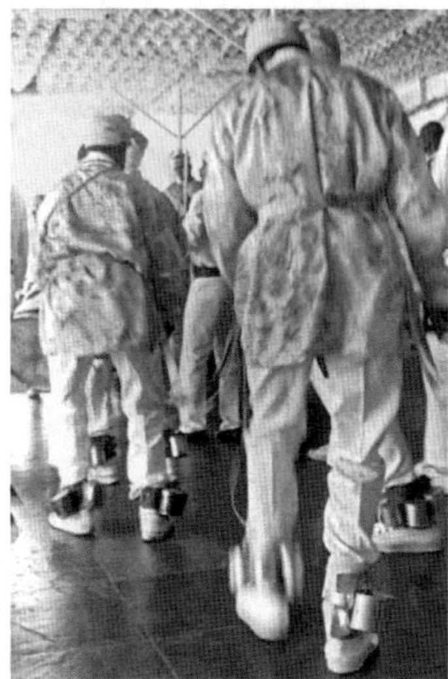

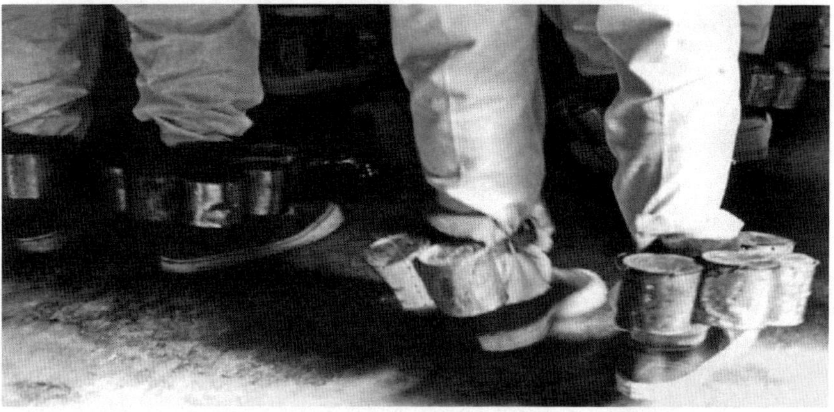

Above on the left:
Mastro hasteado - Festa do Divino Espírito Santo
Pirenópolis - GO 1994 (Hoisted Mast - Divine Holy Spirit Festivity).
Author's archive.

Above on the right:
Mastro hasteado no terreiro de Dona Efigênia (Hoisted Mast in Ms. Efigenia's terreiro)
Festa de Nossa Senhora do Rosário - Belo Horizonte, MG - 1996 (Our Lady of the Rosary Festivity).
Photo Eustáquio Neves.

Below:
Pés com gangas, 1996 *(Feet with gangas).*
Photo Eustáquio Neves.

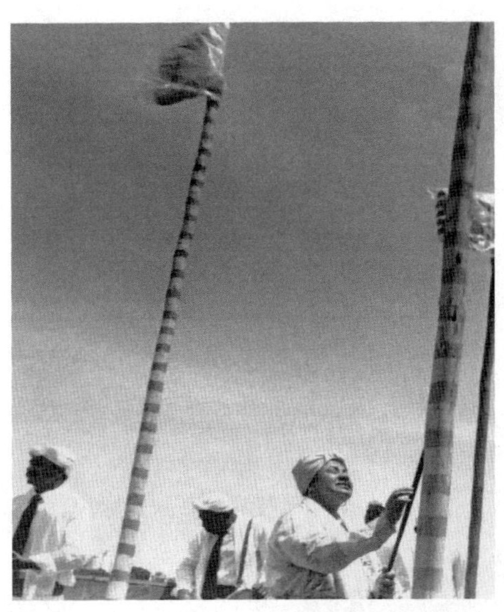

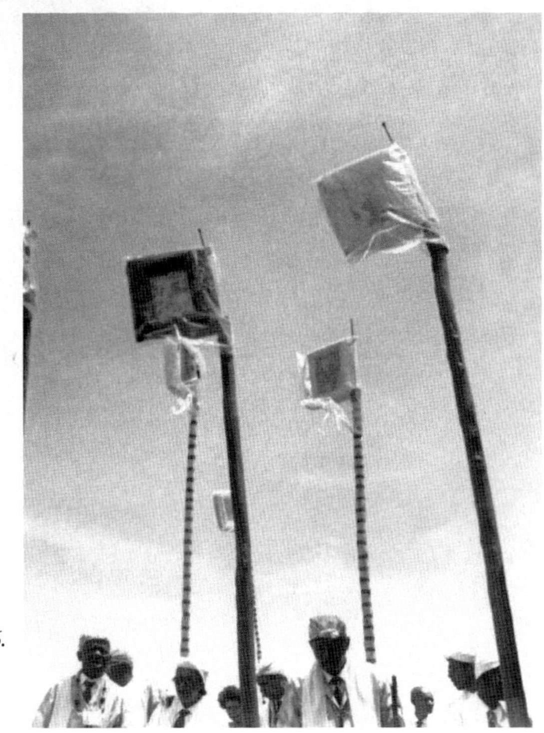

Festa de Nossa Senhora do
Rosário *(Our Lady of the*
Rosary Festivity)
Terreiro de Dona Efigênia 1996.
Belo Horizonte - MG
(Ms. Efigenia's Mozambique).
Photos Eustáquio Neves.

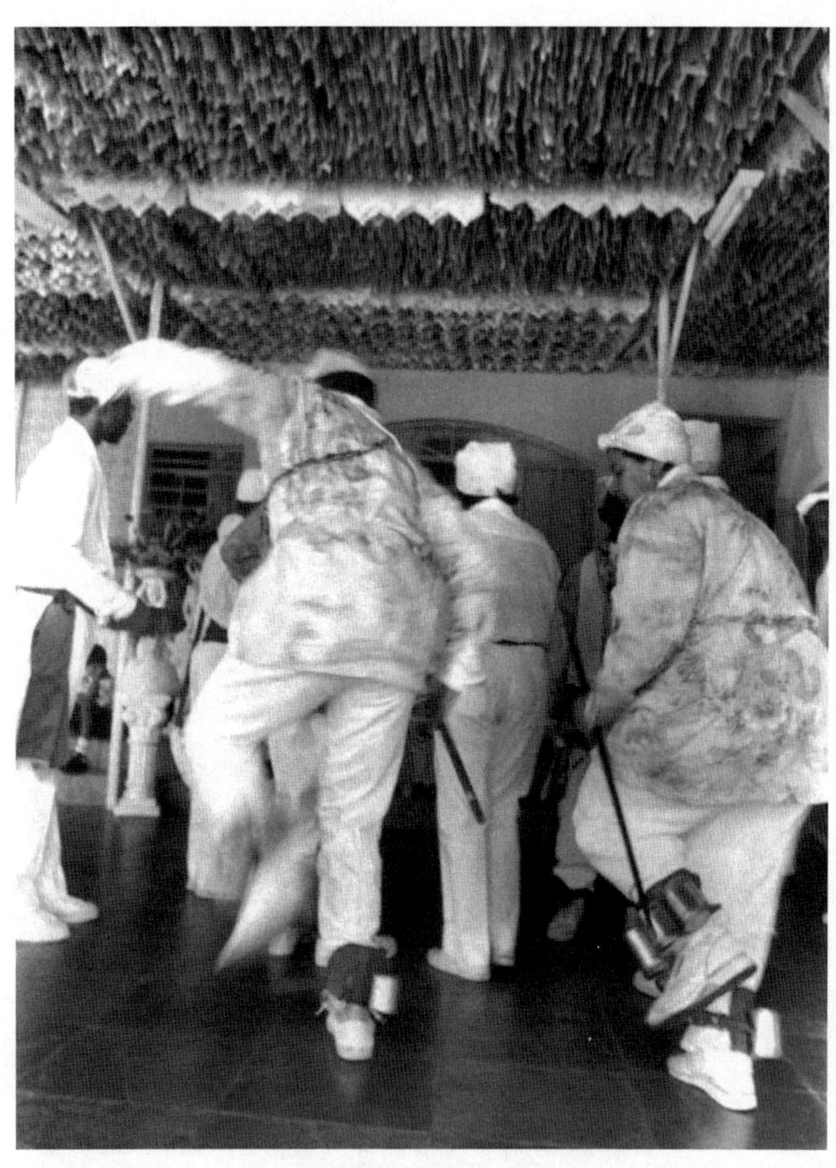

Moçambique de Dona Efigênia
Belo Horizonte - MG
(Ms. Efigenia's Mozambique).
Photo: Eustáquio Neves.

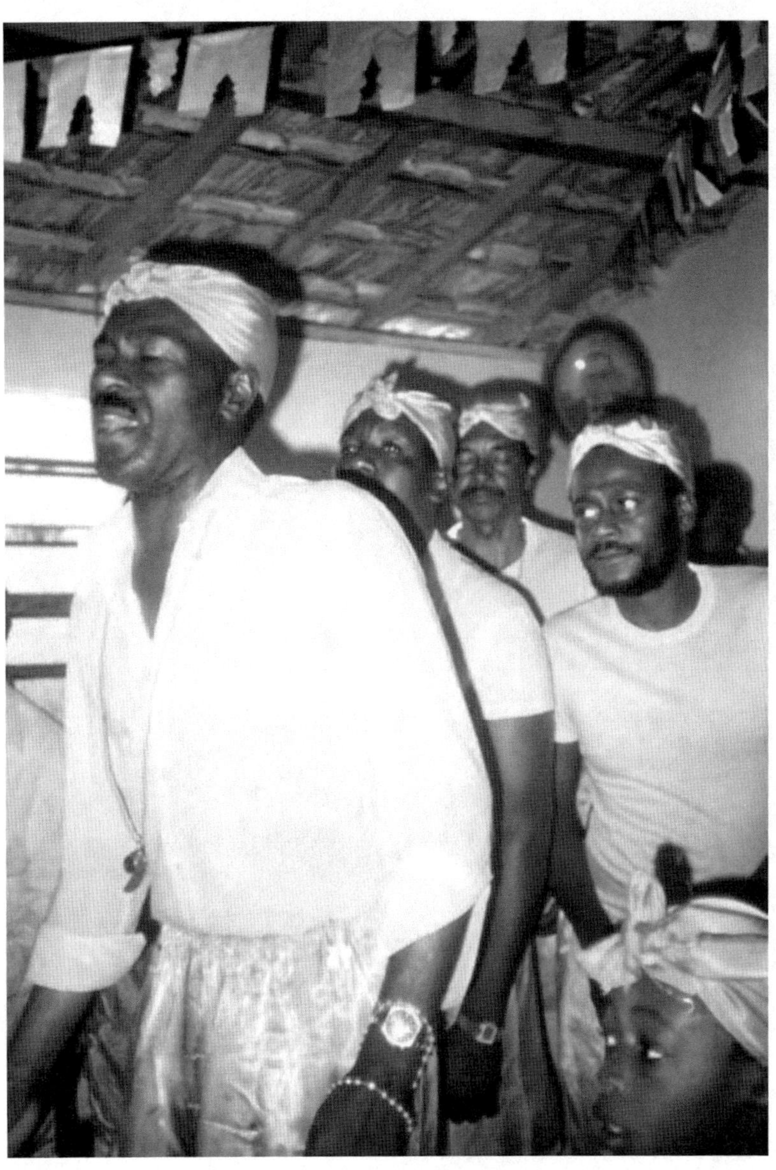

Capitão Joaquim (*Captain Joaquim*)
Guarda de moçambique dos Arturos,
Contagem - MG.
Photo: Eustáquio Neves.

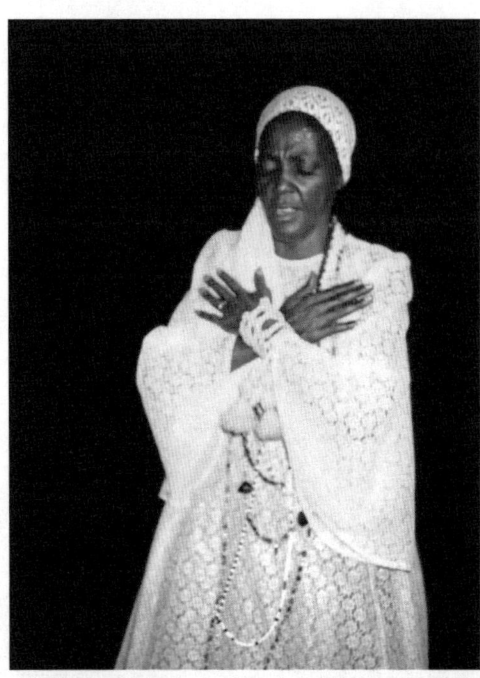

Sebastiana, *umbandista and captain of Mozambique, Bom Despacho, MG - 1987.*
Author's archive.

Saudação ao congá, *Terreiro de Umbanda*
Pai Joaquim de Aruanda
Brasília, DF - 1988
(Hail to conga, Father Joaquim's terreiro)
Author's archive

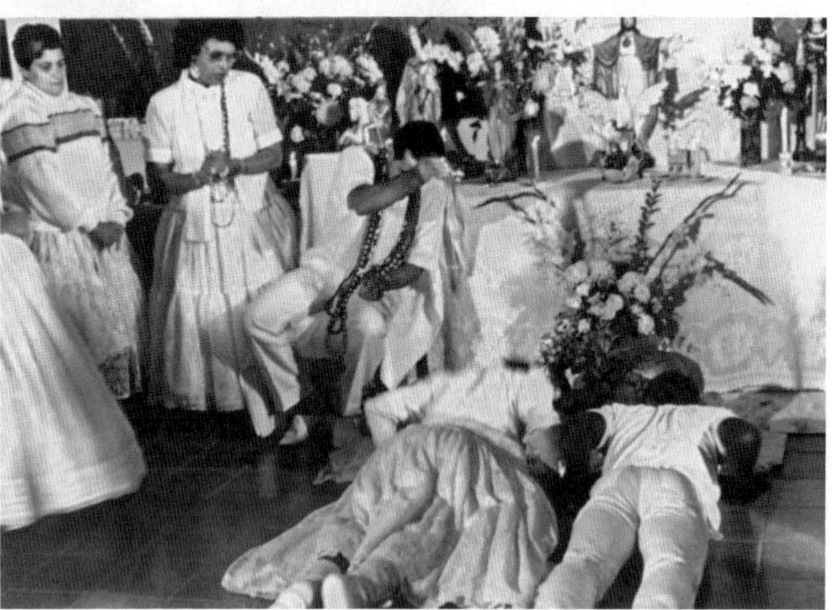

72

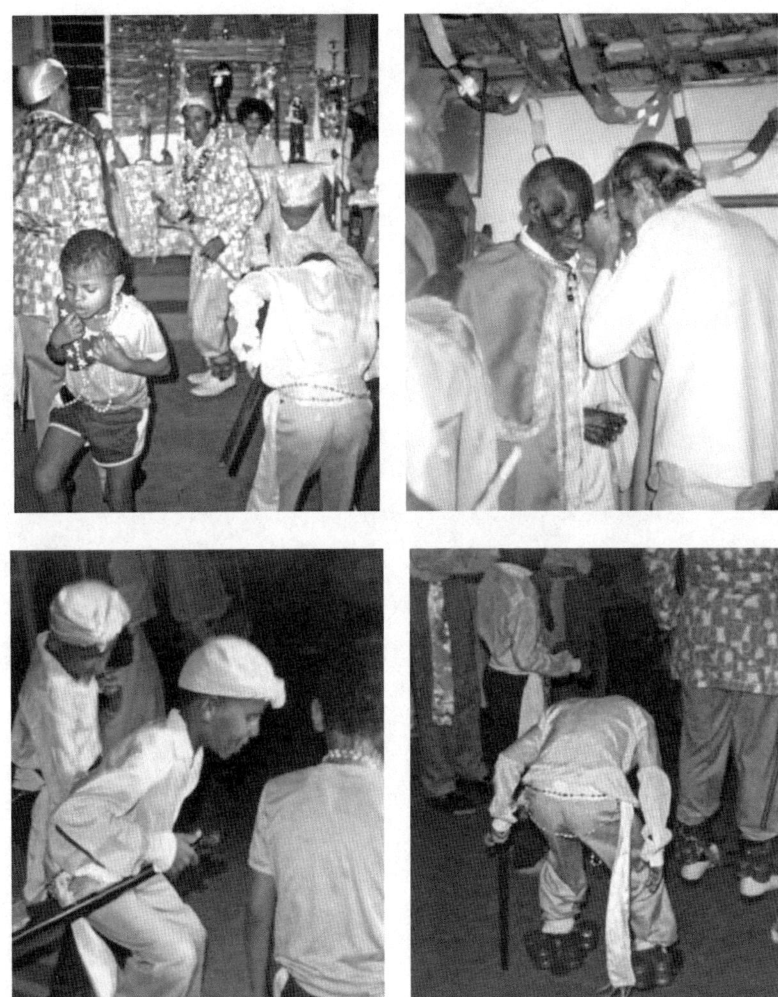

Perpendicular posture.
Above on the right:
Congado dos Arturos - 1987
Author's archive.

Above on the left and below:
Moçambique de Dona Efigênia
Belo Horizonte - MG 1987 (Ms. Efigenias's Mozambique).
Author's archive.

Convex posture.

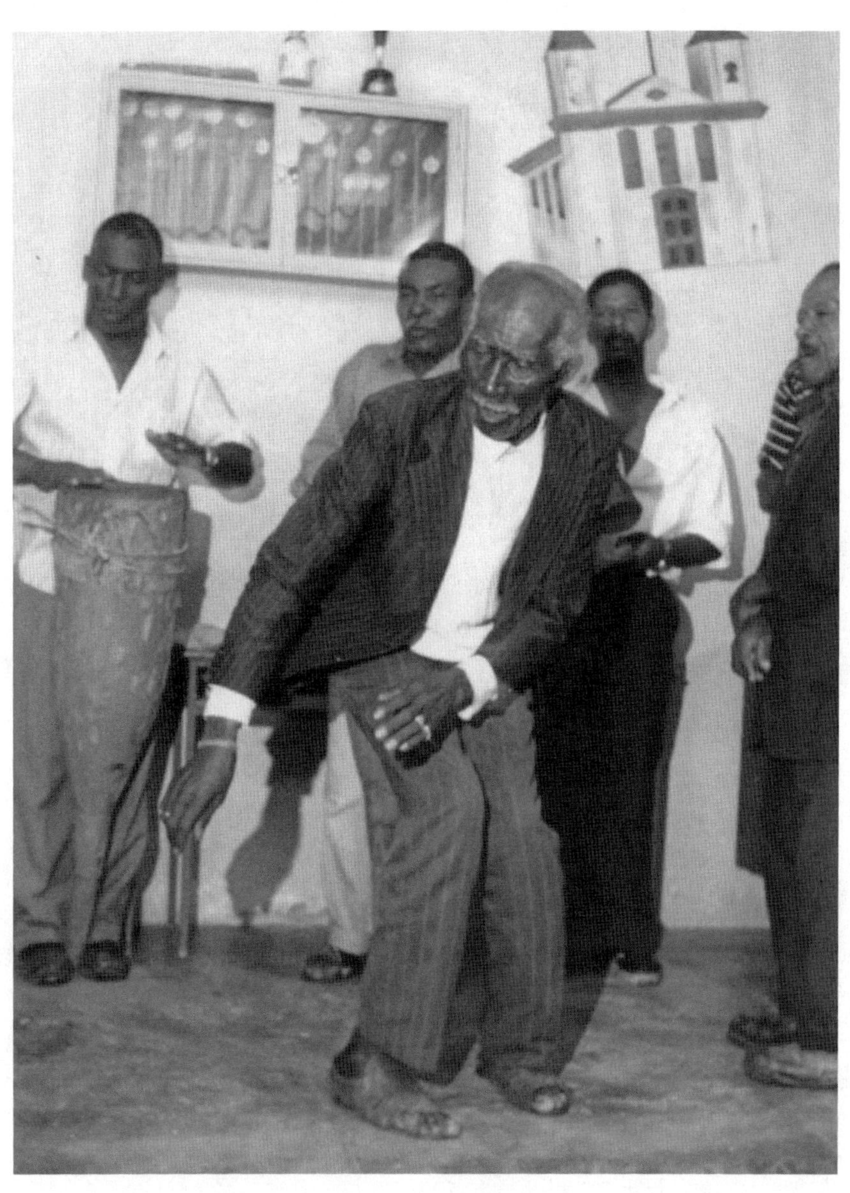

Candombe dos Arturos
1996
Photo: Eustáquio Neves

5 Passages of Sensitivity – The Inner Movement

The inner movement was one of the most exciting aspects observed in our research; it explains a lot about the meanings of dance movements. In the community of Arturos, their inner dance was evident in their *Congado*. The conversation with the captains of Arturos reveals the connection between life and the dancing body:

> *Um pouquinho que eu sofri … a gente vai sentindo …*
> *(The little bit I suffered … we can feel…).*[1]

The breaks are filled with memories of the slavery period. At this very moment, Antonio turns his eyes to the ground. Then, his eyes rise and reach horizons:

> *Alembrei do tempo véio*
> *Esse tempo já se foi*
> *Essa gunga num é minha*
> *Essa inguma é de vovô*
> *É inguma do Rosaro*
> *Foi vovô que me ensinô*
> *Todo mundo chora gunga*
> *Eu também quero chorá*
> *Essa gunga vem de longe*
> *Ela vem de bera-mar*
> *Aí meu Deus, tô no meio do mar marinhero,*
> *O que será de mim, oh meu Deus*
>
> *(I remembered the old times*
> *Those times are gone*
> *This gunga isn't mine*
> *This inguma is grandpa's*
> *This is Rosaro's inguma*
> *Grandpa taught me*
> *Everybody cries gunga*
> *I also want to cry it*
> *This gunga comes from far away*
> *It comes from the shoreline*

---

1 Captain Antonio (Congado dos Arturos), 1987.

Oh my God, I'm in the middle of sea, oh sailor
What will happen to me, oh my God)[2]

In the course of the memories emerging in the images of the chants, the body of the *congadeiro* is transported to feel the other, the one who represents the enslaved ancestral. The received inheritance consists of a mixture of pain, longing, melancholy, and revolt; but the devotee filters and transforms it into strength to overcome his/her own legacy.

In the *Congado*, Our Lady of the Rosary centralizes faith enabling each individual – with the group's strength (living and dead) – to belong to a given space in the great *gira* of the world symbolized by Mary's rosary:

> *Our Lady calls me … In Mary's Rosary, let's sail*[3] *"That's the best thing in my life, I will die in the drums of Mary's rosary, if it is God's will. We pray for Our Lady of the Rosary, Preto Velho, Maria Conga, Mother Mary, Father Joaquim … we make a deal with all of them … Our main influence is Our Lady of the Rosary. We stay there … with our memories.*[4]

Our research repeatedly led us to an immense heart connecting together various manifestations and aggregating a cultural resistance. In each one of them there was a story that placed and characterized the festivity in question:

> *Maracatu is a story of the fields, created in the slave houses by the people working in the fields (cortadô de cana, tiradô de quadra, cambiteiro, carreiro, mestre de açúca, ciscadô de bagaço). There is a certain energy in that field … Maracatu was born from the sugarcane bagasse.*[5]

The *bagasse* is a residue, an essence from which the body is extracted. In the *maracatuzeiro* aggressive and sexual senses are merged, and there is an alternation between the states of stupor and readiness. The quiet man, when invested with this body, becomes a dazzling warrior.

Either in the *Congado*, in the *Maracatu*, or in the *Umbanda giras*, the body is shaped by an inner journey located in the developments presented by each festivity. The warrior emerges in every celebration, because the stories notably marked by oppression have boosted and generated festivities. *Observing the religiousness of the poor and the black people in America, we find that the ability to celebrate in a casual manner is more frequently seen among the populations to whom neither suffering nor oppression is unfamiliar. These things suggest that the real celebration*

---

2   Mozambique's chant.
3   Mozambique's chant.
4   Testimony of José Francisco Lourenço candombeiro from Fidalgo (MG). 1987. 1987.
5   Testimony of Master Salustiano (Maracatu Rural Piaba de Ouro, Tabajara.PE). 1992.

does not disappear against tough reality, injustice and evil, but it is materialized in the most authentic way, recognizing and overcoming these negative realities instead of avoiding them.[6] The spaces of the festivities are the battle fields where victory must be achieved. Therefore, the war becomes a festivity that is the war itself.

The period preceding the festivity day is marked by preparations and rituals that take a long time, so that the foundations may be established and reaffirmed. The foundations are precepts: they generate knowledge on the origin and reasons of the existence and permanence of each manifestation. Regardless of the manifestation, this is the moment in which, within this context, the body and space are prepared. Actions denote expressive movements without any purpose of exhibition. Gestures are filled with intensity, as that is the moment when people absorb the foundations through various work dynamics. The action and gesture represent the strength, which means that they gradually receive the body foundations. The dance movement is prepared from the contact with an original world, acquiring a coded language and being exposed to this world whose daily life is full of threats. Softness allied to certain strength originating from an elaborated inner path is observed in these ritualistic gestures that are performed before the festivity: *We have no Macumba, we have Worship.*[7]

By entering the festivity, we see an inner dance that the eyes cannot see otherwise than through something identified as a magical thing. Along with the performers of this dance, we found that there is a process, or even a method, resulting in this magic. Three aspects interact in this inner path: (1) memories, with their fields of images; (2) the movement of emotions and affections; and (3) sensations. Once this path from the inside out is executed, there is also the reverse movement, or, more precisely, the movements generated by the chants, the music, and the invested objects. The path travelled in the present time and space thereby returns to people's heart as a materialization that motivates and confirms the sense of being alive.

Going back to the time when each person was placed in the festivity, we found that their initial actions were aimed at breaking with the everyday world; these ritual-actions aimed to achieve a state of emptiness, neutrality and concentration. This was an individualized moment, even if the person was engaged in a group action. When preparing the space, tuning of the instruments or even during inaction – when the person remains in silence in a corner – an internal change is

---

6   *Harvey Cox* - A festa dos foliões - um ensaio teológico sobre festividade e fantasia, (The Feast of Fools: A Theological Essay on Festivity and Fantasy), *1974.*

7   Divina, candombeira from Jaboticatubas (MG), 1988. The reference to the word Macumba is used in a negative sense, related to black magic.

processed. In *Umbanda* and *Candomblé*, many of these actions are well defined as they are explicit parts of the foundations. The herb bath is an example. It is used to remove the impurities of the body in order to open the chakras, consequently strengthening the matter. It is an act involving the perception of the person's own body. This and other preparations are deemed essential to receive the *orisha*.

Invocations are marked by the internal actions of commitment, moved by faith and affection. This moment is foreshadowed by chants, music and movements, according to the language of each manifestation.

The memories punctuate all the steps arising from a collective memory, whose values substantiate each festivity. The stories are always related to family relationships, as if they were the mediation to reach the Divine. These stories often travel to the time space of the origins:

> *Originally, the orisha is a deified ancestor that, in life, established bonds to ensure a control over certain forces of nature, such as thunder, wind, etc. The transition of these exceptional beings, the holders of a powerful asé, from their earthly life to the condition of orisha usually occurs in a moment of passion, whose legends preserved these memories... These deified ancestors would not have a natural death... They would undergo a metamorphosis in those times of emotional crisis caused by wrath and other violent feelings. What was matter in their bodies disappeared, burned by this passion, leaving only this asé, pure energy state.*[8]

When an *orisha* is on the earth embodied in one of its *filhos-de-santo*, we witness this strength in the body. However, any detailed description of the movement does not reveal to which extent the body is taken. The body sweats, snorts, increases in volume and width. It expands itself. There are pulsations, dynamos, backward movements and impulses. This whole body-emotion makes us astonished before we are able to understand anything.

Through the masters, the holy image guardians, and the captains we obtained various reports of images bringing detailed descriptions of scenes which were part of their dreams and which could be strongly experienced during the festivity. These internal images affect the emotional force, whose release causes physical sensations. The whole body starts to vibrate an inner process. This is the subtle energy field related to the movements, a language of sensations pronounced before the representation of forms. Different sensations of chills, warmth, pricking, tingling, among others, are felt strongly in the the whole body or its specific parts. In the festivities, whereby the incorporation occurs, these feelings are attributed to the proximity of the entities that the person receives in his or her body:

---

8   *Pierre Fatumbi Verger* - Orixás: Deuses Iorubás na África e no Novo Mundo, (Orisha: les Dieux Yoruba En Afrique et ao Nouveau Monde) 1981.

In the manifestations without incorporations, sensations are often related to a contact of the person with the forces coming from the ancestors and saints of devotion.

The physical sensations are not always considered pleasant. When they are repressed, people complain about the pain in their heads, backs, or other body parts, wishing to experience them in a more satisfactory manner. After these energies pass (when the person does not suppress them), a feeling of well-being is eventually reached.

In the overflow of emotions like aggression, fear, and rebellion, their expressions are not always fully transparent, as they occur within a dynamics in which they soon change. The feeling of devotion ("dedicate yourself to someone or an entity") becomes complex in this part of the inner path. Devotion here is presented as a major force element, because it enables the devotee to overcome the boundaries of the oppressive space and build another space in which the feelings of freedom and equality are achieved.

Salve o Cruzeiro do Sul
Aonde os anjos tem que rezá
Onde os filho chora de tristeza
E as alma vem nos consolá
Levantei coroá, levantei coroei
Vamo pelo ar, vamo pelo ar ...

(Hail the Southern Cross
Where the angels have to pray
Where children cry of sorrow
And the souls come in comfort
Raised crown, raised crowned
Let's go through the air, let's go through the air...)[10]

The organization of the festivity takes a long period. All times and locations are important because they are parts of a journey during which people embody the roots of the festivity. The roots of the festivities are in the displacement of emotions and affections; hope is the core that enables the transformations from death to life.

---

9   Testimony of Carlos Alberto da Costa (Umbanda - DF) 1995.
10   Congada's chant - Arturos.

Usually related to the healing of diseases, the promises occur in a number of festivities. The person promises to "play" in a given *folguedo* or fulfill the obligation through a ritual. Having a *Boi* as a promise (related to St John) or being a king in the *Congado* (linked to Our Lady of the Rosary) are examples. During the festivity, the *promisers* – either at the time of making or paying a vow – assimilate the forces of the festivity assisted by *foliões* or *filhos-de-santo* that intercede with the Divine.

On the day assigned for the celebration it is possible to see the result and the completion of all the works previously performed. Therefore, it is not a mere public presentation, it is a meaningful act: it is the sharing of the strength and the *axé* with everyone that is present. The dances, songs and chants are the emanations of these forces.

At the end of the festivity (it may last for days), people are found to be much more energized than tired. In fact, they are invigorated:

> *The meaning of João do Mato is work, union. The memories… the heart… it beats faster. A great strength seems to exist, and work is not tiresome at all.*[11]

The old masters refer to the progressive loss of the fundamentals. This is demonstrated by the absence of preparations and the consequent fragmentation of the festivity. As for the quality of the movement, we observed a substantial loss that we attributed to the fact that the body no longer has a response coming from the inside. The dance ceases to be shared in order to be exhibited. In these cases, the external factor becomes more important and the festivity gets out of its context and place to become a "folkloristic demonstration". We witnessed several groups with impeccable costumes, a meticulous choreography, and everyone knew the history of their origin and development. However, their bodies had nothing to say, they just played, as if the images and memories no longer circulated through the body.

A significant cut

In the Valley of Jequitinhonha (MG) we met a *Boi de Janeiro* that stubbornly survived. In the backyard of the house, the doll *Maria Tereza* and the structures of the *Boi* lied near the garbage, dressed with poor dresses and adorned with old papers. Alfredo, the owner of the *Boi*, told us he did not know anything about it, except that it was a mission: *I received this Boi from my father, as an inheritance. My grandfather already did it. It is my duty to continue.* There was poverty

---

11 Testimony of João Batista da Luz - Arturos, 1987.

all around and people were seemingly apathetic. Each one took his or her place in a slow, concentrated time: the *Boi, Maria Tereza* – each one taking his or her instrument. The snares began to beat, the movement was shaking the dust and life was sprouting. The *Boi* went out to the streets as it always happened in the past. But today it is not received in the houses and even the local population did not want to share the celebration. There was no great visual appeal, the music and the movements were simple. However, a pulse remained in those bodies along with a surprising strength: the bodies were connected to an inheritance that sharpened their senses. There was a certain quality in movement, as a story amidst wreckage and indifference still permeated the body of every *folião*.

It was observed that in the transition of the sensitive there are several levels scaled between unconsciousness and consciousness. In all of them, there is an inner availability linked to the commitment of the person to perform a task. This is marked by the integrity of the person, as he or she exhibits his or her own inner reality, irrespective of its acceptance by the external environment. The movements extracted from this body have particular value.

The fundamentals imbued with secrets are passed on to those people who are able to keep and take them forward. It is a learning process that enables the receiver to open his or her inner journey. Thus, there is an elaborate process from which the images in their minds gain representation in the body, outlining the vibrations, sensations and feelings.

As for the secrets, it is up to the researchers to deduce their meanings when we dive in the communication of the body. A body inducing us to find the secret passages of a movement originating from memories.

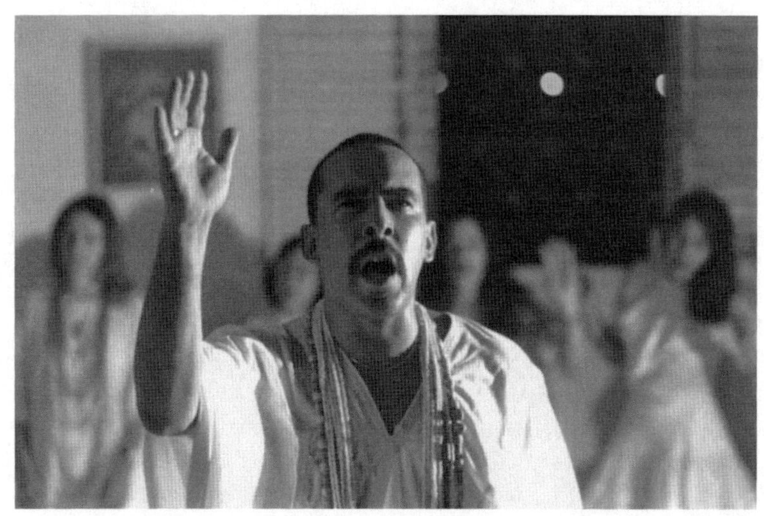

Pai de Santo *Carlos Alberto da Costa*
Brasília DF - 1995
Photo: Juan Pratginesto's

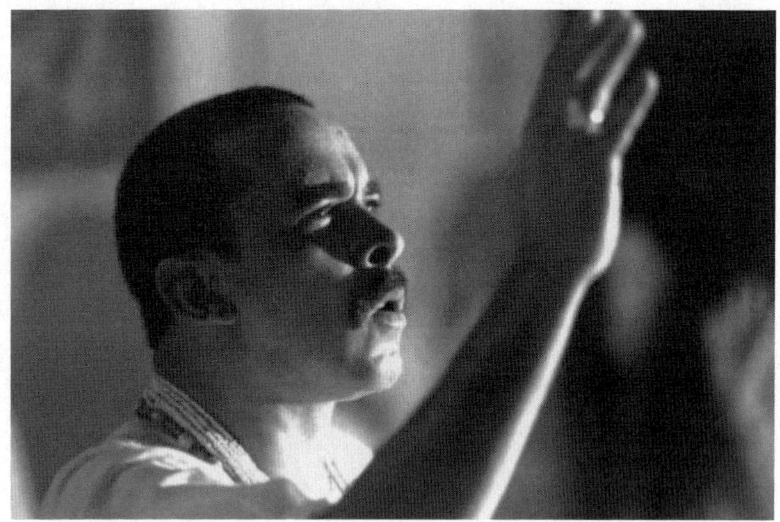

Pai de Santo *Carlos Alberto da Costa*
Brasília DF - 1995
Photo: Juan Pratginesto's

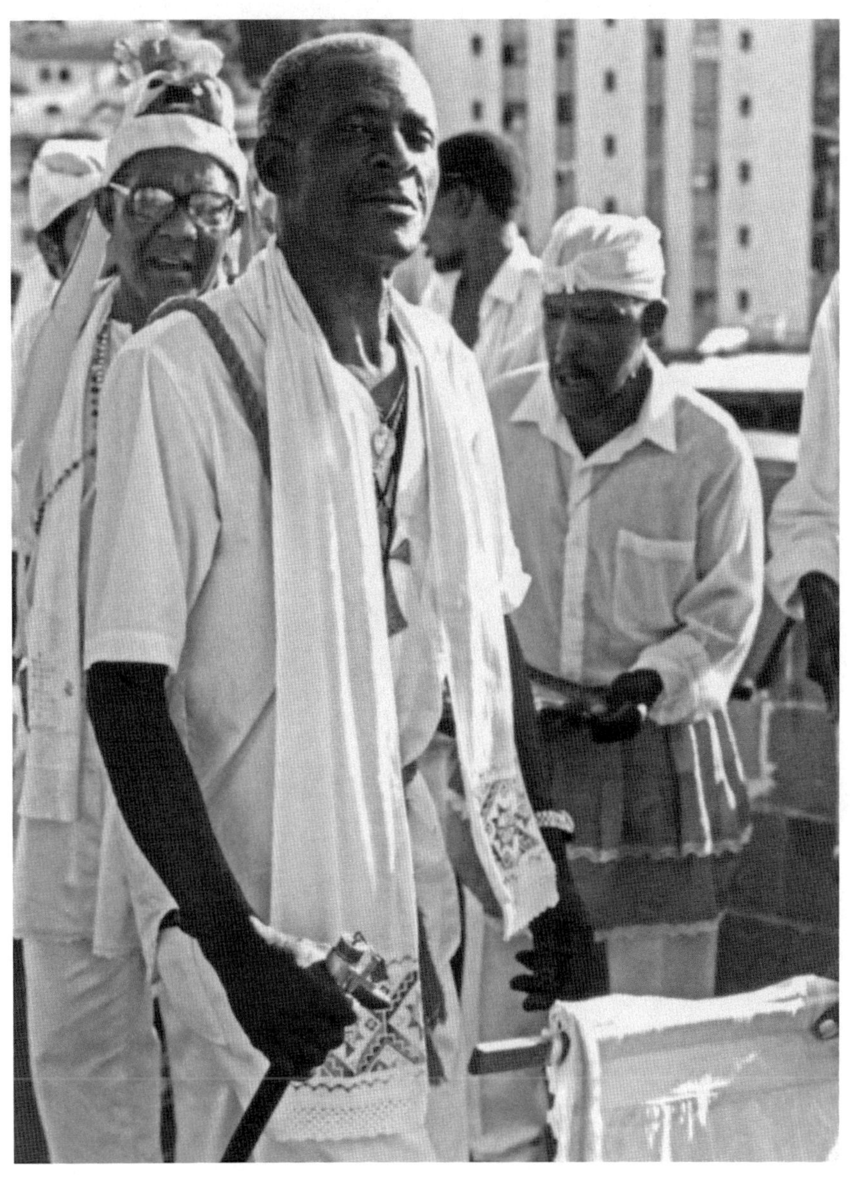

Antônio - Capitão do Congado dos Arturos
1996
Photo Eustáquio Neves

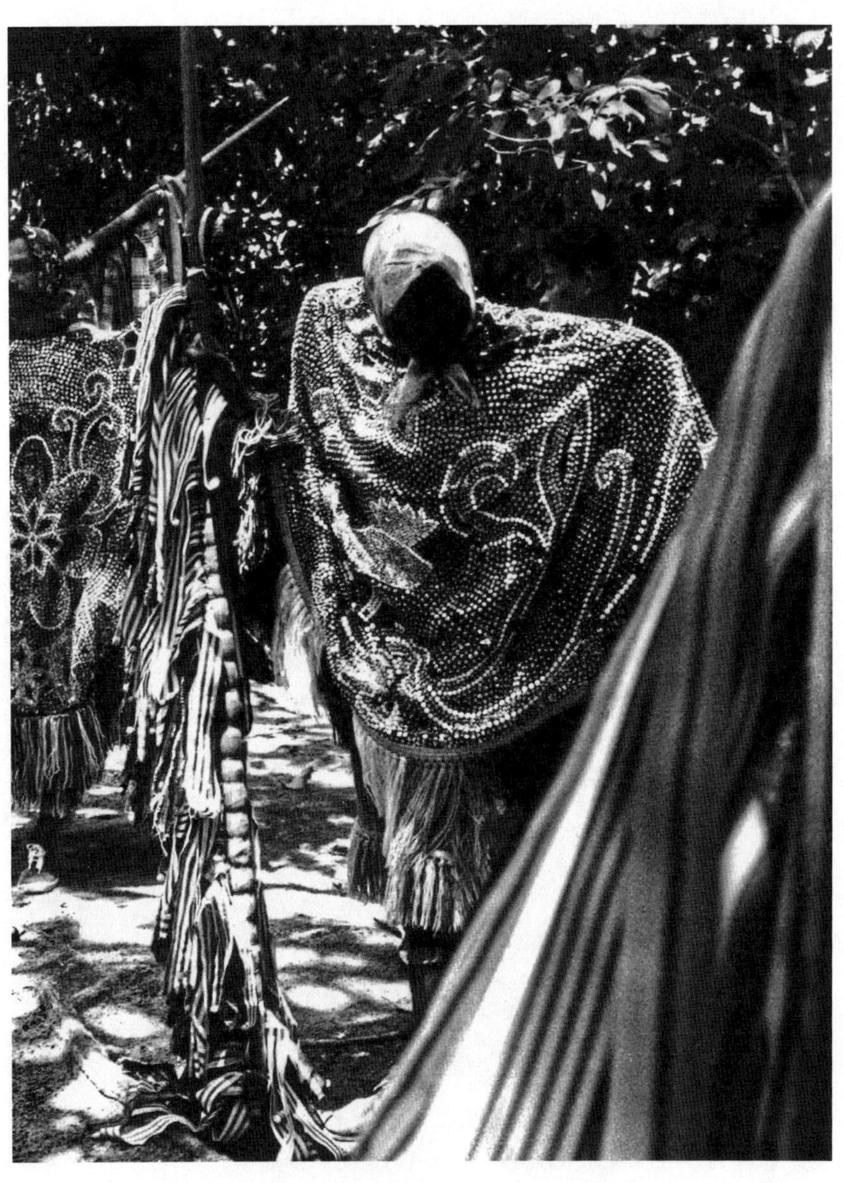

Caboclos de Lança
Maracatu Rural Piaba de Ouro
Tabajara PE - 1992
Photo: Author's archive

6 Features of the Form

Brazilian cultural manifestations have different forms, with distinct regional accents. The investigations and experiences of several of them, shared with our body in the dance, led us to infer their main features. We point out some of these features that are important tools for the dance practice and for the view aiming at a continuous discovery.

6.1 Essential factors of the forms

Essential factors of the forms consist in the conditions that the body acquires in the broad context of form. The senses in the body, the pulse, and the acts of driving and punctuating up to the acquisition of a dynamo, characterize an approach that is present in different manifestations of popular culture.

In practical terms, we have observed the need of a systematic work on these factors in order to enable the development of the form of this Brazilian body.

6.1.1 The senses in the body

Our researches emphasize the importance of muscle tension levels, an indivisible factor of the movement forms. In this movement, the relationship of the body with the environment translates a life story.

Across the network of popular culture manifestations (the main focus of the research), their performers present a life story that reveals the need to resist to many clashes. First of all, they are the warrior bodies. Experiencing them as characters, it is observed that the body only fits the form when it acquires density – an increased tonus with elasticity. The life-festivity meanings are articulated through the movement, causing the body to relax and commit. Its premise is the "tonus of resistance" that is mobilized with the "tonus of support".[1]

---

1 Professor Klaus Viana, in his practical dance classes, applied the terms "resistance" and "support", to distinguish the quality of movements when these were performed with the intent of the muscles and the intention of the bones, respectively. Experiencing these issues as a student the different qualities of tonus became clear, helping me to research in my own body and in reading the bodies of the others. Therefore we use "resistance" and "support" to describe some levels of muscle tension as those are words related to the execution of the movement in the body.

It was also found at every festivity that there is a group of people sustaining the fundamentals – as if retaining them in their bodies – and a group boosting them, articulating the meanings through their bodies that carry out the most extrovert movements. In the dynamics of their dances, we witnessed the dialogue between retaining and articulating. We observed that these aspects materialize the festivity and that, through the tonus, each person embodies and materializes it, too. Therefore, one may say that the materialization of the tonus is the action of embodying the senses.

In the *mozambiqueiro*'s body there is a predominance of the "tonus of resistance", while in the body of the *Congo* dancer we found a predominance of the "tonus of support"; they are imbued with the roles of their respective *guardas*. The *guarda* of *Congo* has the role to lead the way, prepare it and make it more dynamic. The *Congo* pulls the *Mozambique* consisting in the *guarda* that brings the crown, the saint, and the fundamentals of the rosary devotees.

The *bandeireira* of the *Folia de Reis* holds in her body the flag and the Three Wise Men; disguised as clowns, they boost the space ahead with their acrobatic feats. At times, the *bandeireira* (flag carrier) looses her movement and uses body movements with the "tonus of support" to show the flag. Meanwhile, the clowns remain concentrated, maintaining the fundamentals at specific points of their bodies, resisting.

The characteristics and the nature of each *orisha* representation makes it clear how much the tonus acts in their identification. Among other aspects, it was observed that the "tonus of resistance" is incorporated in the body that receives *Shango* (the one bringing justice), while the "tonus of support" incorporates in the body that receives *Oshosi* (the one bringing balance between man and nature).

The outcomes of the research led to the following interpretations:

In the "tonus of resistance" the muscle action is a protection, safeguarding and defending the body from the external environment. In the intention of the body to resist there is a force of restraint and the movement flow is under control. The body presents a dense image. The performance of these movements identified with this tonus in the field research revealed an intention of the body to sharply penetrate the space. Although the reference of this tonus is in the perception of the muscle, in its maximum level we felt like if the bone were "piercing the flesh".

In the "tonus of support" the action of the muscles isto find a support, having a reference of density in the space surrounding the body, with the predominance of a quick change in the support of the muscle groups used during the movement. There is an extroversion in the nature of the movement, showing that the free flow is active. Upon experiencing this tonus through these movements it was observed that the reference lies in the perception of the bone, particularly through the joints.

In the stories told by this body there is an evident load of drama, providing an immediate response of muscle intensity. Gradually, it reduces and modulates the expressions drawn by the movement in the body without losing its essential character, that is, resistance. In the low tonus moments, the body is in a state of readiness, revealing the presence of resistance even when the body may seem surrendered, absorbed due to its attitude.

6.1.2 Pulse

The body pulsates, throbs, senses

The first beats of the drums, the tambourine, snares, and many other instruments sound with their tones, rhythms, and musical constructions, vibrating in the space-time of the festivity, following the path of the *Congado*, the *Boi*, the *ciranda* (Brazilian dance and musical style), the wave of the *frevo* (Brazilian dance and musical rhythm) … The instrument prompts the body to pulsate.

The pulse constitutes the music vibrations which are captured by the body in the visceral and diaphragm regions and which radiate to the solar plexus until it takes over the whole body. Initially, there is an air filling, as if the torso were opening its spaces to receive the pulse. There is expansion and retraction in the diaphragm region, drawing a specific throbbing image.

This initial movement, called pulse, enables the heating of joints and strengthens concentration of the body. The pulse is the heart of the movement, an establisher of the dynamics of each dance.

When the instruments start to be played, there is a unification of dancers and musicians through the pulse that acts as an internal generator providing force.

The varieties of pulses are related to the directions (inside out) of the body in relation to the space. Therefore, the pulse establishes the movement of the body's balance axis.

We assigned meanings to the pulses in the following way:

– Pulse vertically (mast-axis stressing). Ex.: *Mozambique* (MG), *Ciranda* (PE).
– Pulse horizontally (often associated with some dances of female *orishas* in which the pelvis performs the infinity symbol movement). Ex.: The *Candombe* (MG).
– Swinging pulse, to the sides (sustains the center of the body so that it allows for a movement of the legs on the sides without weight transfer). Ex.: *Caboclinhos* (PE).

– Swinging pulse, back and forth (torso front and back are equally stressed during the movement). Ex.: movement of the *caboclos* in the *Boi de Matraca* (MA).

When the pulse is well established (there are rituals where the pulse is worked for a long time), a strong presence is stressed throughout the body, as if the pulse were preparing the body for the in and out movement of impulses, flows and punctuations.

6.1.3 Acts of punctuating, impelling, and flowing

The performance of the body in its relationships with the movements is characterized by punctuations, impulses, and fluidity, a result of all its integrative actions (called *dynamo*).

Punctuating is when certain part of the body marks the space, involving a leaving and returning to the balance axis. The relations of contact of the feet with the ground stimulate the stressing of various body parts in the development of body language. Punctuating is often linked to the pace marked by the parties, drawing pauses that modulate the choreographic route in space.

Impulse is a release of an accumulated force that needs to come out from the body. The movement is directed at a specific point in space, involving the whole body, where certain parts draw the action that closes the process.

In the *Candombe*, it was observed that the impulse was a part of its structure, which is why it was predictable. When the captain of the *Candombe* enters the circle to sing, his movement is characterized by a single act of impelling. The act of silencing the drums also needs the impulse in the body of the captain in charge. The captain follows toward the drums; the act ends when the elbow, shoulder, or hand ceases one of the drums. The body models the instrument and one of the above-mentioned parts leans on it. Therefore, the cycle of starting and closing the chant, repeated throughout the duration of the *Candombe*, is characterized by the body through its impulses.

In the *sambadas* of the *Rural Maracatu* the impulse, as a structural element of the form, is similar. When the sound of the orchestra is interrupted, the *caboclos* are impelled to jump and fall, remaining on the ground. Then, there is the *loa*, the challenge chant of the Master. At the end, the *caboclos* are impelled to leave the ground, jumping or spinning, and then standing up again.

In the *Candombe*, the body of the captain determines the act of opening and closing a cycle; in the *Maracatu*, this pace is set by the music. However, impulse is a factor that characterizes the form of distinct manifestations.

Unpredictable impulse

The flag of the Divine arrived at the house of a woman who had no feet, only two stumps that she used to walk with difficulty. At a certain distance of the flag, she stopped. Her whole body was vibrating, moved by the encounter with the sacred. Within the same bars, she gained momentum and fell down on her knees, holding the flag.

It was observed that the impulse starts in the "core" of the body. To gain momentum, the individual has to reach this center and then go, in a single act, outwards; in these occasions, a specific part of the body stands out.

The dynamo

At certain times, the body enters a continuous flow of movements full of impulses and punctuations. The pulse is kept as if it were helping the breathing to regulate the amount of energy released in every movement. The sense that we found to locate this process resembles a conversion of mechanical energy into electrical energy, as the body becomes stronger. One movement consecutively generates the next one. The speed of this process in which there is an intertwining of internal and external movements occurs in a highly stimulated body, as the dynamo is established in the individual when he or she reaches the apex of his or her integration with all elements of the festivity; it is also harmonized with the participant's group. This fluidity process is usually developed during the days when the *giro* of the flag occurs in the middle of an *Umbanda gira*, in the hot noon of the wave of the *frevo*, that is, at the moments that require the overcoming of limits. The body of the *folião* or devotee, through the dynamo, has to breathe to move with pleasure until the end of each day.

6.2 Specific dynamics

Specific dynamics consist in the development of certain characteristics of a form that are incisive in a manifestation. Such characteristics open a process with a content that goes beyond its own specificity, when something belonging to its essence becomes a part of the body nature, continuing to be developed in other forms.

It is important to recognize the main dynamics in each manifestation, as it is the axis of development of the movement form.

It was also observed that the *ginga* and the Incorporation/Disincorporation dynamics print a peculiar capacity to the body in relation to its plasticity.

6.2.1 Ginga

The *ginga* may be understood as a situation in which the body enters an interaction with the space, being ready to provide immediate and convenient answers to the faced circumstances. *Ginga* is a movement matrix containing all pulses, directions, and punctuations resulting from diverse states awaken by the body.

The structure of the *ginga* may be described as follows: the individual's legs are initially spread apart, in parallel; then they alternate their position, one goes backwards while the other goes forward. The legs are never crossed; the figure of a square is constant. The knee of the front leg is fully flexed. The base is firmly built to the extent that the feet continuously move towards the ground. The arms also work with alternation: the arm that is ahead of the torso is always opposite to the leg that is behind it. During the opening and closing of the body (defense) there is a constant mobility of the arms, repeating the transitions where the torso alternately opens and closes. As the base acquires roots, the body reaches a higher balance, favoring the torso flexibility and agility. In the continuous rotation of arms and legs in the body alignment in X, the structure of the movement within the square acquires a rounded shape. The dynamics of the *ginga* works with the expansion and reduction of its movement. An attentive gaze is an important factor, as it interacts with the axis and the unity of the body.

Without the *ginga* there would be no *Capoeira* and/or *Capoeira players*:

> *The ginga is what differentiates Capoeira from other types of fight; it aims to study the opponent and the "match". It is used to prepare and strike attack and defense blows and it is responsible for the esquivas and molejo (Capoeira different blows), decisively helping the reflex as the capoeirista is in constant movement. A good capoeirista is recognized for its ginga style, that is, if he has rhythm, easeness, range of motion and malice*[2]

The *ginga* synthesizes a tense situation established in Brazil:

> *Capoeira was born from a compelling need of human protection against inhuman attacks. It consisted of agility exercises of persecuted people aiming to escape the cannibalistic fury of the merciless slave owners attempting to capture poor black people to submit them to the empire of their will.*[3]

There is an implicit content in the *ginga* determined by deceit. A set of relationships must be developed through it in such a way that the opponent cannot predict the movement that is about to emerge. Therefore, the individual does not reveal the intention that is already in his or her own body. At the same time, there

---

2 *Hélio Campos* - Mestre Xareú, *1990.*
3 *Hélio Campos* - Mestre Xareú, *1990.*

is a wit to unveil a transition in the opponent's movement, creating conditions to penetrate it:

> *In the back and forth movements of the ginga, the players/fighters seek more than to induce the opponent to an error; as Master João Grande once said, they keep on waiting for a hole to get into their opponent.*[4]

When the *ginga* is in the body of an individual, people call him or her a *mandingueiro*, because this body is worked with sagacity and intelligence. The cleverness of its performance can be seen as a ruse. Despite the fact that the *ginga* occupies the entire body and space around, the torso and upper limbs create drawings in the movement with a hidden meaning, aiming to hypnotize the opponent's body in order to dominate it.

When one tells that the *ginga* is a Brazilian way of moving, we note that it is necessary to analyze its foundations, that is, what caused the generation of this movement matrix. Its disguises are the reminiscence of the times when it was necessary to cover up a fighting body. Today, this memory is still printed in some bodies. *I like to remember that Capoeira appeared in Brazil as a fight against slavery (Master Pastinha)*[5]. When an individual uses the *ginga* without cultivating its main features, that is, its uniqueness in each person's body, no memories are established in his or her body.

In life you got to *gingar* a lot, all the time – this is the advice that every *Capoeira Master* repeats on a daily basis.

The *ginga* represents a great synthesis of *Capoeira*; the masters set out their basic principles as follows:

> *Always keeping a foot back... always keeping the balance, remaining as long as possible in contact with the ground ... Being patient to study the opponent, being able to act in the best moment.*[6]

This legacy of *Capoeira* crossed skies, seas, and lands reaching the entities of *Caboclos*, *Marinheiros* and *Baianos* in the *terreiros* of *Umbanda*. The *ginga* can be also found in the captain *Zé Bengala* that leads the *Congo of the Arturos*, but not in other captains, as they do not have the *ginga* in their bodies. During the field research we observed that it was not a choreographed *ginga*. It emerged in the

---

4   Anonymous report "Capoeiragem e os seus principais cultores; a ação da Policia, de Vidigal a Sampaio Ferraz" (Capoeiragem and its main followers; Police action from Vidigal to Sampaio Ferraz) - Vida Policial - Rio de Janeiro, March 27, 1925.

5   *Cezar Barbieri - Um jeito brasileiro de aprender a ser (A Brazilian way), 1993.*

6   *Cezar Barbieri - Um jeito brasileiro de aprender a ser (A Brazilian way), 1993.*

body during the incorporation of the entities, such as those found in this captain during his act of leading the walking of the *Congo*.

There is another type of situation in which the *ginga* is incorporated in popular manifestations through direct contact with the *capoeiristas*:

> *The presence of Capoeira was noticed everywhere, especially in popular festivities, where it is present until these days, although totally different from what it was in the past. In every Largo festivity, profane, religious or secular-religious, Capoeira has always been present.*[7]

In the *Rural Maracatus* from Pernambuco, the *Caboclos de Lança* develop a movement form based on the *ginga* during the *sambadas*. In the *sambadas* some movements were found to be very similar to *Capoeira*'s. The music, however, had no relation with it, and none of the *Caboclos* we met in the field research reported to be a *capoeiristas*.

In relation to the step of *frevo* from Pernambuco, we found the following statement regarding the incorporation of the *ginga* as a possible matrix that gave rise to this dance:

> *The Ginga of Passistas (dancers) is a initial point for their steps… From a dynamic point of view, that was all that the passista of Recife kept from the Capoeira. Naturally this statement may surprise some people, as it was affirmed that the movement comes from Capoeira. The truth, however, is that no pictures, drawings, or detailed descriptions of capoeira show any strike or action that allow the establishment of similarities with the steps of a frevo dancer (passista). However, more than anything that it could represent as a natural heritage, the soul of Capoeira has been found…*[8]

It was concluded that this movement matrix resulting from so many meanings and intentions produces a dynamics that gives rise to various movement forms. Much more than a part of choreographic repertoire, the *ginga* represents the possibility of building creative relationships between bodies through an acute and refined perception. Learning the *ginga* is not a matter of practice – one has to experience it.

A few years ago in São Paulo, at the intersection of Estados Unidos Ave. with the 9 de Julho Ave., I observed some street children selling candy. Attentive to the traffic lights and watching out for their younger siblings, they twined their bodies around the cars seducing potential customers for buying. The torso punctuated, twisted and writhed. In defense and attack, with money and offerings in hands, the boys played a game of survival. The liveliness in the gaze by the exercise of

---

7   *Waldeloir Rego* - Capoeira Angola Ensaio Sócio-Etnográfico (*Capoeira Angola, a Socio-Ethinographic Essay*). *1968*.

8   *Waldemar de Oliveira* - Frevo, Capoeira e Passo, *1971*.

92

peripheral view interfered in the whole body as if it were tuned. Through wiliness, the boys led the movement of hurried glances. With rhythmic precision, the whole body of the children was articulated and, at the exact moment, it retreated to the sidewalk to wait for the next turn. This was the most perfect *ginga* I have ever witnessed.

6.2.2 Incorporation/Disincorporation

The dynamics of Incorporation and Disincorporation researched in Brazilian rituals turns it into a factor that provides essential data to understand the language process of a full body.

Although the approach is not focused on beliefs or religions, there is no doubt in relation to the sensitivity of the theme. However, the importance of investigating the body in trance (starting and finishing this movement) was observed, especially when certain data began to shape the course of this reading. The examples include the revelations of some *pais-de-santo of Candomblé*, when they say that the *orisha* or saint lies within the person despite the belief in the existence of an active supernatural force.

This idea is reinforced in the *Umbanda* as shown in the following statement:

Ninety percent of the Entity's doctrine depends on the doctrine and evolution of the medium. In other words, the entity evolves according to the evolution of the fundamentals, as well as culture, knowledge on itself, and life struggle.[9]

The veracity in relation to the body receiving or not a Spirit was not a relevant information (provided by the initiated ones) to the research. The study focused on verifying the presence or absence of a significant change in the body of the individual; such change would be credible based on his/her performance in relation to a remarkable development of an expression when an entity was "riding" his/her body. Therefore, the research did not focus on Spirits, but on the embodied self.

The approach to *Incorporating* and *Disincorporating* refers to a body predisposed to materialize a range of contents and meanings by experiencing an escape from its own axis. During the Incorporations, a union of various bodily images is established in one single body. On the reverse of this act, there is a development process resulting from coexistence of "gaining body" and "losing body". Metamorphoses occur (plasticity is an irrefutable argument) before our eyes, leading us to believe that "an entity is coming to earth."

---

9   Carlos Alberto da Costa - Umbandísta.Brasília (DF), 1995.

The fact is that this dynamics reveals how the nature of the body and its resources are still unknown. The statement by a *pai-de-santo* that an "artist is a potential medium" (*Raul of Shango*) denotes a common sensitivity to both, necessarily flowing in different streams.

Regarding the body connected to the Spirits, the existence of a huge prejudice and fear before its expressed sensitivity was observed. Seemingly, many of the reactions, gestures, and movements that may emerge from our bodies have not yet been scrutinized, possibly due to the fear of discovering that there is a trapped trance within each of us. It is something strange that we do not want to know. Therefore, further study and research is necessary in the field of dance to point out that the unconscious world, residing in the incarnate body, allows little knowledge on it. This barrier may be due to the greatest of our fears, that is, the consequences of the strength that the body keeps locked. The fear of a "disorganized" movement leads us to choose a certain standardized or fixed form, precisely for being within a predictable framework.

It is important to note that prior to the momentum of the incorporation the individual had already undergone a series of preparations. During that time, the individual had contact with the archetypes announced by the entities, as the medium still had no revelation of the peculiar characteristic of the entity, even if he or she had already seen it in dreams and waking state impressions. Finally, the physical aspects of the entity, the landscapes it inhabits, and even its emotional data, remain a mystery. The entity will only become known after its incorporation. From such moment the concreteness of the history embodied in the entity begins to be reported, with senses and emotions taking shape. The development of the entity will occur to the extent that there are successive processes of incorporation and disincorporation, putting the entity in union with its medium in order to work.

In the prelude of the Incorporation, there is an outer dance that connects with the environment and fills the space. It was observed that the gaze of the medium turns inward, leading to a deep internalization and reducing external actions.

The precise moment of the Incorporation is the momentum in which the medium "loses his own body" to acquire "a new one". This fact evidences the union between the body of the entity and the body of the medium receiving it. The processes of losing, gaining, and connecting are observed in this stage. Input and output of contents, which are mixed to generate impulses, streams and punctuations, are observed in the body of the medium:

The mechanics of incorporation requires the communicating entity or Spirit to involve the astral body of the medium, operating in three parts: psychic function, sensory function, and motor function. These are the three necessary conditions to process the mechanics of Incorporation.[10]

According to the mechanics of Incorporation, people describe distinct sensations in the integration of these fields, varying according to the entity and the medium:

Sometimes it's a push, just ahead … a shock. I feel as if experiencing a shock. Each one feels it in a different way.[11]

My legs tremble, I feel like I was going to fall; in my feet, I feel a very great heat, they start to sweat. I feel numbness in the spinal column. My head tingles. There are different sensations for each phalanx. The sensations are also conducted to the points where the chakras are located. It is like all your energy went to those vibrating points (related to each entity). It is like if you had felt a mutation on these chakras; it is like being stung in the backbone. Then the incorporation takes place.[12]

During the movement the so-called dense physical body is extrapolated, making it clear that it is being incorporated. The "axis-mast" bends, rotates, tumbles. The individual experiences a movement of loss of centration, as it is necessary to leave an axis to acquire another. The "sacred" part of the body oscillates, curls and propels. The Incorporation always comes from the sacral region:

That's exactly why we are called "cavalos" (horses), because it is said that the Entities ride us. This is the point of greatest vibration. This part of the backbone is critical for the incorporation, as the Entity stands up from it.[13]

Before the entity is incorporated, the following movements are expressed by the body: shacking, trembling, vibrating, and surrendering. These movements punctuate the forehead, shoulders, elbows, knees, shoulder blades, ribs, and other parts of the body according to each entity and its medium. They both carry the sense of getting in and out of a stream filled with punctuations.

The movements of the sacrum are quick and strong, involving stretching and bending the hip as well as spirals and rotations. The gradations of the pulses vary enormously. Sometimes the impulses stretch the sacrum on the heels. In other actions, the movement is subtle, with a well delimitated area receiving and generating the transformation. Always involving the hips, the sacrum is like an electric shock that resonates throughout the body.

---

10 "Umbanda, Uma religião brasileira'"/*Magazine- São Paulo: Escala, ano I.*
11 Umbandista - *Campinas (SP), 1995.*
12 Carlos Alberto da Costa - umbandista, Brasília (DF), 1995.
13 Carlos Alberto da Costa - umbandista, Brasília (DF), 1995.

In a seemingly disorganized and unbalanced form – translated as a circumstance experienced by the body to enable changes – the whole body acts in an incisive manner without losing its unity. When the entity is adjusted to the body of the medium, the back of the hands often rests on the sacrum; there are cries and other actions coming from a single center, reinforcing the "axis-mast", so that it is well stuck in the ground. When the process of incorporation is initiated, the body of the medium is modeled with all the contours of the assumed identity. In other words, the entity is incorporated.

The body language of the act of Disincorporation is similar to that of the act of Incorporation, but with one difference: there is an action of removing something from the body. Feet penetrate the ground, hands propel to reach the ground as if something slipped through the fingers, the head turns around and throws up. The impulses cause the body to move through small jumps.

When the movement is ceased, the individual that is closer to the medium often helps him or her to return from the state of Incorporation by calling the person by his or her name and uttering the following sentence: *(Name) your guardian angel is calling you.* Investigation on this third element participating in this dynamics – the guardian angel – provided the following report:

> *It is an invocation of the Spirit of the person back into himself/herself as the other (the Entity) is leaving. Because there is an exchange. However, the spirit of the individual remains there all the time, bound by the navel, as if the individual stayed outside, but stuck to the umbilical cord (referring to the body of the individual). In short, the individual's spirit gives way to another spirit, but it remains connected to its umbilical cord.*[14]

The touch of the hand and the induction of certain movements are used by those who assist in the individualized process of the medium, both in the Incorporation and Disincorporation. Differences in the performance are observed, when the entity is incorporated for the first time and when a series of incorporations have already taken place in the same medium:

> *When you begin to incorporate the entities comes abruptly, shaking you, throwing you to the ground. People have to support you, holding your back. As you experience these processes of incorporation and disincorporation you strengthen your chakras and your energies, then your entities begin to adapt to your regular physical condition. A connection with your regular way of life begins to occur. The spirit comes very hectic and, over time, not only you become physically structured to support this spirit, but also this Spirit becomes indoctrinated and starts to behave in a milder way. There are certain cases in which people cannot even perceive that an incorporation is going on. Because you prepare yourself physically, psychologically,*

---

14 Carlos Alberto da Costa - umbandista, Brasília (DF), 1995.

This dynamics supports an understanding of the process of constructing the performer's character, when the proposal is to live it in the flesh from an experiential content. This is neither about "journeys" nor mystification; it is about "landings". The field reference presents the reality of an internally performed work that is gradually built with the effective participation of the body-subject. Ninety percent of the Incorporation depends on the medium; the same is true for the performer when he/she is developing a character. The other portion, corresponding to the entity in the *Umbanda*, may be compared to the interference of the innate talent of the performer.

In the complex mechanism of the *Umbanda* – where an energy flow acts on the physical, emotional, and mental bodies interacting with the spiritual entity – incorporating is equally important as disincorporating. In both cases, the body has to undergo an unbalanced condition. The chaotic movements gradually merge until reaching a conceived form. The body was reorganized and re-balanced. The power acquired by the body to reverberate an intimate content in direct relation to a collective unconsciousness makes the individual act very differently from his/her normal behavior. But this reality of the incorporated subject eventually intervenes in his or her daily reality.

The medium does not choose what to incorporate. This is something that does not depend on the person's preferences. The individual gives up his/her self-image in order to receive what is necessary in his/her body.

The dynamics characterized by the incorporations and disincorporations and the sums in this process of self-discovery happens in those individuals who make themselves available to receive the incorporation, aware that the reins are in his/her own hands.

---

15 Carlos Alberto da Costa - umbandista, Brasília (DF), 1995.

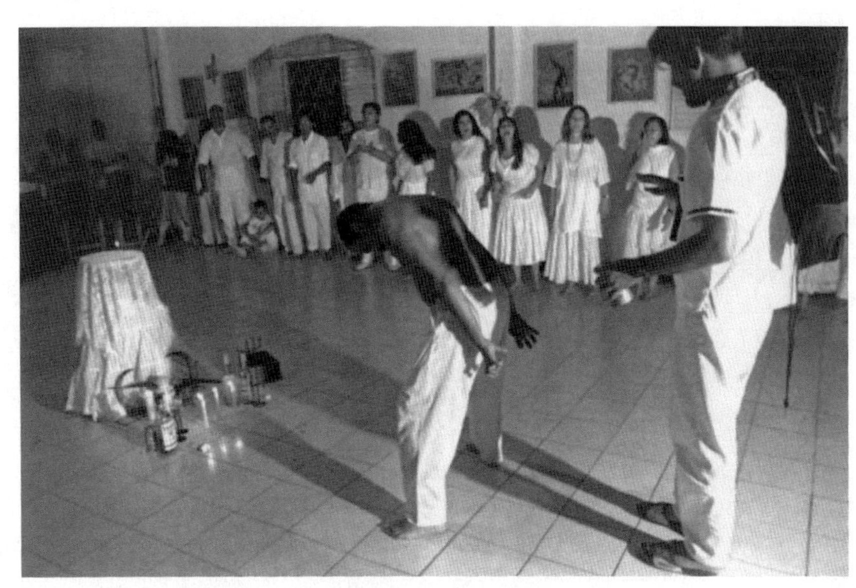

Incorporations of Eshu
Carlos Alberto Costa - Umbanda
Brasília DF - 1995
Photo: Juan Pratginesto's

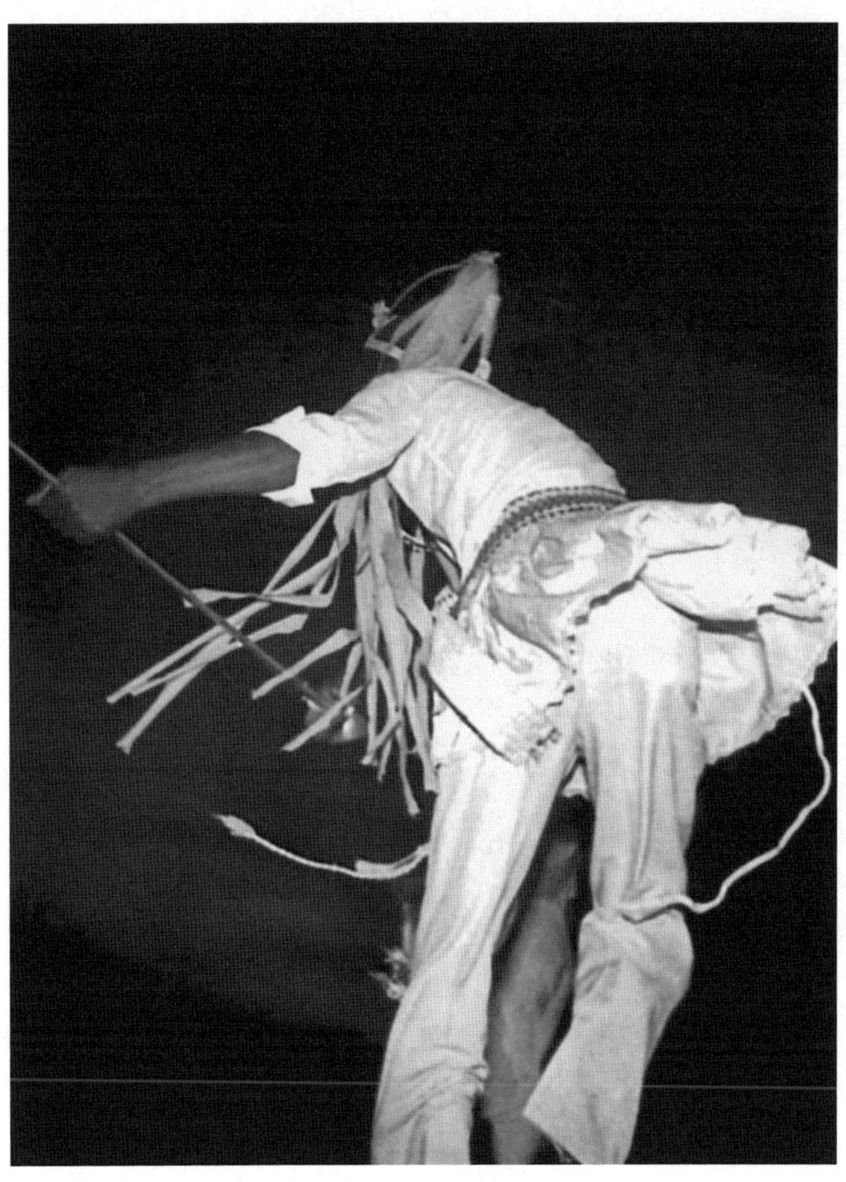

Dançante de Congo
1996
Photo: Eustáquio Neves

7 Confluent Elements

Há uma festa sem começo
que não termina com a morte.
Um antigo brinca no terreiro
Auê, sê benvindo!

(There's a party that has no beginning
and that is not ended by death.
An elderly plays in the terreiro
Hey, welcome!)[1]

7.1 Playing Singing: Pronunciations of the body

The sound of the instruments, the chant, and the language of movements that create dances are merged in actions that show a single inner path. We often find ourselves in the middle of celebrations listening to the body and seeing the sound:

Canta, canta, minha gunga
Num quero vê ninguém chorá
Aruanda tá cantano
Eu também quero cantá

(Sing, sing, my gunga
I don't wanna see anyone mourning
Aruanda is singing
I also wanna sing)[2]

The *gungas* are percussion instruments played with the feet. The chant demands the *mozambiqueiro*'s body to work with strength in harmony (from the feet) – let the *gungas* sing. Unveiling every piece of history, the devotee keeps dancing and singing:

Essa gunga vei beira-mar
Correu mundo, correu mar
O meu pai mandô avisá
Qu'esse gunga não pode pará
Pró Rosário de Santa Mariá,
Ela vei de Angola
De Angola vei prá cá

---

1   Edmilson de Almeida Pereira - A árvore dos Arturos (The Arturo's tree), 1988.
2   Mozambique's chant - Congado dos Arturos (Arturos' Congado) (MG).

Eu sô fio de Artur
Ele mandô ela vim falá

(This gunga comes from seaside
It traveled through the world, through the sea
My father sent a word
This gunga cannot stop
For the Rosary of Saint Mary,
She came from Angola
She came here from Angola
I am Arthur's son
He asked her to come here and tell)[3]

Feet start to beat, accelerating the rhythm and working along with the drums to fill the sound space. In this scenario of *Mozambique,* the space is represented in the *gungas* and characterized in the speeches during the chants.

The image of a ritual, a session of *Capoeira* or a *folguedo* is materialized in the individual before he or she can in fact see it:

> *Those who really like it…when the berimbau is played…they go crazy, they go after it. It's like a person who loves Bumba-meu-boi, when he/she listens to the bexiga.*[4]

The qualities of instruments with their tones and rhythmic diversity, associated with the statements of the chant, are embedded in every circumstance of the manifestation.

The sound of the *berimbau* indicates the type of Capoeira's play and characteristics of the circle (called *roda*). Chants follow the *berimbau's* beat. If the beat is Luna's, this means that it is a masters game; if it is a Cavalaria's, it means warning: the arrival of a stranger in the circle.

When the drums of the *Congado* sound "Serra Acima" (up the hill) and "Serra Abaixo" (down the hill), they reveal hard times of the past; and through these rhythms and chants, they seek strength to overcome such moments. These sounds are considered "powerful songs" and, in certain circumstances, they mean a challenge:

> *One cannot sing like that, you cannot think and sing. You have to look. I am carrero, it's time to start singing Pai Carrero. When we are tired, we start singing "Balaim de fulô", then "Balaim de fulô" saves us.*[5]

It was observed that the participation of the whole body in the action of "starting to sing" begins with the feet. Changes occur in the balance of the body when

---

3   Mozambique's chant - Congado dos Arturos (Arturos' Congado) (MG).

4   Manoelzinho, maracatuzeiro (PE). 1972.

5   Sebastiana, captain of Mozambique, Bom Despacho (MG), 1987.

the "powerful songs" start; there is a higher precision of gestures and the body becomes ready for action.

In certain occasions, during festivities of *Congado*, several groups with different types of instruments, rhythms, and chants perform at the same time. Such situation requires increased attention, particularly by the captains; they must keep their whole body-ear in a state of alertness:

> *So we know everything they are singing over there, and they also know what we are singing. As a captain, I got to pay attention to whom is singing, because they suddenly tell about a dangerous person that is coming; so I got to run and catch my sword.*[6]

In this case the chant announces danger, calling for action that is prepared in the dance with the sword, whose function consists in protecting the devotees by neutralizing possible negative energies:

> *We feel, we feel, we feel. We know about the upcoming radiation; we know if it is good or bad. We ask, inside our heads. When it is good we feel that positive flow inside; and when it is bad it causes that painful feeling in here (points to his heart). So you have to know how to sing so that this painful feeling disappear.*[7]

Investigation on the meaning of being able to sing reveals the existence of an association with the fluency of movement in the dance form. Those who can sing can dance with the same skill and vice versa. To be able to sing is to be able to open a sounding board all over the body, printing deep feelings to the air vibrations:

> *When I go for visits all around I always try to treat well my fellow man, the captains. I know how to approach them, I can sing. Sometimes they are spiteful to me, but I sing so beautifully and eventually we become friends. Thank God! But we have to be careful.*[8]

The development of an inner strength expressed in singing and dancing determines, for example, the choice of a person to be captain of the *Congado*. When a captain is baptized,[9] he/she acquires responsibilities on the movement that his/her chant could trigger, because his/her resonance chamber was expanded, differentiating the tones that make words blessed and articulated. Thus, *if a Captain is not baptized, no chant enters him/her.*[10] Moreover, the body listens to the word that comes from the

---

6   Manoel - Congado of Dona Efigênia, Belo Horizonte (MG), 1987.
7   Sebastiana, captain of Mozambique, Bom Despacho (MG), 1987.
8   Sebastiana, captain of Mozambique, Bom Despacho (MG), 1987.
9   The so-called captain's baptism is related to the transmission of knowledge on the foundations; thus, it refers to the devotee's inner path.
10 Captain Mário - Arturos, Contagem (MG), 1995.

intangible; then it appears in chant and orders – in the rhythm – the act that must be pronounced for purposes of peace or war.

The chants, also called *pontos* or *loas*, have as many roles as the circumstances may require:

There are plenty of chants for a person to sing. That's the way poor people handle suffering. Sometimes, for someone who has everything, it means nothing; but for us, that means a lot.[11]

When we're weeding without singing, we get even more tired. The pace of the hoe is developed through the chant. The hoe is used to make a drum, and the song comes from there.[12]

The "playing" or "challenging" chants often symbolize something that is the counterpoint of what is expressed in dance. In the *Batuque*, some chants allude to the ethereal space while the dance approaches the earth through stomps referring to fertility rites:

Cadê meu benzinho
Ele foi passeá
Entrô no balão
E foi pro ar
Foi pro ar, foi pro ar
Entrô no balão
Foi pro ar.

(Where's my hubby
He went away
Got in the balloon
Then, he flew to the sky
He flew to sky, he flew to sky,
He got in the balloon
He flew to the sky)[13]

In the *Candombe*, the challenges suggest the person to show his or her strength, as shown in the following *ponto: swallow, put your feather in the air*. The articulation of the chant in the body is connected to the drums and with a deep contact with the ground.

Following the path of the working tools integrated into the movement of the whole body, what was actually desired to be extracted from reality was unsuccessfully investigated: the sound or the movement. Thus, the work of a *Congadeiro* with a *patangome* was observed: his arms go up, then down, and the tool

---

11 Lira, crafts woman and batuqueira, Vale do Jequitinhonha (MG), 1988.
12 João Batista (Festivity Capina João do Mato) Arturos, Contagem (MG), 1987.
13 Canto de Batuque (Batuque Chant).

is connected to the breastbone. The *Congadeiro* continues to perform movements of sieving; he holds the tool in his chest and maintains the movement of sifting, pouring. Meanwhile there is a succession of twists and punctuations; the feet slide and penetrate the ground. The use of percussion instruments that are similar to the *patangome*, called *guaiás* and *querequechés* (among other names), is common to different manifestations. These instruments are made of metal or straw in different shapes and sizes, containing seeds inside. Many people who use these instruments claim that the secret of the movement lies within them.

The *Candombe's* drums deserve serious consideration by the devotees, as shown below:

> *Tamborete sagrado, com licençá, oê!*
> *Tulitinho de pau que Deus amô*
> *E que Nossa Senhora abençôo*
> *Crivo, Santa Maria, Santana*
>
> *(Sacred drum, excuse me, hey!*
> *Tulitinho de pau loved by God*
> *And that Our Lady blessed*
> *Crivo, Santa Maria, Santana)*[14]

This chant of the *Candombe* reveals the names of the sacred drums.[15] According to the myth, when leaving the sea Our Lady jumped and sat on the *Santana*. The drum – as well as Our Lady's moving abode – means the entire *Candombe*. The chant is moved by the drums and energized by five voices.

In the *Candomblé*, the drums are named *Rum, Rumpi* and *Lé*; they are played by the *Oghans*. The instruments are responsible for the pronunciation of the Divine. The *Oghans* are persons devoted to the instruments; they are cared for and fed. As an entity, they transfigure themselves into a body that calls for another body to merge and dance.

The act of being able to play requires that the individual's hands – materializing the traction – celebrate with the energy or spirit of the instrument.

Regardless of the instrument, being or not in the body of the individual expanding the dance form, a juxtaposition of singing, playing, and dancing is always present. Changes occur in relation to the structural conditions of each manifestation. The *Rural Maracatu* each act is well punctuated. The sound of the orchestra, the movements of the *caboclos de lança*, and the *loas* of the masters are roles performed

---

14 Ponto de Candombe (Candombe chant) – Fidalgo (MG), 1987.

15 There are variations of the name of the Candombe drums, such as Jeremias, Santaninha and Santana.

by different groups of people. However, they are interdependent parts of cycle. A good *Maracatu* master has participated in all these roles.

The manifestations – like the *Folias* and *Bois* that are present in all parts of the country – exhibit great musical differences. Regional accents are reflected in different instruments and in the rhythmic differences. It is possible to hear some chants with the same content from north to south, but with differences in musicality. This shows that the movement extracted from different pulses made the body flexible and preserved the unity resulting from the interactions.

In several regions of Brazil a drum is present, feeding a rhythm. There are so many musical timbres that it is difficult to classify them. The body lulls songs, in on-beat, pause, and off-beat of existence:

> *Eu não sei se eu canto ou choro*
> *Com alegria será milhó*
> *Se eu cantá*
> *Alivia minhas pena e minha dôr*
>
> *(I do not know if I sing or cry*
> *with joy it will be better*
> *If I sing*
> *It relieves my pain and my sorrow)*[16]

7.2 The act of investing

Clothes don't make the individual, we gotta be what we are.[17] The accuracy of this sentence illustrates the essentiality of the garment without the connotations with fantasy. The same is true for the objects or instruments used; their roles override any reference to them as props.

Investing themselves through the clothing of saints, *mozambiqueiros,* or any garment characterizing the roles of individuals in the festivities, requires a journey in search of knowledge. The identification of the act of investing is due to the importance assigned to the objects and garments when these are rooted in the grounds of the festivities. In this sense, when the individual puts the garment and takes the object, it also means that he/she is taking possession of a sum of meanings magnetized by the antiquity of these acts and filled with stories.

A small piece of blue cloth may be transformed into a *mozambiqueiro* skirt as well as into a bandanna. These parts of the costume represent the integration of the individual to the mantle of Our Lady, which covers and protects. The

---

16 Canto de Batuque (Batuque Chant).
17 Sebastiana, captain of Mozambique, Bom Despacho (MG), 1987.

importance of dressing up with this garment lies in the person performing the act and in the moment he/she takes the right and duty to be a vassal of Mary.

Regardless of luxury or austerity in relation to the garment, its value lies in the act of the person merging to the founder matrix of the sacred. Through incorporating or dealing directly with the *orisha* (*filho-de-santo*) and tying the rag to the torso, the individual commits to carrying out the work as a child or caretaker of the saint.

In this act, even when small pieces are used, an effect is produced on both who is performing and who is watching it, leading them to understand what the individual starts to represent.

When Our Lady was walking through the world, she cried when she witnessed the suffering of captive men. When she fell on the ground, her eyes sprouted beads of tears. Rosaries, crowns, and instruments used in the torso, head and hands of the *congadeiros* are made of vegetal beads. They cover the body with mythical fragments:

> *The more tear beads of Our Lady, the better is the balance of the mozambique.*[18]

The quantity of details often leads to elaborate garments that present more details than necessary. Such situations are present in the perfection of the *orisha*'s garment when an individual, after the initiation, incorporates it. From head to toe, there is a volume that covers it, showing in details the whole "performance"[19] carried out in the body.

In the *Caboclos de Lança* of the Rural *Maracatu*, it was observed that the elaborate garment turns them into a mystery and a synthesis of the festivity:

> *It has so many clothes, it has to have socks, a pair of shoes, a belt, a flower, a long-sleeved shirt, a colorful collar with sequins and beads. A large bag... the rattle... a colorful spear with ribbons... a hat named funnel, looking like a wig... that flower in the mouth, that's a secret of it, a protection... and the flower smells.*[20]

Elaborate garments require the participation of the individual, so that they may be produced. The *Caboclos de Lança* often embroider their collars and make the wigs in the funnel. These tasks demand dedication and patience. During initiations in the *Candomblé* people learn by manufacturing various pieces of their

---

18 Sebastiana, captain of Mozambique, Bom Despacho (MG), 1987.
19 Workmanship is related to Initiation. It corresponds to a set of rituals providing the person passing through this important transformation with knowledge. The stages of this process are symbolized in the costumes.
20 Manoelzinho Salustiano – maracatuzeiro (PE), 1992.

orishas and learning their meanings. These actions consist of rituals in which the individual is in an auspicious condition to receive and print inner senses related to garment. Therefore, there is also a gap, as people see the meanings of their inner *orishas* represented in the clothes and objects. When participating in the ritual execution, the individual gains the power in the act of investing.

In the *Umbanda*, an almost reversed process in relation to the traditions was observed (in which the individual knows about his/her act of investing). When the medium incorporates an entity for the first time, there is no representation in relation to its clothes and objects. The entity will reveal to the medium what he/she should wear in dreams and during the *giras*. When an entity is incorporated, its nature is gradually revealed. According to its way of acting, the entity requests the pieces that will compose its garment. The medium becomes aware of the meanings when he/she begins to wear and use what is determined by the entity. In this case, the individual is invested by the development of the entity, whose construction comes from the time it has been manifesting in connection to the dedication of the medium. Certain combinations of clothes and objects may seem absurd, but an absolute consistency can be observed when one investigates the history of the entity and the act of investiture of the medium. In this process it was also observed that materializing a garment or object consists in shaping content and establishing the meaning of each moment. Magnetized by the word, one single piece becomes meaningful:

> *I came here to put my strength, the strength of my cape on all of you with the permission of Oshala.*[21]

The Physical Structure resulting from a symbolic anatomy is more evident when the body is wearing the elements that are part of the festivities. The movement of the invested individual may be seen in the parts of the body.

The head is the top of the ornate mast; an uncovered head is hardly seen. Heads tied with cloth, in turbans, carrying skullcaps with mirrors and ribbons falling to the shoulders, with feathered bonnets, hats made of leather, metal or straw are often seen. The movement of the head is a determining factor of what the devotee wears.

Two examples of heads that have opposite expanding and restraining movements are observed: the *pendoada* head and the crowned head, respectively.

The *pendoada* head usually presents different elements of the landscape of the festivity's origin; these elements are worked in the sense of expanding the

---

21 Eshu Tranca-Rua incorporated in Carlos Alberto da Costa (DF), 1988.

movement of the head. In the *Caboclos de Lança*, the rough and sharp sugar cane becomes the colorful and flexible wig made of tissue paper:

> *The peasant walks with straw hat on his head, but the caboclo doesn't; the caboclo wants a funnel, he has to have it. He seems to be carrying some hanging cane. When the cane is hanging it looks like a cabloco with a hat… The caboclo, moving that wig, has to show some evolution.*[22]

The function of the crowned head consists in supporting the divine power on earth in the space of the festivity. In various processions, the crowns are in the heads of those investing in the roles of kings and queens; the crown gives them modesty and a deep inwardness. The crowned head is lifted up due to an almost immobility.

The flag, which is a key element in the organization of various types of procession, comes out of the torso: *It is the guiding flag because it moves ahead guiding the steps.*[23]

The guiding flag is a piece of cloth with a simply or richly elaborate print of the beloved blessing symbol. Investing the flag means showing the print, carrying it throughout the festivity, indicating the paths, and opening what lies deep inside and that makes the external movement. As the flag is the dominant artery of the festivity, it requires the *bandeireira* to have authority and serenity. Between holding and releasing gestures, the conductor cannot fail to keep the sacred object. A guiding flag should never fall.

The devotion of the *bandeireiras* has a long history. The flags are brought to their chest a high number of times, causing them to become increasingly alive.

In the lining of the hips, a piece of clothing that categorizes many Brazilian manifestations is present: skirts. Made in different colors, volumes, lengths and styles, they reinforce the movement of the sacred part of the body, that is, the sacrum. The straight skirts emphasize the verticality of the *Mozambique*; small ruffled skirts of the *Congo* show the free flow of horizontality. The voluminous skirts of *Candomblé* highlight the ins and outs of the *orishas* in the body. In the hands of a *Pomba-Gira*, the skirts represent weapons and veils; these entities also wear seven skirts to unveil each moment of their *gira*. In the case of the *Pomba-Gira*, it was observed that investing up skirts occurs at the moment when they are undressed.

However, the skirt as a skirt has no meaning. It is necessary to know the investiture in order to find a proper skirt. When a laywoman expresses her mediumship (= sensitivity) in a terreiro, it is said that "she must wear a white skirt", which means that she needs to be initiated in that rite.

---

22 Manoelzinho Salustiano – maracatuzeiro (PE), 1992.
23 Manoel, congadeiro, Belo Horizonte (MG), 1987.

The hands stimulate the movement of the whole body, meant to protect, save, and lead. Through the hands, the swords, spears, and sticks are invested, reinforcing the verticality; each one represents an accurate centration tool in its form.

The stick is the magic weapon of the movement. In its form, the size of the upper part is larger than that of the bottom part. The stick canalizes high energies, enabling them to be brought to the ground; it requires precision of character by those who will move it.

Without the sticks, the captains of *Congado* and the masters of *Maracatu* are neither captains nor masters. In the *Congado*, when a captain dies, his stick cannot remain static; it must be passed on to another person who is able to invest oneself with it:

> *You have to know how to hold the stick, how to handle it, otherwise… When defending the others or at war, the captains turned the stick into snakes and wasps. The stick gives a signal. Then you have to use it correctly and make the meia-lua, so that you don't get stuck in one place; otherwise you will get stuck. I signal using the stick so they know what I am doing there. You have to know how to take the stick; otherwise, you don't show anything, don't sing, do nothing, you see? … Everything falls to the ground.*[24]

Covering oneself to become someone else

People who perform the *Boi, João do Mato*, and the *Mascarado* (among others) disappear within the structures, greenery or masks to give life to a representation. The whole subject becomes the core of another form. Their identities are hidden to enable the magic of the investiture. The characters are surrounded by mystery; their main characteristic lies in the identification that we want to give them. During their performances, they exhibit movements of disgust and attraction converging to empathy with the audience as they accept all kinds of provocation. A greater freedom of attitude is observed when the individual becomes the "core" of another form – a kind of behavior that is not authorized when he/she is uncovered.

In the course of the festivity, the act of investing reveals the transition from the concealment to the revelation of what each individual assumes in his/her body. The invested body flows towards the human being as a creator being in time and space.

7.3 Buildings of space-time

The festivities surround the progress of time that is expanded by memory. During the festivities, the sacred takes the space and makes the displacements converge

---

24 Sebastiana, captain of Mozambique, Bom Despacho (MG), 1987.

in various rounded shapes. The trajectories – with their stops – turn into gears of a wheel that goes beyond the physical space:

lê! A roda do mundo é grande, a de Zambi[25] inda é maió

(hey! The wheel of the world is big, but Zambi's is bigger)[26]

At each point of the space worked by the rite, there is an invocation to past forces, which are to be updated in the present. Therefore, it is an occupation resulting from the re-elaborations of space-time. These re-elaborations of space-time promote the nomination of the ritual known as *Gira, Giro*, Rosary, or *Roda*:

I was fourteen when I learned the Folia of the Divino. I learned it from João Gonçalves Pereira; he had learned it from his father; his father had learned it from his grandfather. So I think it is a very old thing that comes from the dawn of the world.

Formerly there was the giro consisting of two flags spinning around for twelve and eighteen days, respectively. It was so beautiful, all those people following the flag. There were the singers of Folia that was sung throughout the night, sometimes eight, ten days in a row. No one could notice the time passing. But today there is no Giro do Divino like in the old times. We still make a Giro during two or three days in order to preserve it.[27]

As it happens with this Folia, a decrease in the length of the path traversed by the devotees was also observed in other manifestations. However, there are essential spaces that are preserved. The remaining sites present the recurrence of the time when there was greater circulation of the sacred. These spaces are insistently taken and marked by a rounded shape.

The meaning of opening the Rosary in the *Congado* or opening a *Gira* of *Umbanda* has a direct relation with specific points in the space that keep and receive the memory of those who perform the rite. The opening also represents the possibility of dynamic spaces involving both inner and outer movements integrated into the smallest actions. Thus, daily spaces are converted into sacred spaces presenting an organization related to the required time of occupation, in order to enable the memory of ancestors to be reintroduced in the present. Rosary, *Gira, Giro*, or *Roda* are ended in the same site where they start. In the closure, the present time is well situated and the future of new festivities is designed and kept in an enigmatic space-time represented by the altar or the *conga*.

---

25 Zambi = God.

26 Ponto de Umbanda (Umbanda chant), Capoeira from Congado.

27 Mr. Zeca, folião of Divino de Turmalina (MG), 1988.

7.3.1 Landscape and scenarios

The festivities surround plenty of landscapes (consisting of their characteristic scenarios). Imagination merges with various living grounds of a reality that is trodden at every festivity cycle. Although some spatial treatments are unique for each site, it was observed that some of them are similar in nature and function. It is possible to affirm that there is a recurring Brazilian scenography from north to south and east to west. It consists of the *conga*, the *terreiros*, the kitchen, the paths with their crossroads, and the cruises. These spaces are interconnected and merge into one another. For example, in the *Umbanda* and *Candomblé* the space of the *terreiro* is extended to the *camarinhas* and houses of the *orisha*.

In this approach, the spaces are inserted into the bodies of the individuals through the interconnection created in rituals. The body connected to the space is the result of a path that leads men towards their own integrity.

The festivity is developed from the core – represented by the *Congá* – in the territories of the house and on the streets; gates, arches, and crossroads delimitate each crossing.

Congá, Conjá or Altar

The *Congá* is a small – but important – space housed next to a wall of the *terreiro*; it includes images of faith and affection represented by the saints, entities, and various objects chosen to be the tools to generate the strength of the movement. Candles, lit in an act of firmness, illuminate the intentions placed in the *Congá*.

The image of the patroness, the reason of this festivity, is surrounded by many others that form the celestial universe with the Holy Cross centralizing the space. Converging in a single point, the *Congá* closes and opens like the devotee's inside. Before the *Congá*, the devotee absorbs it, becoming little in the inside – that is to say, in the entrails – and then expands, widens from the cardiac plexus, pushing this movement to the extremities (from top of the head to toes). The *congas* are usually thoroughly crafted and adorned with various meanings, from the ground to the ceiling; its visceral part is the one with the greatest volume of the represented divine forces.

The *Congá* is a projection of a world which is grater and better than Earth; it is the receptacle of pain and hope, the protective source caring for each step of the devotee. It is a space that assigns a geographical location to the individual, representing his/her right to occupy a place in the world:

> *Ó Senhora do Rosário / Ai que vai abençoá / Abençoao mundointero / Abençoa esses filho do Congá*

(Our Lady of the Rosary / who shall bless us / Bless the whole world / Bless these children of Congá)
(Loa of Congado)

Defumai o Nosso Congá / Defuma os filhos do Congá

(Fumigate our Congá / Fumigate the children of Congá)
(Chant of Umbanda).

As the core of strength, exposure and concealment of the foundations, our altars always present a double entendre:

If you are Catholic, you hail Jesus Christ, Saint Barbara, Saint Ana, Our Lady of the Rosary, Our Lady of Aparecida. If you belong to Umbanda, then you hail Obatala, Nana Buluku, Oshun, Ogoun … It doesn't matter, what comes from our heart is okay.[28]

The *Congá* is the spatial location where the festivities start and end. There, the Rosary, *Gira* and *Giro* open and close.

Terreiro

The *terreiro* virtually loses its connotation of an open-air, flat, wide space of land, becoming the space for freedom of expression in each festivity. Therefore, the status of *terreiro* is defined by the type of ritual. *Terreiros* can be either placed directly in the land or on a pavement; it can even be located in a building's floor. A *terreiro* is characterized as the place that accommodates the *Congá*, having an empty space to be filled with different dynamics. As a great scenic space for Brazilian cultural manifestations, the *terreiro* may be multiplied in different representations. From a caboclo's village to a gypsy tent and then to a slave ship on the open sea. The *terreiro* is the existential laboratory of the Brazilian people.

As a part of the foundations, the *terreiros* are built in locations considered as "strong places". The ground and the ceiling are carefully maintained, so that the space may be the *Gira*'s mothership. This type of *terreiro*, often closed with the doors open, centralizes each festivity. However, there are other open-air spaces that are called *terreiros* as well. These spaces are located in front of houses, in yards, or next to churches. The choice is not random. The chosen locations are those that – similarly to the spaces where the masts are raised – have some history, a humus that strengthens their settlement.

We observed that in several places the construction of a *terreiro* space gains some ramifications, such as the various rooms where sacred settlements can be found. At the same time, however, we observed a restricted space of a street

---

28 Manoel, congadeiro, Belo Horizonte (MG), 1987.

becoming a *terreiro* as a result of a human fence formed by members of a *Candombe* group. At that time, the *Candombe*'s drums evoked the *terreiro* from ancient times when the ground was unpaved:

> *Eu fui carrero / hoje em dia sô boiadero / Eu dancei nesse Candombe / Dentro desse terrero. Vovó não qué / Casca de côco no terrero / Prá não lembrá / Do tempo do cativero*
>
> *(I was an oxcart driver / now I am a cowboy / I danced in this Candombe / In this terrero. Grandma doesn't want / Coconut shell in the terrero / She doesn't want to remember/ her times in captivity).*[29]

Kitchen

Most kitchens are located next to the *terreiro*, often enframing what happens outside.

The kitchen is the space of affective coexistence and coziness that excites memories. With generosity and abundance, many kitchens still use wood-burning stoves with an endless fire; coffee is always poured and there is always some smoke in the air. Chants, fragments of dance and several stories that seemed to be lost in time find their places in the kitchen. In this unique space of the house, during the preparation of the ritual meal, people fight against oblivion and bitterness. Festivity lasts long and the kitchen can never stop.

We experienced the activities of the Arturos' kitchen both during the special festivity days and in everyday life. Always open, it is a meeting point, a place of transitions, but it is also a place where one can stay for a long time. We collected precious data there, experiencing the transitions in time that made us wonder, for example, what would *Batuque* be in the past. The power of femininity, which has its territorial domain in the kitchen, manifested itself during a regular afternoon, when Grandma Carmela's kitchen became a *Batuque*'s space in its sophisticated sensuality and mystery. It was not possible to casually capture it with such intensity in any other space.

The crossing spaces

The crossing spaces are doors and gates that define the spaces of the house and crossroads where the paths cross each other. Besides, other passages are worked, next to the central point of the event: the arches. Made of leaves, with various combinations of paper flags or flowers, the arches reinforce the differences between the

---

29 Candombe from Fidalgo (MG), 1987.

places. The treatments to these divergent spaces are often associated to the balance and harmony of the festivity.

Doors and gates are considered as the housekeeper's dwelling. In *Candomblé* and *Umbanda*, the *orisha* or *Eshu* is fixed in the entrances, playing the role of protector of the *terreiros*. During the festivities, not only *Eshu* but also other keepers, such as *Ogoun* and *Oshosi*, are invoked: they shout and move through the crossings, while being incorporated. In other manifestations, the gate is always carefully crossed, never turning your back on it; it results in the movement called *meia-lua*. These borderlines are respected in the entrances and exits, endowing the routes with meaning, as they reaffirm the need to recognize the ground on which one is standing.

We may invoke the *Congado* as an example. Let us see how the transition occurs through these spaces based on the words of Sebastiana, captain of the *Mozambique* in Bom Despacho:

> *When I get to the gate, I tap the stick three times, here and there, I perform the meia-lua, go to the gate and excuse myself. I turned my back, then I entered; right after me, my group entered head-on.*

The magic thing about these crossings is related to the movements that promote the opening of the paths. According to Sebastiana's words, we verify that the movement *meia-lua* is also performed as a request for permission to pass through a crossroads:

> *Performing the meia-lua means to cut off the evil that lies in the crossroads. If you do not know how to pass through it you will keep turning around all the time, never reaching a church. Someone may use Our Lady's power to get a flag and leave it in the crossroads. And how can I pass over Our Lady? So, I have to pass over without stepping on her.*

These spaces are often associated to an open dimension, to darkness. They are tapered and may turn into a hole restraining the route. Nevertheless, those who know how to contour the crossing spaces are rewarded with the flow of the paths.

The difference of the arches lies in the opposite direction of the gates and crossroads.

While these are permanent in daily life, absorbing the whole burden coming from the land or sky, the arches are set to dilute negative energies opposite to the foundations of the festivity. The arches act on the negative energies that people carry in their bodies, letting off steam. Besides, the arches organize the paths and round the festivity space. There often is a superposition of gate and arch previously settled with bamboos or made of people, raising their swords or sticks at the gate during the moments of great movements.

The insiders of each manifestation salute the crossroads and know how to get in and out of them. Otherwise, in the absence of crossings, the space would be uncovered, without keepers to take care of it. To non-insiders, these crossings provide a feeling of being penetrated by another world, proposing a different way to set foot, especially when the space to be recognized demands the repeated performance of the *meia-lua*.

The cross

On the streets and in some spaces of the house, it is common to find a wooden cross fixed in a circular cement base. This symbol is also called *Cruz das Almas* (Cross of Souls). Festivities are held in these spaces in honor of the *foliões*, the *filhos de santo* or Our Lady's children who passed away:

> *Salve o Cruzero do Sul*
> *Onde os anjo tem que rezá*
> *Onde os filho chora de tristeza*
> *Nosso Senhô vem nos consolá*
>
> *Hail the Southern Cross*
> *Where the angels have to pray*
> *Where the children cry in sorrow*
> *Our Lord come to comfort us.)*
> (*Loa of Congado*)

The cross is marked by a feeling of loss. At the same time, however, the strength of this space comes from the devotee's life memories that were left behind by those who have been in that place.

The *Boi Janeiro* of *Maria Coqui*, from the city of Rubim - MG, visits the cross of the cemetery late in the night, at the big hour. This is what Maria tells us about this moment in which chants and dancing are present in honor of the merrymakers from the "other side":

> *Many things happen… everybody sees a lot of things. Here, you see a bird while chanting. When it ends, all disappears.*

The paths

The more interior and peripheral the landscape is, the more it turns into a scenario that merges with the festivity. Now, the old dirty roads are covered by asphalt and vehicles, narrowing the space for the development of *Giro* or Rosary.[30] As a result, the festivities lose much of the characteristics of their courses; the paths suffer changes, being transformed by the imagination. It is possible to say that the paths in this urban model become an obligation instead of a journey to other worlds.

The same path is usually repeated in each festivity by each group in their location. The *folias* of Divino, Saint Sebastian and *Reis* still exist in the heart of rural areas. On farms and in small isolated houses, the flag is received with reverence manifested in chants and dances. Traveling night and day, the flag's *Giro* absorbs the sunrise and sunset. The colors of the day and the shades of the night are absorbed by the parties and time is fully experienced. In the resting places, the previously defined hosts prepare the space to receive the group. In these resting places, we can find the *terreiro*, the *congá*, and often the craft of arches. Welcoming rituals and *catiras* often occur over there. At sunrise, the flag returns to the paths, often in a hurry, so that it can visit every familiar house. At each stop, there is a circumstance consisting of a new landscape and new characters that are closely related to the sacred, demonstrating, through this bond, the peculiarities of their expressions. The flag is received and then delivered, it continues to travel through the paths. The Divine, kings and saints, enable the merrymakers to take the roads without any fear or disapproval; they interact with the world outside as their bodies are previously "shielded". Tiredness is overcome because the rhythm of the movement helps them keep the pulse. In each track, attentive devotees carefully watch the mishaps trying to move them to open the passages to the invisible that reaches the flow of the festivities. Thus, a group of people, under heavy rain or a scorching sun, restores the past history of the paths, respecting and honoring them.

The strength of these movements, which add up fragments of each visited house, provides the revitalization of the senses and sharpens the perception of those who participate in the wanderings. Notably, these long walks frame the most striking phenomena, which are difficult to register in the field research, namely – the experiences stored in the body of each merrymaker. The body updates these experiences when its own clarification is, for some reason, triggered. The *Giro* composition lies in the sum of these various paths. Following these parties makes us participate in these experiences written in the body. By virtue of this process, we become owners of our own bodies, as it were, understanding what the *Giro* really is.

30　We aim at reading the body as a source connected to the original space of popular culture manifestations. However, we recognize that the changes in the space – influenced by urbanization and modernity – may lead the body to re-elaborate its forms of relation with the space. For the purposes of this work, we focused on the analysis of the source-body connected to the original spaces.

In the urban space, tracks, rails, stones, mud, dust, and vegetation are lost; eventually, the original landscape, which modulates the pitch, makes it possible to elaborate one of the richest and most expressive choreographic ramifications of religious manifestations in the countryside.

7.3.2 Choreographic ramifications

Occupying all the spaces proposed by the festivity, the bodies have an expression that qualifies the performance of each act, causing *Giro*, *Gira*, Rosary or *Roda* to become dances permeated by circumstances. Therefore, we assume that choreographic structures are presented in all of the sacred paths. When opening a gate, when settling, in the relations between people, the rite calls for a harmonious spatial arrangement and a specific language of the movement. The spaces are interconnected, because the choreographic report performed by the devotees in a given moment is a result of earlier times and spaces in which the body was worked on.

João Lopes' *Mozambique* is still traveling through the dust of the outskirt streets of Belo Horizonte. Devotees have performed a series of *meia-luas* in the various crossroads they have crossed. The structure of the procession has been maintained, keeping a compact formation of the group: the flag ahead, followed by the commanding captain and *caixeiros* surrounding the other captains and vassals. Long ago, they have left the altar of the chapel where they made the commitment to follow through in the name of Our Lady of the Rosary. All of this happened at a time when the *gungas* were fully played. The step is now slow, the *gungas* set the pace smoothly, and the body absorbs the chant, gaining concentration. There is no monotony, only an apparent tiredness of crossing the dark paths.

Up and down the hills, the *gungas* beat and the chant never stops:

Vô descê praqui abaixo, com Jesus de Nazaré (I am going downhill along with Jesus of Nazareth…)[31]

In the most difficult moments, the captain in charge of the chant requests an incisive entrance of the movement:

O Rosário de Maria chorô serra abaixo (Maria's rosary cried down the Hill)[32]

On the corner of a street, a boy from the neighborhood jumps ahead of the procession, performs an aú[33] and "hail the flag", vibrating his whole body. He follows

---

31 Loa de Moçambique (Mozambique's chant).

32 Loa de Moçambique (Mozambique's chant).

33 Offensive-defensive movement, similar to a somersault, in which the capoeirista throws his body to one side and spins in the air, making a semi-circle with his legs, supporting

opening the way with his feet, with his entire body. João Lopes observes the facts without losing the pulse, receiving the circumstances, as the boy welcomes strength. The stick is raised and the captain turns it, expanding the space of the procession and indicating a new direction.

To get to the house of the queen of *Congado*, the *Mozambique* had to walk next to the railroad tracks. The landscape composes the scenario of the procession, and rough terrains interfere with the choreographic route:

Ê, Angola corre mundo / Ê, corre mar / Essa gunga vai virá

(Hey, Angola around the world / Hey, through the sea / This gunga shall turn)[34]

His feet bog down and get unstuck by getting support on the sides. The *gungas* get heavy.

The arrival at the *terreiro* sets the feet free, calling the queen to compose the procession. The space inside the house is occupied, concentrating voices and movements; nothing stops by space restriction. In carefully dosed, essential movements, everyone fits in the house.

The procession becomes larger, with kings and queens following the *mozambiqueiros* on a partially paved street. Their feet are bound and rebound, eyes reach horizons and heads apparently want to touch the sky. The *gungas* on the right side call, while those on the left beat and call back. And so the *Mozambique* goes down on the ground with the axis of its body establishing itself in twists that, from time to time, suggest spirals.

After such long bounds and rebounds, going deeply down on the ground, up and down the hills, the bodies acquire swing and vibration. The dynamo incorporates the movement of the *gungas*, which from a distance, resembling waves of the sea. The bodies get freed in suspension by going up and down the ground.

The path becomes narrow, and now the space requires greater contention and balance, as the passage is through a footbridge:

Ê, vamo divagá / Moçambique não pode corrê / Ê, vamo divagá / Aô lelé, Aô lelé, Aôlelé, lelêlilelê á

(Hey, slow down / Mozambique cannot run / Hey, slow down / Aôlelé, Aôlelé, Aôlelé, lelêlilelê á)[35]

---

his hands on the ground. (Aurélio Buarque de Holanda Ferreira – Novo Dicionário Aurélio da Língua Portuguesa, 1986).

34 Loa de Moçambique (Mozambique's chant).

35 Loa de Moçambique (Mozambique's chant).

The text above is just a small excerpt from a *Mozambique*'s half-day of live walking. The procession began very early and ends at dusk, intensified by the devotees' faith:

Quem é, quem vai no Rosário de Maria … (Who is, who goes to Maria's Rosary…)[36]

This chant is quite significant, as it is necessary to attend the "Rosary of Mary" in order to understand its choreographic construction that is unique at every single moment.

It is difficult to frame it, that is, to preserve this choreographic development in a fixed space. This difficulty results from the dynamism of the spatial occupation in which the actions implemented in a frame are closed somewhere else. Here is an example: at the gate of an *Umbanda* site, *Oshosi* is incorporated in a *filho-de-santo*. His gestures, chants and cries are accompanied by *ogans* with the conga drums. So we can see a moment of the dance of *Oshosi*, with impulses and punctuations, in a body that acquires the dynamo. In the framework of the gate space, the scenery flourishes. *Oshosi* is reinforcing himself in this space. However, its action is not completed there. It goes through a path within the site, then heads to the *camarinha*. A development of the language of its dance occurs in the path, and it is also interconnected with the movements that subsequently occur in the *camarinha*. In this case, we can say that from the moment that *Oshosi* incorporated in a person until the moment he leaves, there was a single choreographic record. Therefore, the framework was not restricted to the gate.

The choreographic nature of the discussed festivities is not conditioned by the appreciation of an audience. It is a process in which the shapes of movements with their qualities and spatial balance result from the elaboration of a specific content to reveal that body and space are intricate in their relationships.

Penetrating and sneaking away

The words of Captain Sebastiana from *Mozambique of Bom Despacho* are important to clarify the relationship between the devotees and the space in which they move:

For the whole time, it is a war field, a battleground. It is all or nothing. Either you know, or you don't know, got it? That's the tradition. When I dance, four steps forth and four steps back, that is the defense of mine. When I go ahead and get back, I defend myself from the enemy. Then I shake my body, the path is open. Let's go.

This description of the occupation of a space by the *Mozambique* could be the same for different moments of the *Maracatu, Umbanda, Candomblé,* and *Folguedo*

---

36 Loa de Moçambique (Mozambique's chant).

120

do Boi that we attended. A remarkable peculiarity is observed in how the space is occupied, that is, the act of penetrating gets a sense of attack, while the act of sneaking away gets a sense of dodging. The lines that form the drawings are marked by the process of going forward and backward. The circles are strongly delineated through half circles – the so-called *meia-lua* (literally: half-moon) – indicating a means to protect oneself.

Breaking forms

> *The way I play is different from everybody else's. I like to invent things. I am not better than anyone else, but I play... When I perform a meia-lua, I do it differently, I deconstruct it in four, five strikes, just with the meia-lua! When I perform a cabeçada (blow with the head), I divide it into two, into two... just with a cabeçada!*[37]

This *Capoeira* master's testimony illustrates a reference of expansion of the choreographic form that we also witnessed in the performance of other masters of Brazilian cultural manifestations. Therefore, the dancer has the skills to break forms. From the structural elements of a manifestation, the way the dancer moves changes the very form that generated it. Within the flow of decomposing and transforming, the movement is not crystallized, as right after its creation it becomes something new and dynamic.

Maintenance of the structures

Some choreographic structures, such as raising the masts in the *Congado*, are endowed with meaning and ritualistic acts that enable the body to be trained and prepared simultaneously with the space that will receive the festivity.

> *This is the magical moment of contact between earth and heaven. Then, that long mast is trying to reach the sky. It seems to be far away. For example, there is Saint Sebastian, we pray here on earth for Saint Sebastian to hear us. This is as if there was a thread linking here and there.*[38]

During the mast raising, space and body are revived through a kind of verticality that drives and connects the heaven/earth and divine/human polarities.

A man digs a hole in the ground, others carry the mast where the flag is set. Slowly, mast and flag are raised with their base set on the ground. The feet penetrate the earth and the head wants to fly to the sky. The body surrounds the mast,

---

37 Master João Grande, in Barbieri, Cesar – Um jeito brasileiro de aprender a ser (A Brazilian way to learn how to be).
38 Manoel - congadeiro (MG), 1987.

touches it, the head joins the process, contacting the axis that unifies the high and the low. Objects such as rosaries, swords and sticks are put around the mast and brought back to the center of the devotees' bodies.

When the masts are raised, the body and space start a converging and expanding dance, continually moving around the mast. Acts of touching and surrounding the mast are uniform; however, the greatest expression resulting from the intensity of this relationship depends on the dynamo of each one.

The torso wants to expand towards the flag, but the feet do not leave the ground. Spinning and bringing the memory of resistance until the moment to leave, the feet exert a traction force, so that the body can perform the *meia-lua* and interconnect the spaces. Men's feet resisted, making resistance the common memory.[39]

> *Ôô Criolo*
> *Dança essa meia-lua*
> *ô, criolo*
> *Dança com pé no chão*
> *ô, Criolo*
>
> *(ôô Criolo*
> *Dance this meia-lua ô, criolo*
> *Dance with your feet on the ground ô, Criolo)*
> (Chant of Candombe)[40]

Viva Nossa Senhora do Rosário. Viva São Sebastião. Viva Santa Efigênia. Viva Nossa Senhora da Graça. Viva todos os santos que são da cor do céu.

(Hail Our Lady of the Rosary. Hail Saint Sebastian. Hail Saint Ephigenia. Hail Our Lady of Grace. Hail all saints who have the color of the sky)[41]

Losing the paths

Concessions allowing fragmented rites in the places disconnected from their spatial characteristics remove the property of this choreographic nature in which there is a feedback system of the space with the bodies of their devotees. Resulting from social changes, these cases lead to a loss of the sacred foundations, turning the rites into poor choreographic compositions. The dance structure loses

---

39 *Núbia Gomes and Edmilson Pereira* – Negras raízes mineiras: os Arturos, *(the Arturos: black roots from Minas)*, 1988.
40 *Núbia Gomes and Edmilson Pereira* – Negras raízes mineiras: os Arturos, *(the Arturos: black roots from Minas)*, 1988.
41 Hailing the five masts raising of Candombe from Fidalgo (MG), 1987.

its base, showing movement shapes and space occupations without their most expressive senses and values. As a legacy of early times, when the elders used to play in the *terreiro*, many memories will remain on the bodies of those who traveled the paths seeking their own stories.

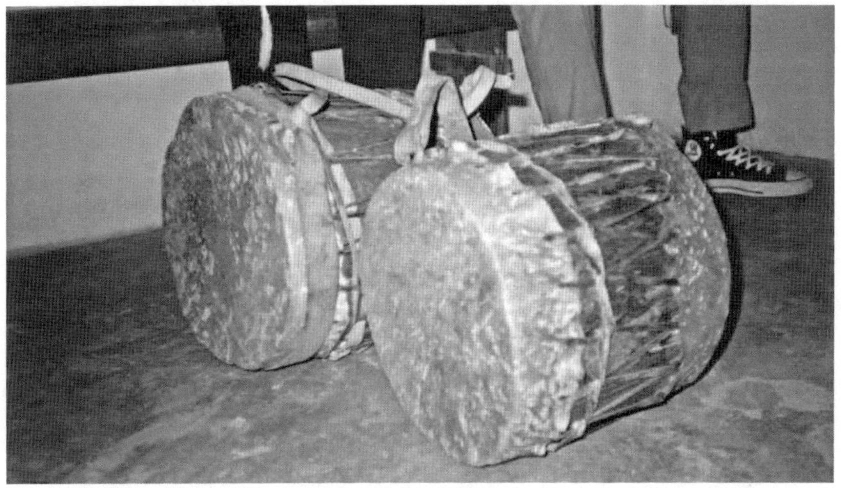

Caixas do Congado
Arturos - 1987
Author's archive

One cannot sing like that,
you cannot think and sing,
you have to look...

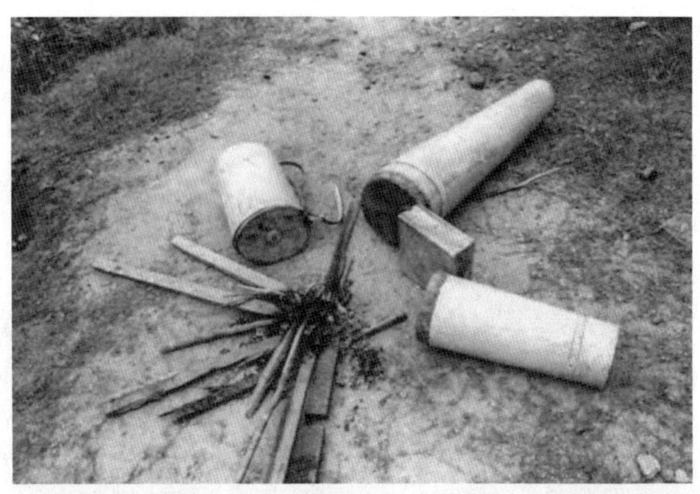

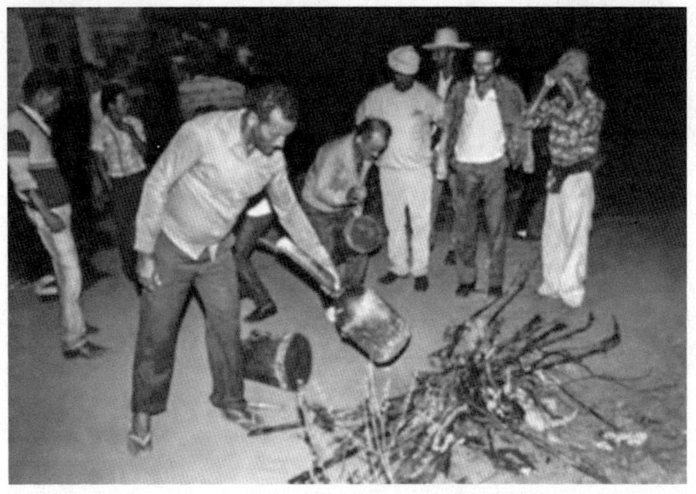

Above:
Instruments of Candombe
Quinta do Sumidouro MG 1988
Photo: Ricardo Oliveira

Below:
Candombe de Quinta do Sumidouro
Instrumentstuning, ahead Captain Antônio Pereira de Almeida, 1988
Photo: Ricardo Oliveira

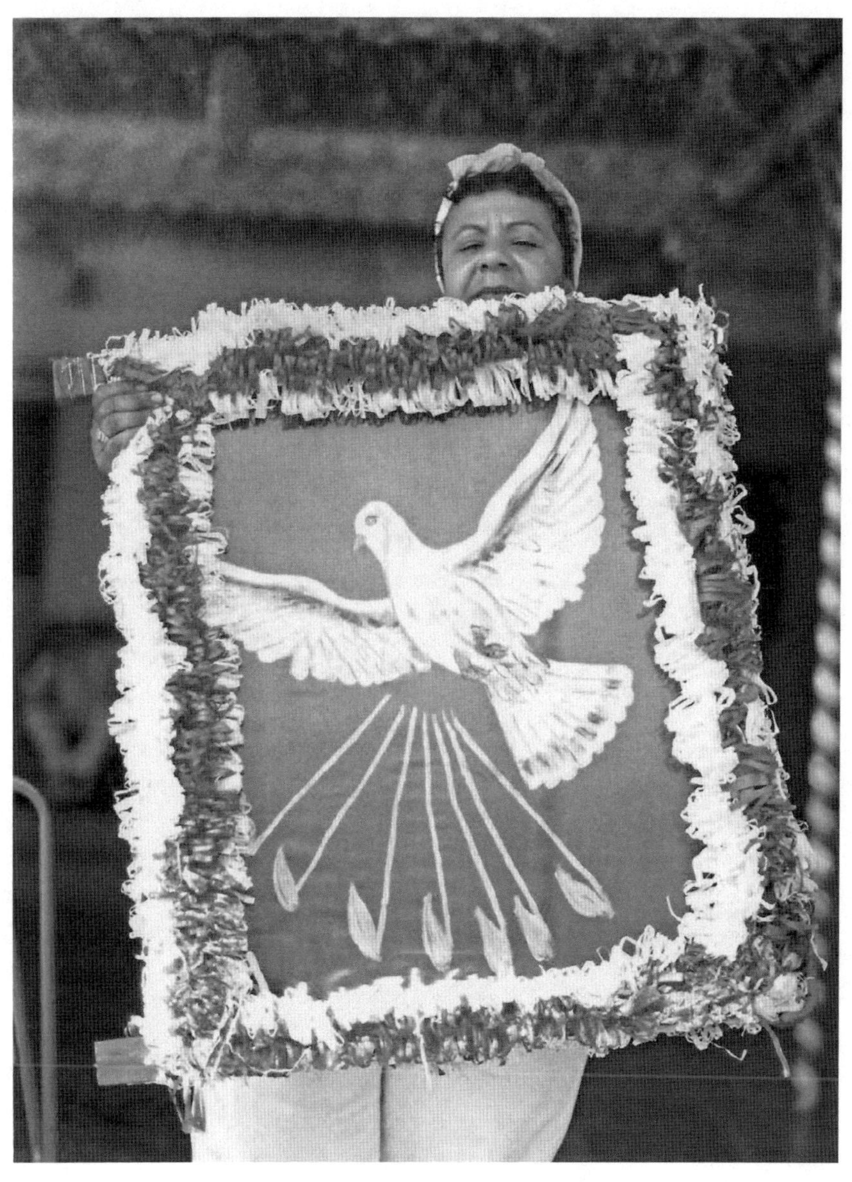

Eni carrying the Divino Espírito Santo flag
Belo Horizonte, MG - 1996
Photo: Eustáquio Neves

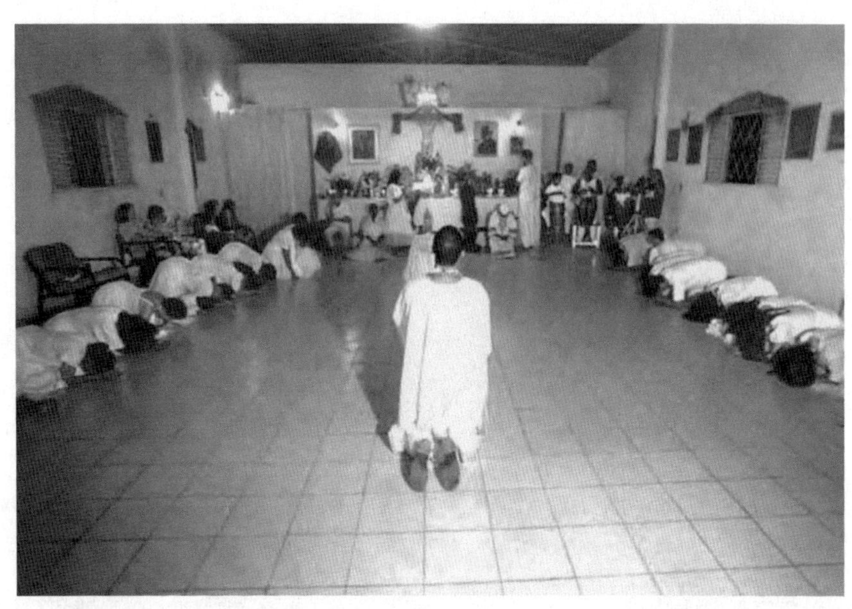

***Terreiro Pai Joaquim** of Aruanda and*
Boiadeiro de Minas
Brasília DF, 1995
Photo: Juan Pratginesto's

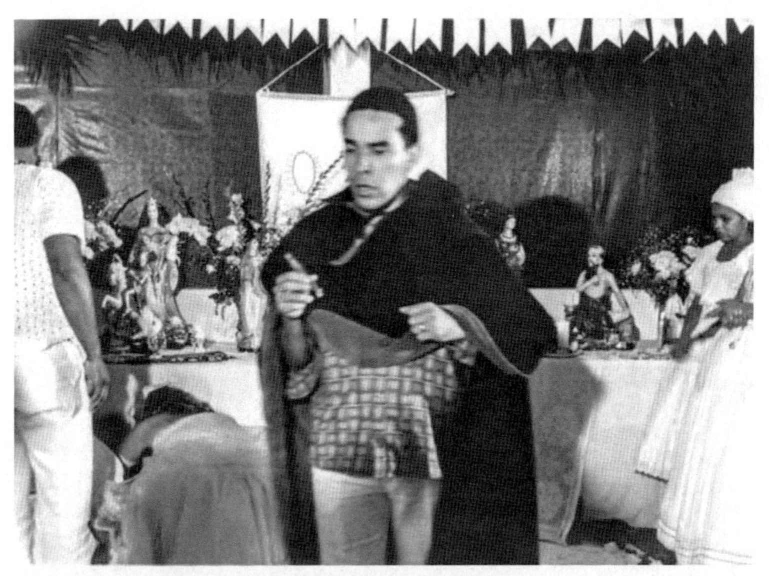
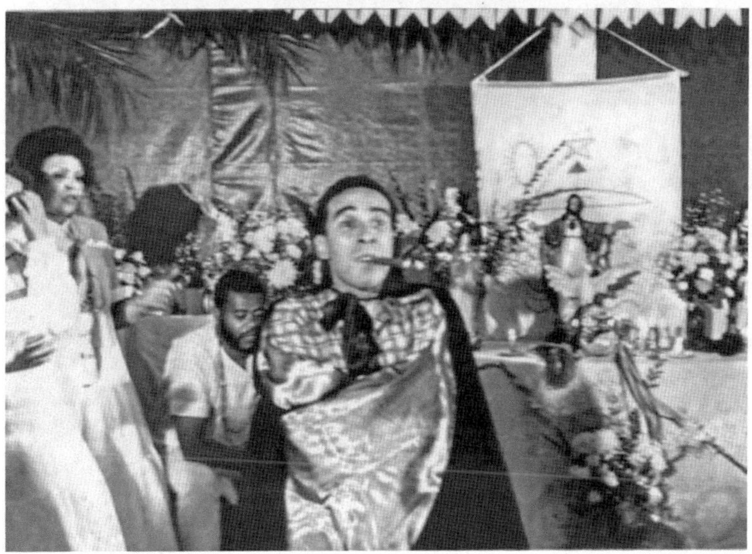

Exu Tranca-Ruas, incorporated in
Carlos Alberto da Costa
Brasília, 1998
Author's archive

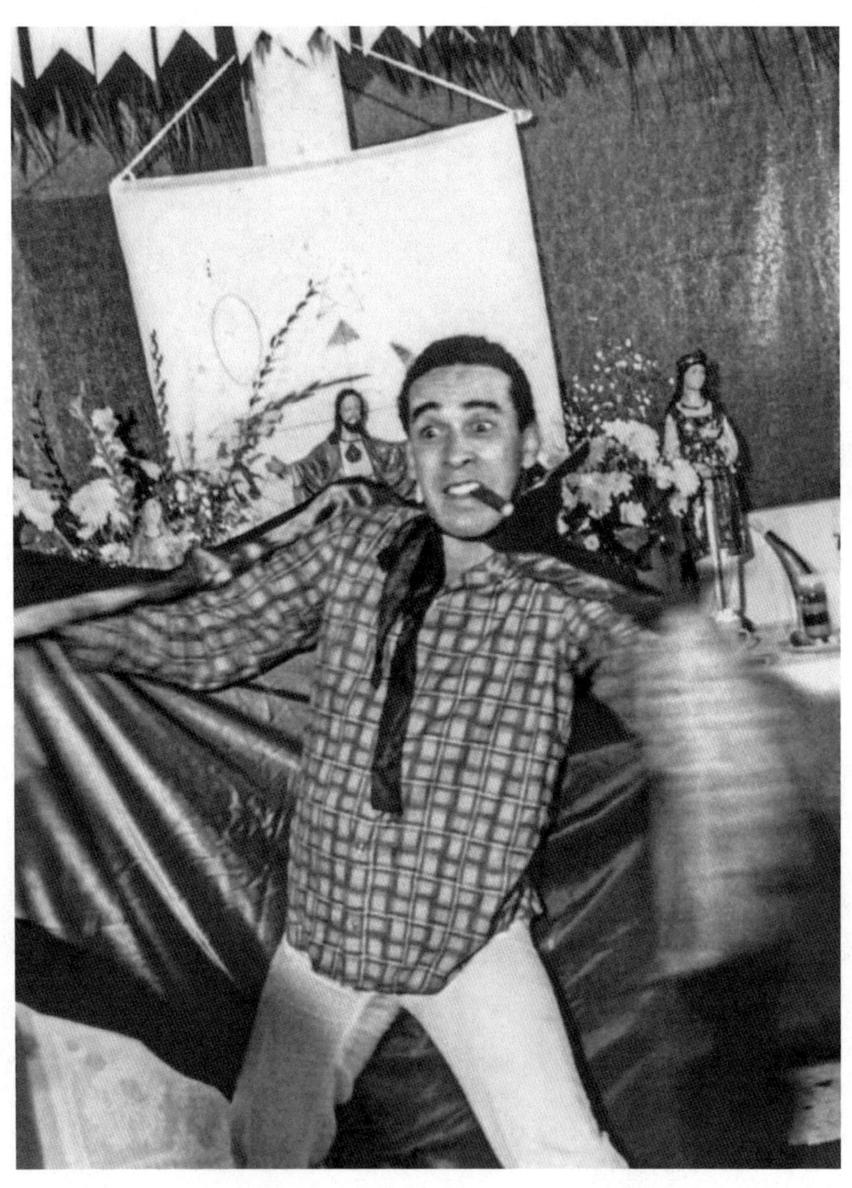

I came to put my strength, the strength of my cape,
on all of you with the permission of Oshala.

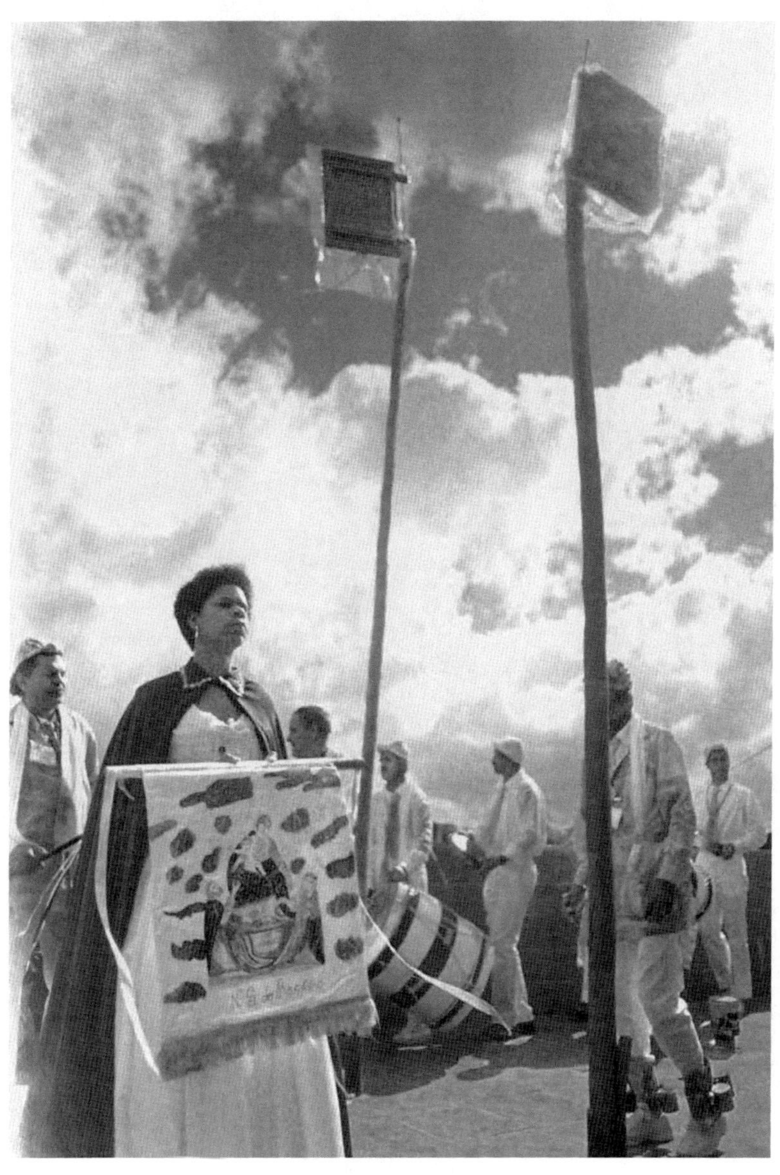

Guarda de Moçambique *around the Mast*
conducted by the Guiding Flag
Terreiro of Dona Efigênia, 1996
Photo: Eustáquio Neves

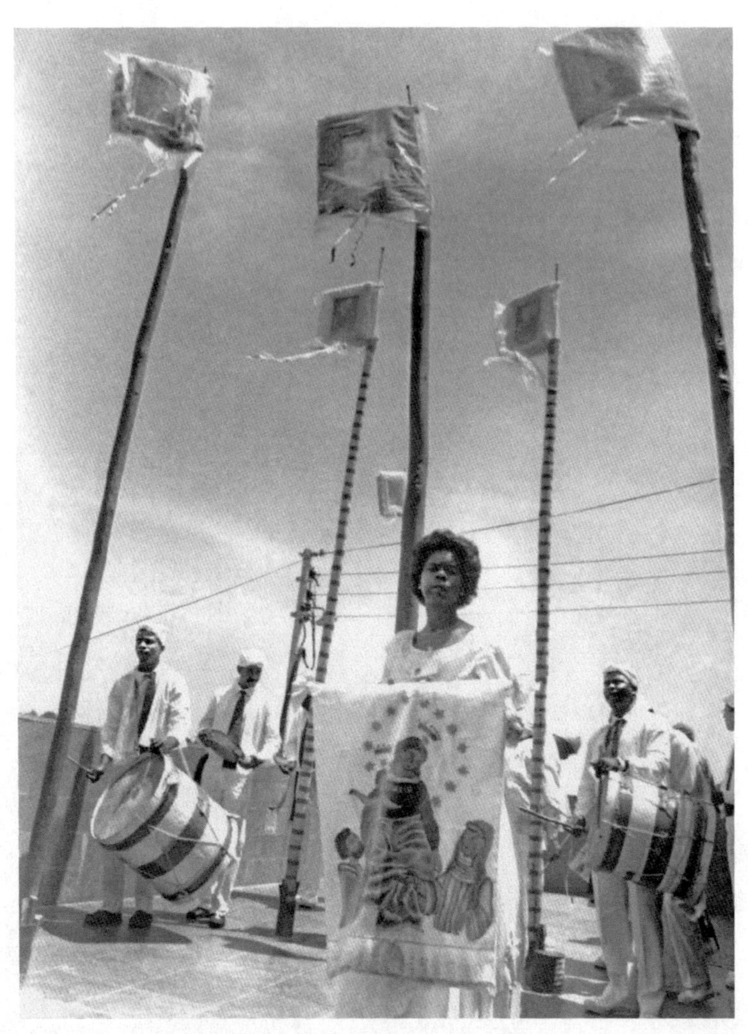

Guarda de Moçambique around the Mast
conducted by the Guiding Flag
Terreiro of Dona Efigênia, 1996
Photo: Eustáquio Neves

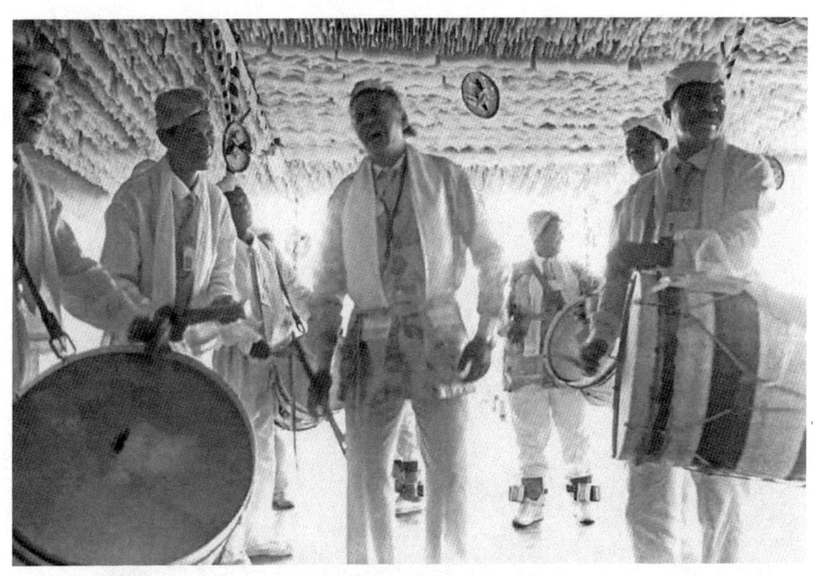

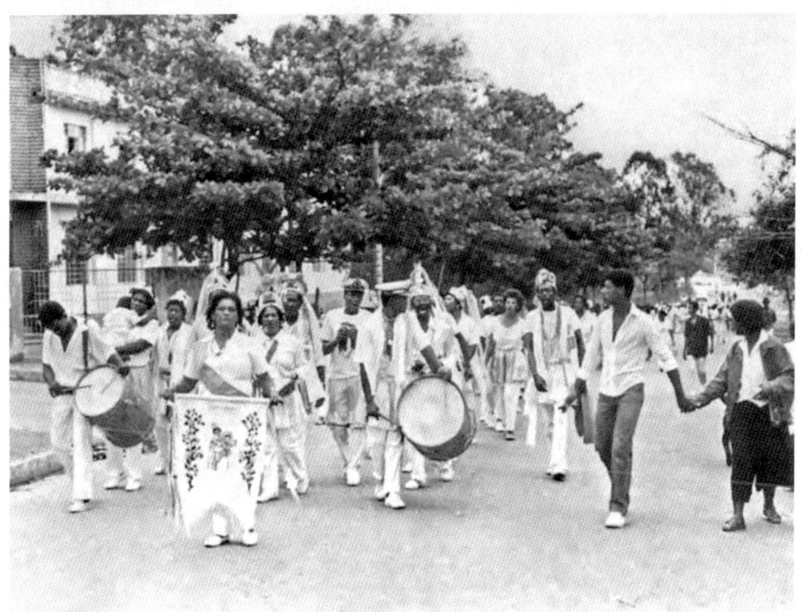

Above, on this page
Arturos, *Guarda de Congo, 1995*
Author's archive

Moçambique, *Terreiro de Dona Efigênia*
Belo Horizonte, 1996
Photo: Eustáquio Neves

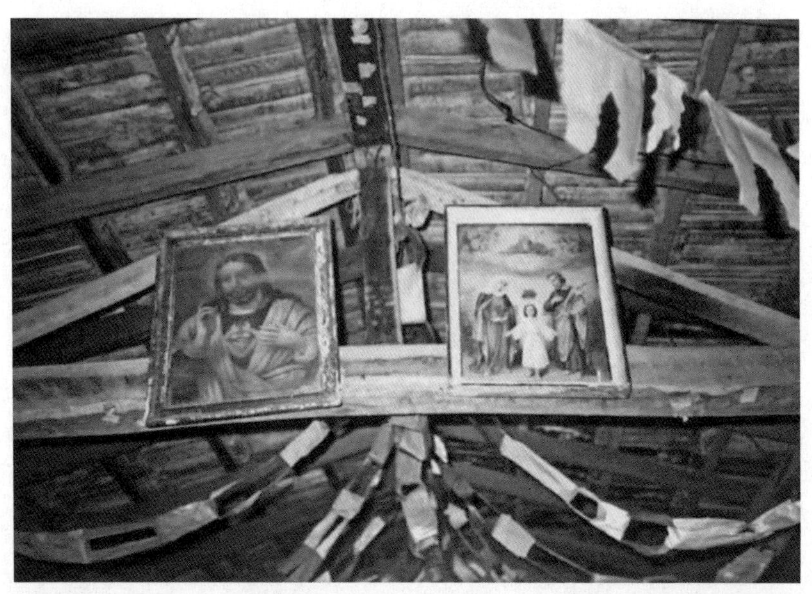

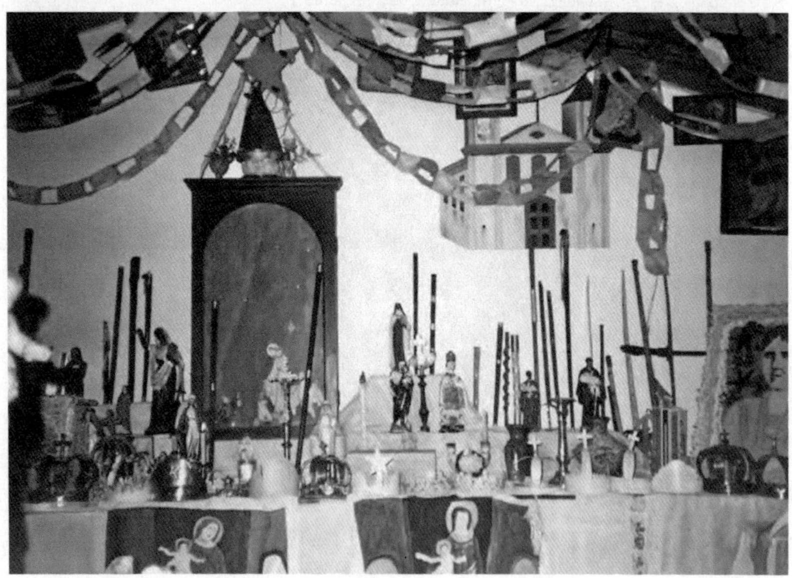

Congá of Arturos
Contagem, MG - 1987
Auhtor's archive

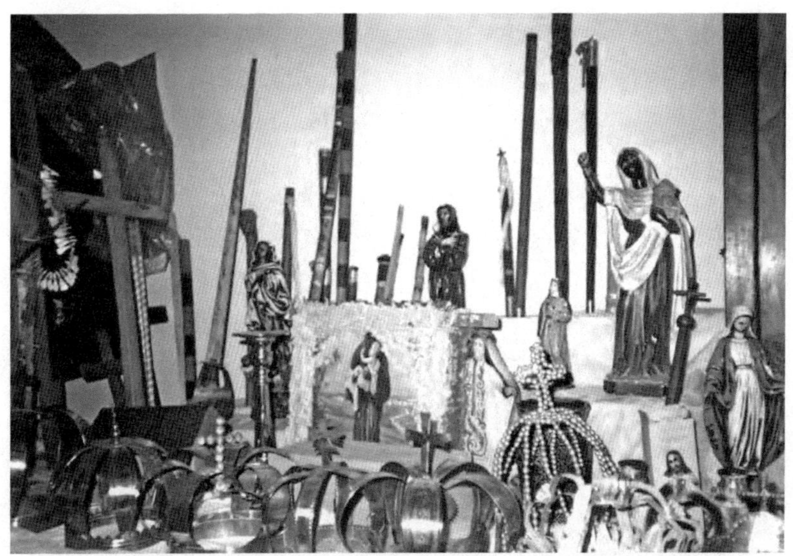

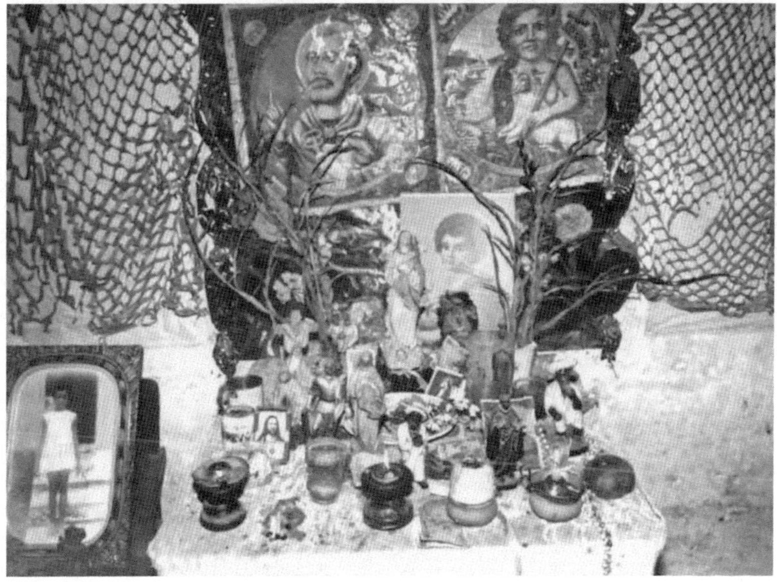

Above:
Congá *of Arturos*
Contagem, MG - 1987
Auhtor's archive

Congá, *house of Divina*
Mato do Tição, Jaboticatubas, MG
Photo: Ricardo Oliveira

133

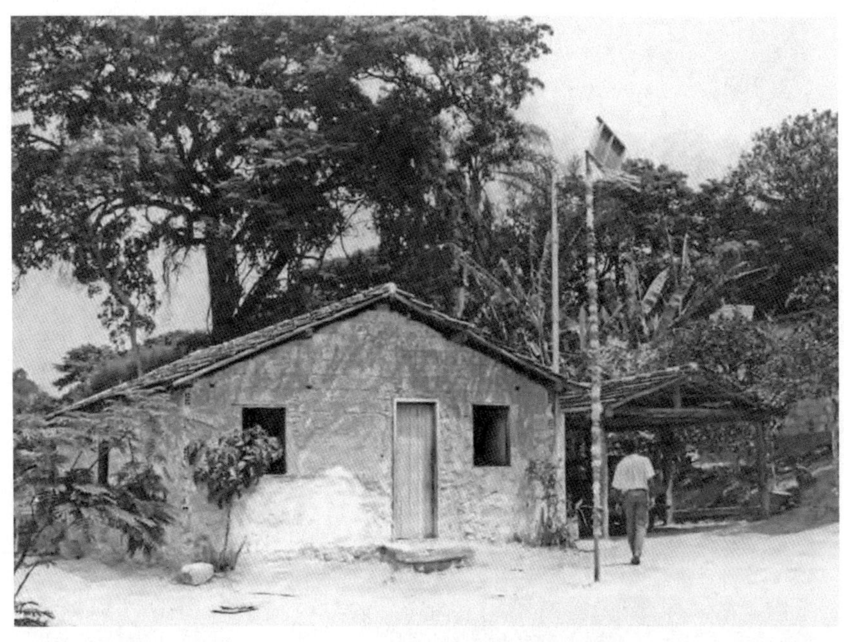

Frente da casa *de Antônio*
(Front of Antônio's house).
Arturos, MG, 1987.
Author's archive

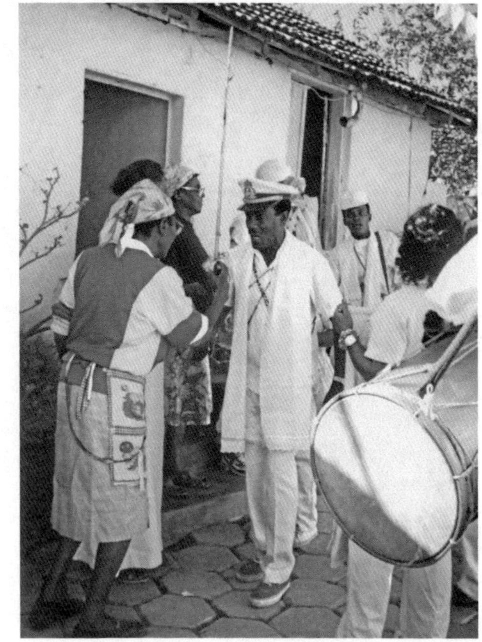

Recebimento do Congo
(Congo is received in the
terreiro in the house of the Arturos)
Contagem, MG - 1995.
Author's archive

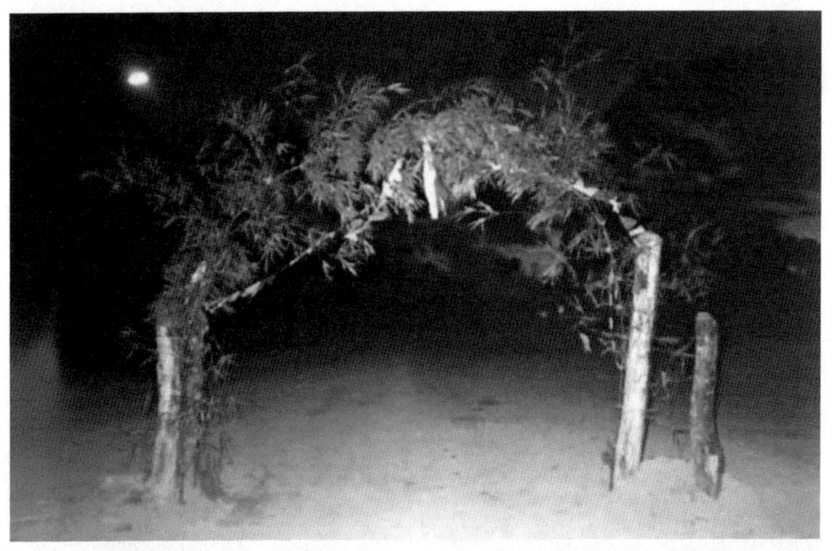

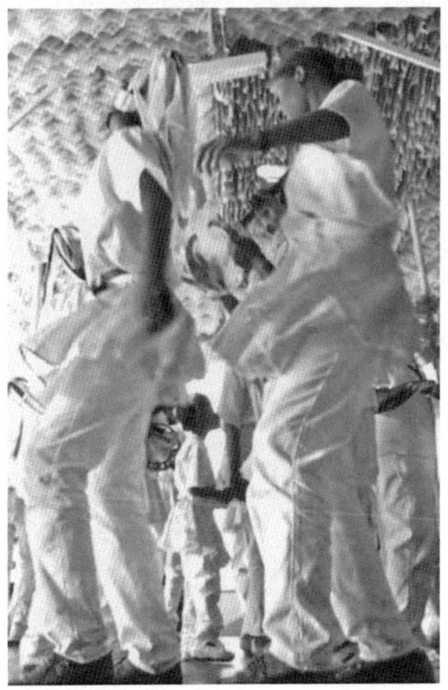

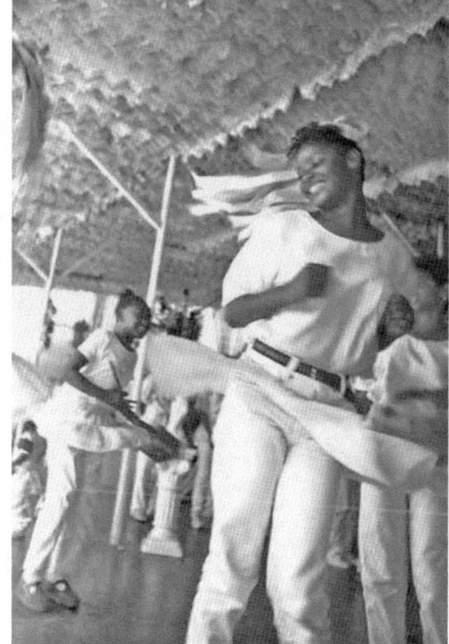

Above:
Travessias, *Arturos Contagem – 1987.*
Author's archive

Below:
Congo, *1996*
Photos: Eustáquio Neves

135

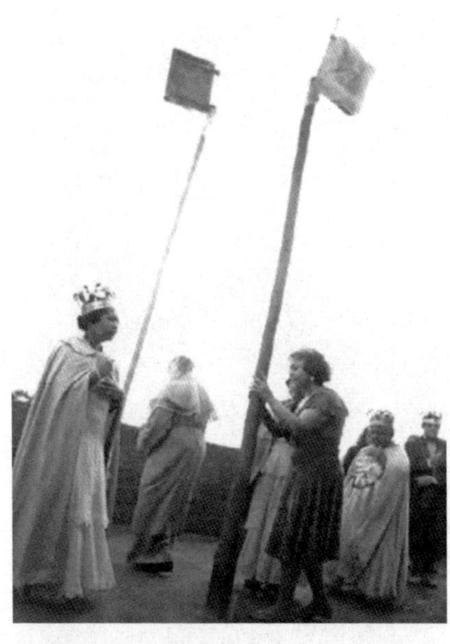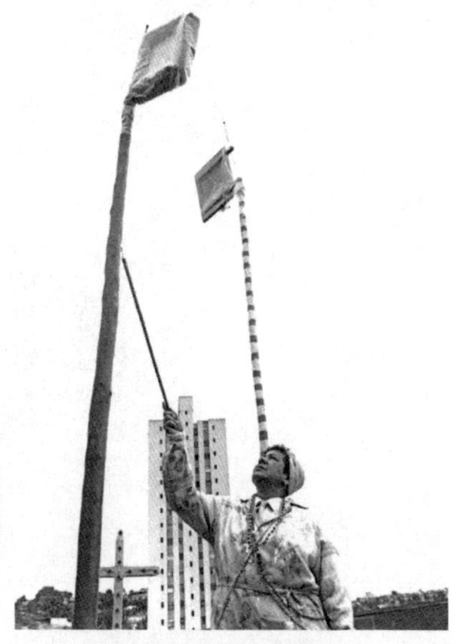

Hasteamento de mastro (Flag raising)
Terreiro Dona Efigênia
Belo Horizonte, 1996.
Photos: Eustáquio Neves.

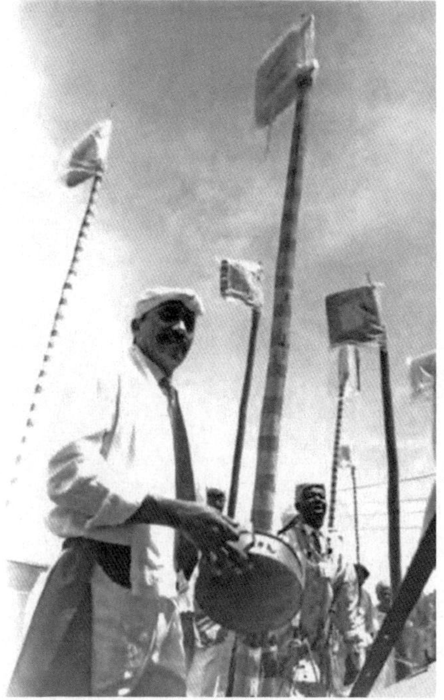

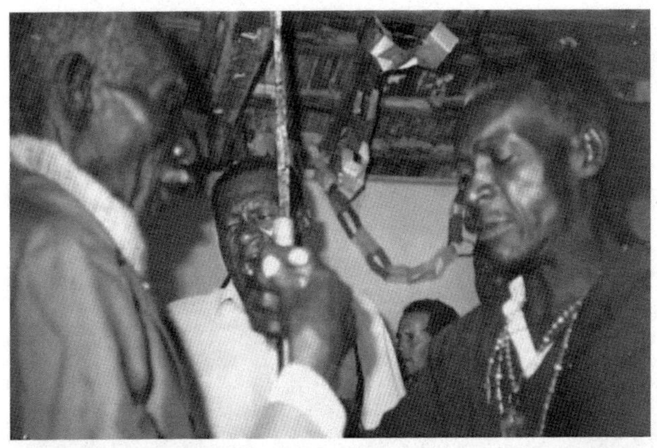

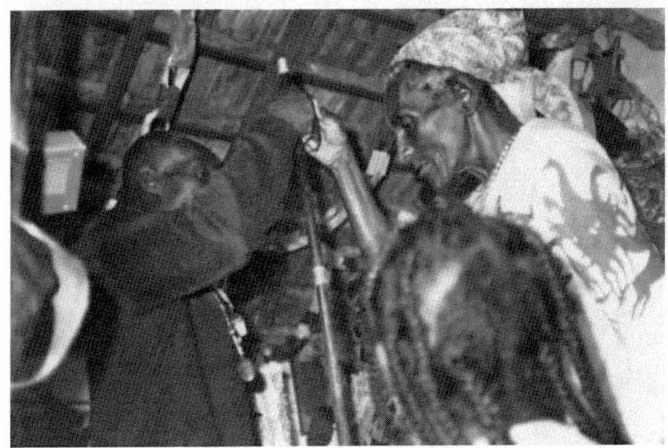

In the beginning of the
Rituais do Congado
(Congado's ritual):
investiture of swords
and stick
Arturos, Contagem
MG, 1987
Author's archive

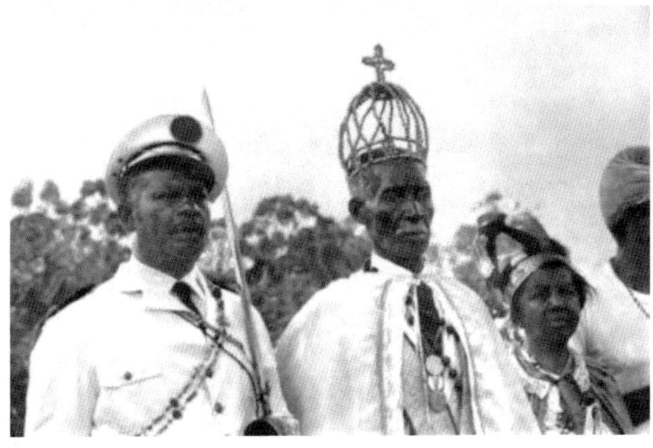

In the middle of the
photo
Mr. Geraldo, *king of*
Congado de MG, with
the crown keeper and
one the queens.
Arturos, Contagem
MG, 1987
Author's archive

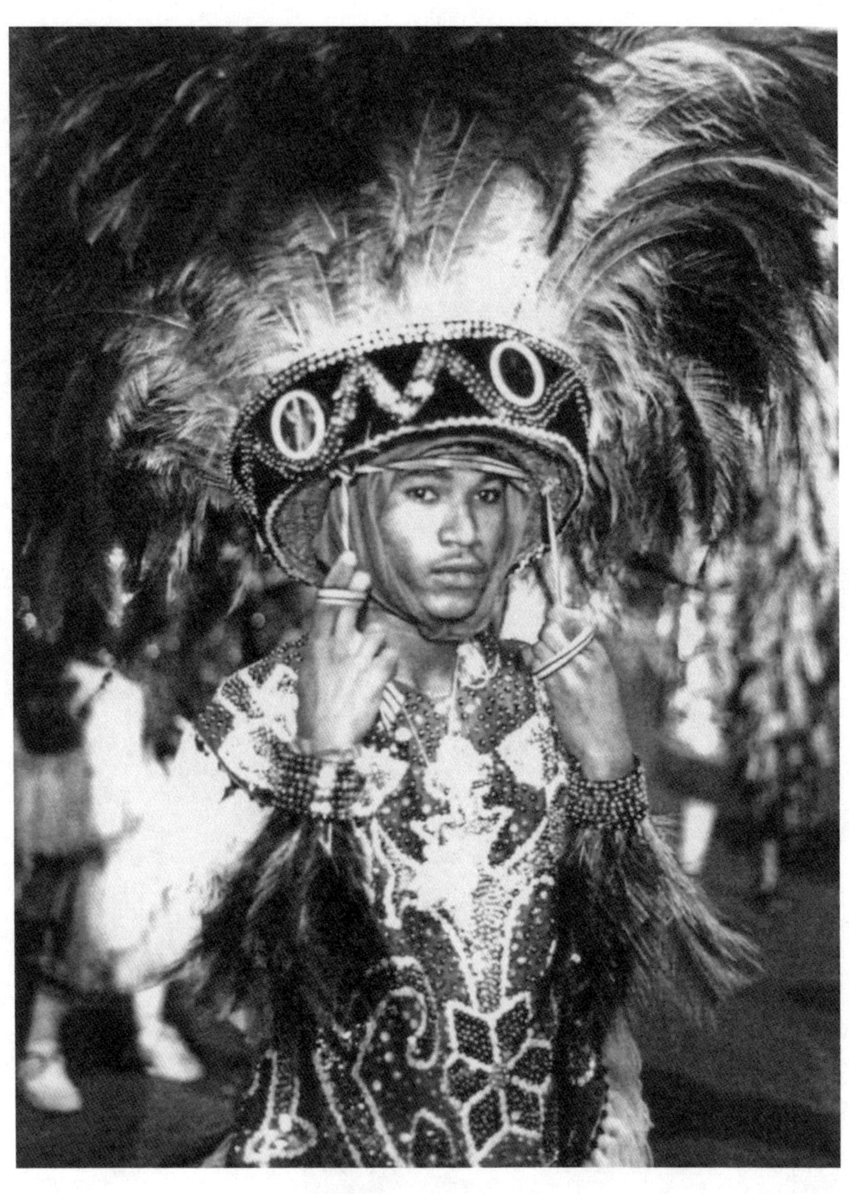

Caboclo de Pena,
MaracatuRural de Tabajara, PE - 1992.
Author's archive

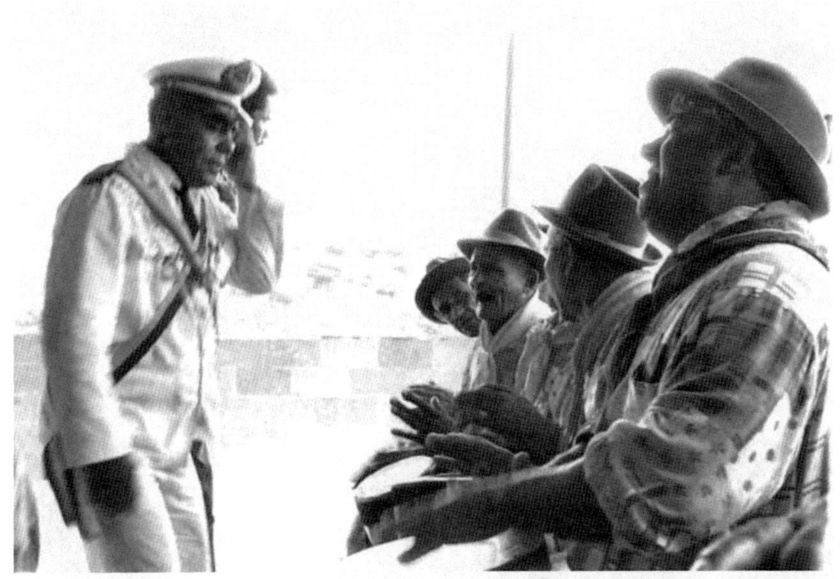

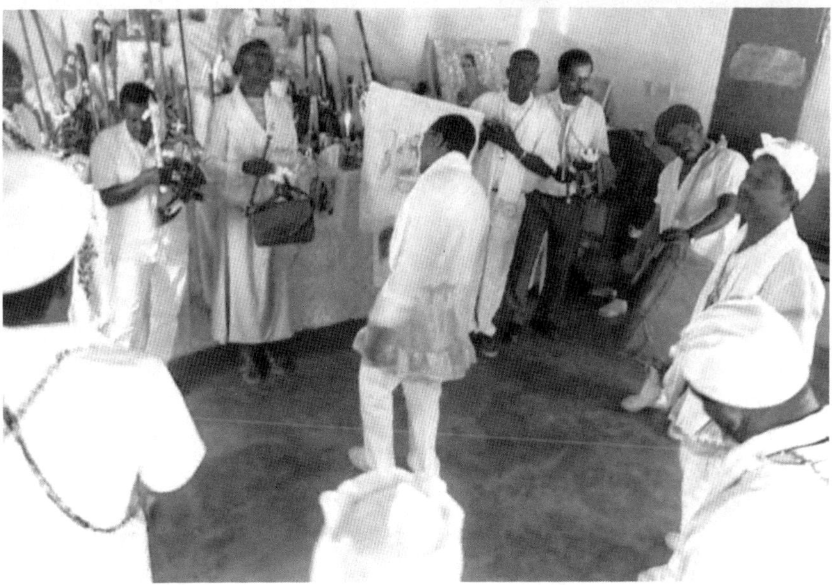

Above:
Candombe, *1996*
Photo: Eustáquio Neves.

Inside the **Capelinha dos Arturos***,*
Congá and terreiro, 1996 (church)
Photo: Eustáquio Neves

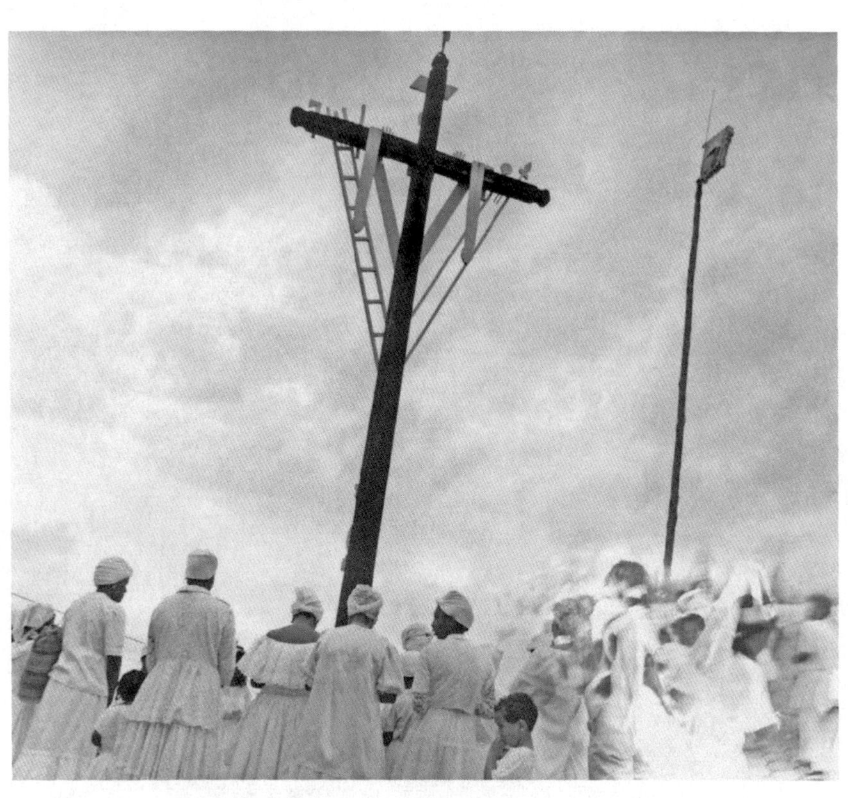

Above:
Cruzeiro, *Arturos*
Photo: Eustáquio Neves

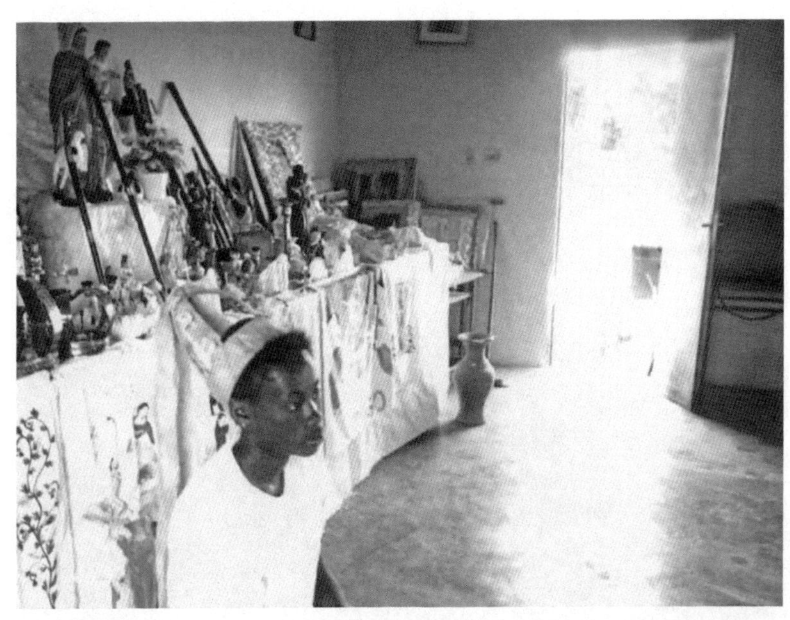

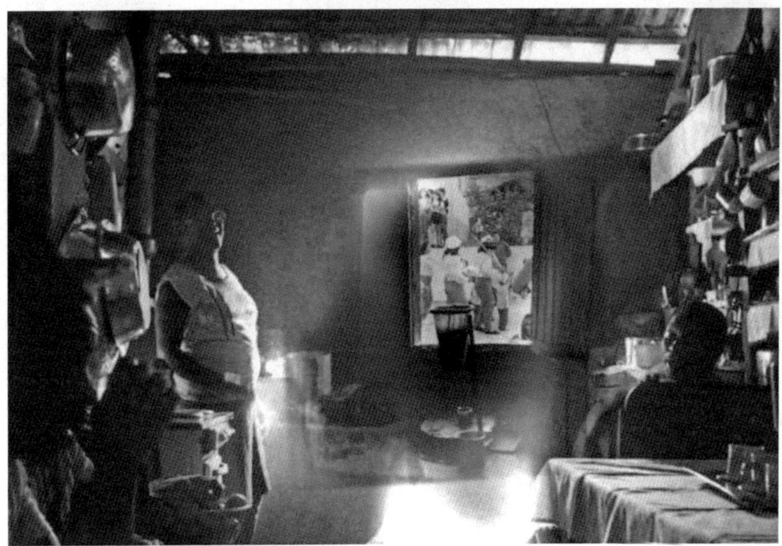

<table>
<tr>
<td>

Above:
*Inside of **Capelinha dos Arturos**, 1996*
(Arturo's church)
Photo: Eustáquio Neves

</td>
<td>

Below:
***Cozinha dos Arturos**, (Arturo's kitchen)*
Feature in the ph3oto Induca, 1996
Photo: Eustáquio Neves

</td>
</tr>
</table>

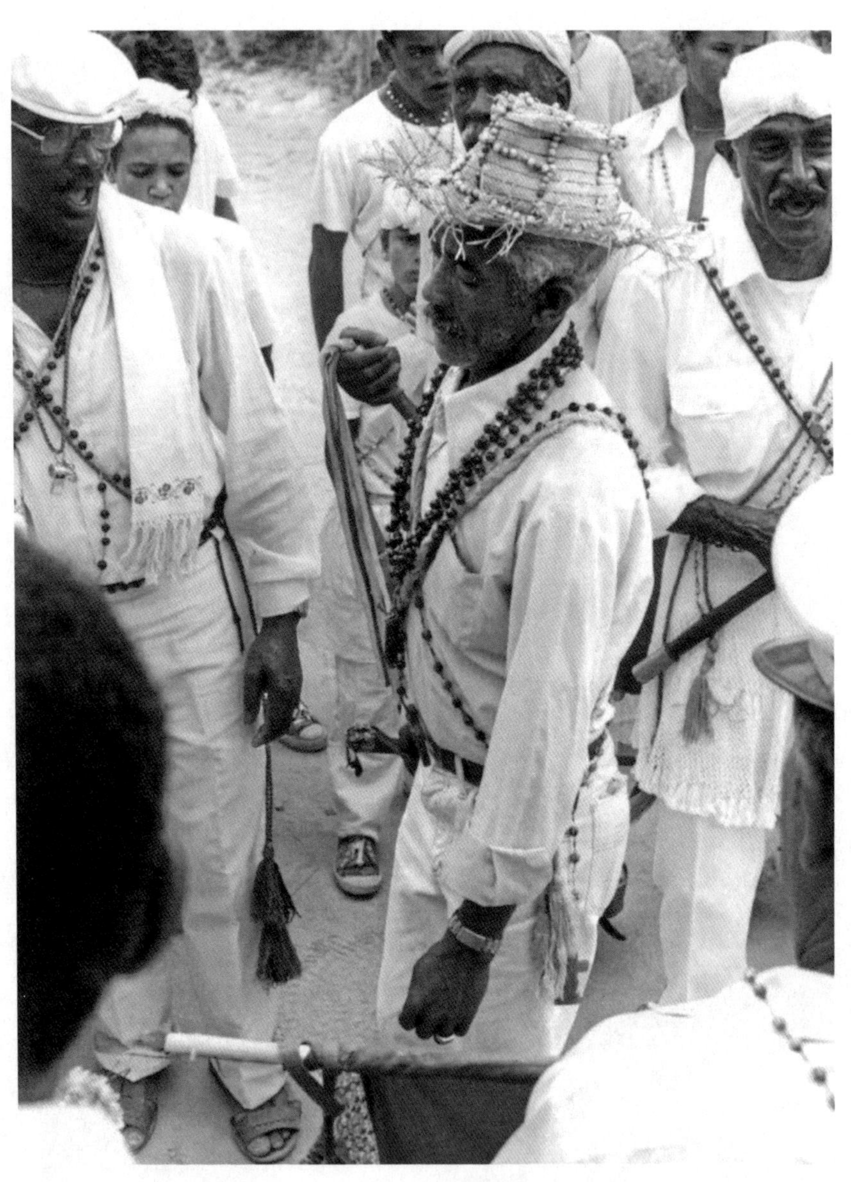

Moçambique de João Lopes
Belo Horizonte, MG
1987
Author's archive

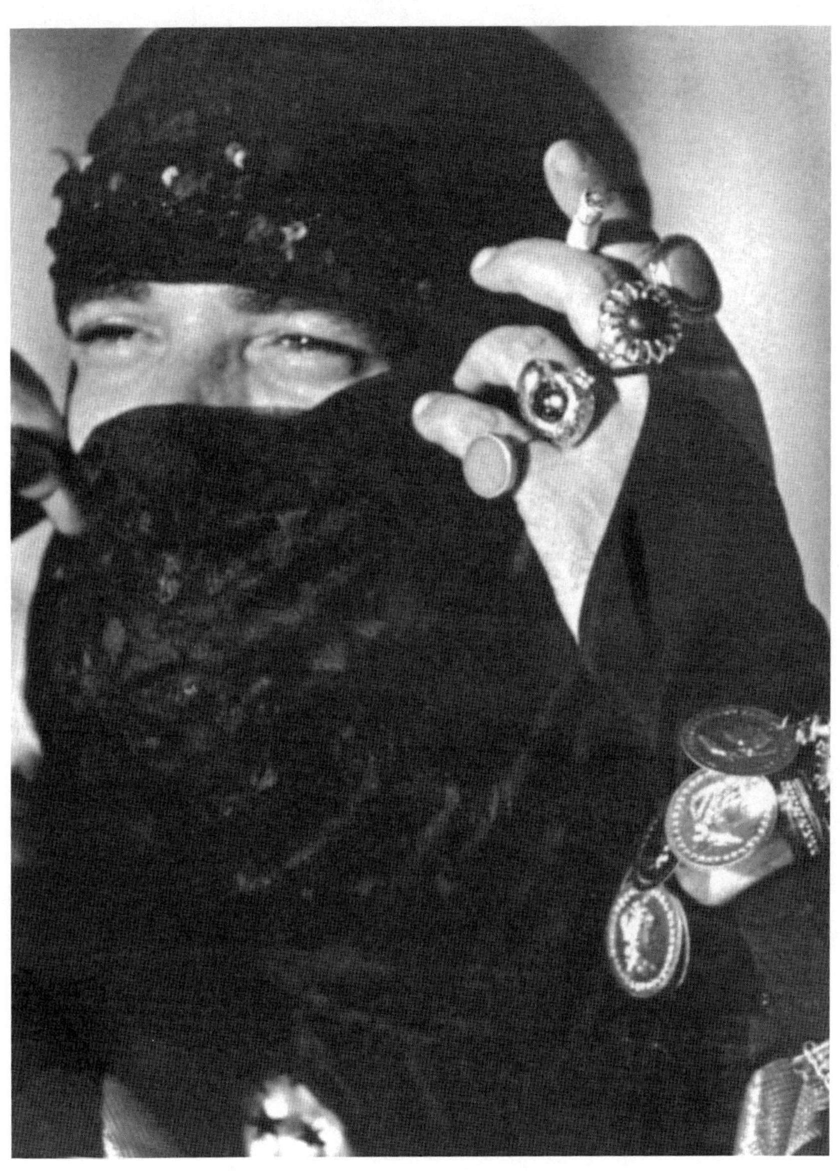

Pomba Gira Maria Padilha
das Sete Encruzilhadas
Brasília, DF - 1995
Photo: Juan Pratginesto's

143

8 Looking Through the Crack

Afoxé belongs to the poor, as well as Capoeira. Maracatu is performed by the poor. Maracatu does not belong to rich men, I haven't seen it before, right?[1]

In the pursuit of the Brazilian characters, we attended the visceral school of rituals and found its extensive movement. We were taken by the feeling of weakness in face of its dynamism, continuously generating shades of compositions that we could not hold in our hands. The moments shared during the rituals provided us with the image of a gaze through a slightly open door through which fragments irradiated as witnesses of important social experiences.

In each research field, we met people who proved to be the masters in life, performing the role of pillars of the groups to which they belonged, without claiming any credit for it. We highlight these people, avoiding generalizations as there are not so many of them around. During the time of our research, many of these people passed away, revealing the evidences of substantial changes that occurred in this school of ritual movements.

We aimed at pursuing certain contents that insisted on pursuing us. Besides, we let ourselves go by the movements emerging from people who dominated an "entire body" process, that is, a body expressing daily life and festivities.

The door was opened and a look through the crack revealed ways of life that were very close to excellence in human relationships.

8.1 The worked body

The keepers of the popular culture model consist of workers, rural workers, garbage collectors, truck drivers, cooks, tractor drivers, among others – groups of poor, simple people who have the skill to turn a hard daily existence into a celebration of life:

We do it because we love it. We spend our earnings in the Maracatu to have the pleasure to see it dancing.[2]

Several voices from those groups that keep the visceral school of rituals with different performances, but similar bodies, resonate in this statement of the *maracatuzeiro*. With a knack for generating a power that is stronger than the contours

---

1   Manoelzinho Salustiano, maracatuzeiro - Olinda (PE), 1992.
2   Manoelzinho Salustiano, maracatuzeiro - Olinda (PE), 1992.

of the body, these people see the dance outside them gaining forms in movements and, with such dimension, they dive in it with their whole body and soul.

The entire body is a result of an interweaving between daily life and festivity. In hard, heavy, underpaid work conditions there is an accumulation of emotions that are converted into pulsations in the spaces of the festivity.

These pulsations produce the dance that is connected to the senses of life. The fruition of emotions allows an expansion that enables people to penetrate the harmony of movement. The physical skills and the callus formed as a result of the daily struggle for survival become more sophisticated due to the special moments of dancing.

There was a time when the bodies of devotees were immersed in nature, in the work in the fields. The knowledge acquired in the fields was mixed up with festivities. The difficulties to survive were not little, but there was a greater integration of the body with the environment. The farming language is rich and space is gained by walking miles. Our analysis evidenced that most researched individuals consisted of rural workers. Their childhood memories were mainly related to daily life with parents, in a structure in which everything had its own place and time was enjoyed by singing, plowing or building fences, while learning the structure of the *folguedo*.

The research on female rural workers in different places and times revealed that their relationship with the festivities became restricted. However, the richness of their body language and the way they mastered their bodies were tools that helped us to understand the worked body. We found that the belief in Divine had remained alive.

The crack of the door brightens, bringing the clamor of the women of the land. There is so much laughter in the fields… One can perceive a sensuality that is spread and the rhythm of those who want to make the day. They are lonely women, always dreaming of affection. Their task is to bring up their children, to help them survive. Here we observe the life conditions of women in the past, emphasizing the differences in the rights and duties in relation to men. However, even in pain, these women do not lose the sensibility allowing them to live pleasurably.

Urgency, rhythm, attention, readiness, and breath are necessary to make the day. An alignment of the posture and proper use of muscular groups are also necessary, so that each activity is fully performed. Cutting sugarcane or harvesting coffee depends on the precision and mastering of various stages of movements: impulses, punctuations and flows must occur in their specific places. The body cutting sugarcane is different from the body harvesting coffee: the roughness and hardness of one opposes to the delight and flexibility of the other. Both demand much effort:

I know how to do every work in the fields. We deal with a lot of things. Sometimes, under the rain, sometimes under a scorching sun. It is good to feel the weather.

The body assimilates the working tools. Such tools intervene in the body language according to their affinities: either through a hoe, a machete or a sieve. The women like to work in the fields, but they express disapproval for being underpaid. If there is work to be done, they won't stop, blurring the boundaries between harvesting and giving birth:

I was harvesting coffee when I had this belly ache. I leaned down. I just had the time to take the cloth, then I gave birth to a boy... Right there, in the coffee plantation.

Although these histories and the work in the fields seem to be very similar, each of these women shows very well delineated personal traits. Amid these heroines, we highlight one in particular. Neiúda is a lonely woman, she does not belong to a festivity group; her body pulsates, but she no longer participates in rituals. She belonged to the *Umbanda*, then she joined several evangelical churches in order to get freed from the devil that had been torturing her for a long time. However, religious conversion was difficult to her:

I wanna see you feel our tragedy.

That is how Neiúda introduced us to her domain, the land that demands work. The strength to be a rural worker is what she inherited from her mother:

Only God worths. We walk throughout the world, we do not know how to get home. God only knows, no one else.

Neiúda is a woman of many losses and scars. There is no space in her body that has not experienced pain. The posture of her shoulders resembles someone who carries a huge burden. Her heavy hands lean on the thighs, but she keeps the axle. Her posture often belongs to someone who keeps the feet behind, as if she was supposed to *gingar* (a *capoeira* movement). Her body speaks with that knack of those who work with the "Resistance tonus". In her hands, "the bone perforates the flesh" in order to reveal, through gestures, the landscapes and the meanings of the stories of her life with an extremely human mark: the days she would not have even a grain of rice to eat; times when she had no house to live or the circumstances of not owning a body, because she remained unconscious for an undetermined period of time due to physical violence. Life of her body passed through many challenges, but she overcome her own misery and now laughs as if she had nothing to lose. There is no room for more tragedies in her life:

If I fail, I die.

However, as if so much pain was not enough, there also were God's trials, who sent a devil to her:

> *He really rides. He leaps on your back. Sometimes I wanted to go somewhere and he said: I will leap on your back, so you will not go. The weight on my back was so heavy that I could not stand walking. But I was stubborn and I said: I will, I will, I will. And I did.*

Neiúda's responsive body felt a tingling and burning sensation that, according to her reports, was due to the presence of the devil that had been living in her wardrobe for a long time. In the last meetings with Neiúda, the devil seemed to be giving up on her, as she told us:

> *That figure that appeared to me was the devil, and he was accompanied by others, and he told me: "honey, not even a thousand devils can beat you."*

> *If you stay alone, you become depressed. If you only think about your problems, if you only sit at the corner, only stay quiet and cry, you'll get even worse. You got to stand up and speak to yourself: I will struggle, I will take the win, because I want to achieve this victory and the Lord will help me. The Lord's hand is not so short that it cannot save; nor His ear is so heavy that it cannot hear. You got to be patient and avoid getting angry, otherwise temptation invades your body.*

During this testimony, Neiúda stuck the machete into the ground, looked at the vastness of the sky and felt thanked for the air she breathed.

With the individual or the festivity as the focus of the research, we observed that the data were intercrossed, resulting in a worked body whose content we can describe as resistance. This is a force that overcomes the weight of the oppression imposed on the body and that emanates from some kind of hope showing human beings that it is worth to struggle for life.

8.2 The "devil" and the saint

Eshu is the master of cosmic magic, whose essence controls the diastole and the systole of the universe, as well as its inhalation and exhalation. Its driving force enables the manifestation of power in action. Besides, *Eshu* is the guardian of the limits, the balance point of the cause and effect movements. Due to its dynamics, *Eshu* is also the mediator in the relationship between gods and men, as showed by the chantings of *Umbanda*:

> *O vento que venta lá, venta cá*
> *Exu é magia em qualquer lugar*

> *(The wind that blows over there, also blows over here*
> *Eshu is magic everywhere).*

This is the most human among all *orishas*; it is neither entirely good nor completely evil:

> *Eshu's ambiguity as a symbol of negative forces (defensive and protective) conveys human conflicts and the search for the balance of oppositions.*[3]

Eshu has good and bad qualities; it encourages both fear and safeness. There is an *Eshu* for each *orisha*, as well as for each human being, as it provides each individual with the earthly and cosmic identity.

Eshu's ambivalence allowed the institutional power, represented by slave owners and Christian priests, to identify it as a symbol of evil and perversity, relating it to the devil.

Therefore, according to the *Umbanda Iniciática*, *Eshu* is the master of cosmic magic, the great architect of the universe; in the African tradition in Brazil, it is a carrier *orisha*, the most respected one, the first to be invoked. For the colonizers, he is the personification of the devil.

Popular *Umbanda* assimilates these references, including the image of the devil; it is, however, a loving devil, which, without losing its ambivalence, is considered as the other face of God:

> *Eshu has two heads…One is Satan from hell; the other is Jesus from Nazareth.*[4]

In the *Terreiros* of *Umbanda*, *Eshus* get closer to the physical matter; they are entities that lived on earth, remaining close to the contemporary man. However, these entities belong to legions that are interconnected to other entities and *orishas*, following a hierarchical sequence until reaching the divine essence.

For a better understanding of the archetype manifested through the medium, let's observe some aspects of the sacred revealed by the entity itself.

The day was neither bright nor dark in its misty appearance, *Exu Rei* (King *Eshu*) took control over the medium Carlos. In his elegant mode irrespective of time, the entity greets, with a serious, solemn voice:[5]

> *Good evening.*
> *We are the reflect of you,*
> *Eshu is a blessing angel,*
> *Eshu is an elemental, the force existing among God, the orishas and physical matter. Nothing is done before pleasing Eshu, nothing happens prior to caring for the earth element.*

---

3 Olôórisá - Escritos sobre a religião dos orixás / *coordinator and translator Carlos Eugênio M. de Moura, 1981.* (Writings on the religion of the *Orishas*).
4 Ponto de Eshu. (Eshu's chant).
5 Carlos Alberto da Costa. Brasília (DF), 1995.

From the unification of the seven upper elementals with the seven lower elementals a trilogy between God, spirit and man emerges. This trilogy generates *Eshus* and *Pomba-Giras* that are designated by Oshala to fight for the power and balance of the seven *chakras* of man:

> *We are under the power of Eshu; for many of us, it is due to the redemptions of debts that I would not call the past debts, but behaviors in past incarnations. Usually, the so-called Eshus were cruel men, and now they return in this form of Eshu to redeem their debts. They still carry the forces that governed them in life and that still hold them attached to this world.*

> *Tranca-ruas was a great lawyer, João Caveira was a great doctor, and I was a great writer.*

Each name refers to a legion as there are many *Tranca-ruas, João Caveiras,* and so on. *Exu Rei* individualizes them, referring to the entities incorporated by its medium:

> *I've been to all four corners of the world. I come from Syria, my real name is DVOGAN ERGÔ. I was a great slave and became a great master, but I was very cruel, so the strength I have to balance the trilogy in people's life is related to balancing myself on the basis of them.*

> *At the moment, I am a part of the house of an Orisha. It allows me to have the strength (through an Oshala and with the love of my medium) to polish my pyramid and follow my way. I redeemed myself, I predisposed myself through an Oshala to redeem my debts, so I travel to all four corners of the world to work with the seven energies. While I guide and clarify I evolve; it is as if I had passed through regression. From a vassal on the earth, I become a king in the spiritual world.*

Exu Rei shows some codes transmitted through its hands to the initiated ones during the ritual dance:

> *If an Eshu dances with hands like this (palms facing the ground relating the fingertips of both hands), he is saying that the balance is serene. If he contours like the waves of the sea (rotating its hands in and out), this means confusion; and if Eshu has claws, watch out, trouble is coming!*

> *But the main meaning of Eshu's dance is the energy that turns around the positive and negative sides. As I work on these forces, my excitement relates to detachment release.*

A reduplication of *Eshu's* values was observed in other Brazilian cultural manifestations, especially in the significant characters embodying irreverence and challenge in contrast to an established order. However, *Eshu* and other similar entities are not exactly static figures, they represent the symbols of change establishing a new dynamics.

João do Mato is a vegetal figure covered in greenery representing weed. It is the character that centralizes the equally named agrarian ritual that was, until recently, held once a year by the community of the Arturos. At a given moment, during the weeding rite, the hoes are intersected, forming a corridor; *João do Mato* is attracted to this space. This means that the strength of weeding workers temporarily overcomes the strength of the weed. In the following dialogues, *João do Mato* acknowledges its defeat, but it says:

They cut my arms, but the root remains.

João do Mato is sent away from there to another community. But a gift is offered to it: a bottle of *cachaça* (Brazilian rum made of sugar cane); *João do Mato* dances, trying to balance the bottle on its head. Then *João do Mato* leaves. The festivity, which was first held in an open space, starts to occupy a confined space. There is a table ritualistically set with flowers that flourished in the destroyed bush and cookies made of the corn harvested in the same farm where *João do Mato* used to live. Balance is achieved thanks to the manifestation of the entity-weed that enabled an effective action of transformation of man and the world that surrounds him.[6]

In the festivity of the Divine Holy Spirit in the city of Pirenópolis (GO), the figure of the *Mascarado* (a masked figure) coexists with other manifestations of popular religiousness:

The Mascarado is a unique figure. A figure that no one knows where it came from or where it goes to … It's just – no chance of being wrong – the expression of freedom. The Mascarado has what men need most: freedom – to speak, to act, to express without any prejudice. Then they go to the public square. Everyone can go, the way they want to go, dressed as they want to; there are no groups, there is no one. Each opened portal is a Mascarado that goes to the street: it writes what it wants, it says what it wants. The Mascarado does not wear a mask on its face to hide its personality, this is so true that in the middle of the folguedo they throw the mask away and continue to be offensive, still angry, saying what they want. So, this is a moment of freedom. And this freedom was granted by the Divine Holy Spirit festivity, the Pentecost festival.[7]

In the arena of the *cavalhadas*, the figure of the *Mascarado* contrasts with the figures of the *Moor* and *Christian Knights* that represent order and holiness. The *Mascarado* appears covered by the mask and clothing, so that the person wearing them cannot be identified. Each *Mascarado* is unique in its design and represents the forces of freedom and contestation, as its actions are characterized by

---

6   We found other references on this rite, named Maromba, in the Community of Agriculture Workers Misericórdia, na Chapada do Norte. Vale do Jequitinhonha (MG), 1988.

7   Testimony of Pompeu Christovam de Pina, Pirenópolis (GO), 1994.

breaking the limits. These characters provoke both fascination and fear. Before starting the fighting ritual between the *Knights*, the *Mascarados* invade the arena: as satirical characters and acrobats, they challenge balance in all circumstances. They exceed the time for which they are allowed to remain in the arena; so it is necessary to kick them out, even using police intervention.

In the rite of weeding and in the Divine Holy Spirit festivity, there is a moment when the conflict is not only a representation; it is experienced by the devotees as something real. Both *João do Mato* and the *Mascarado* – just as *Eshu* – assume the repressed and hidden aspects of human being, living and making all participants really live the scene in progress during the ritual.

Returning to the *terreiros of Umbanda*, the most varied presentations of *Eshu* were observed, evidencing that the accuracy of the performance was directly related to so-called degrees of evolution. The same medium and his respective *Eshu* undergo changes as they work on the *Giras*; therefore, sometimes they present a negative polarity and in certain moments a positive polarity, always considering these two forces.

At a given moment of their development, many *umbandistas* admit the need for some mediums to express their own content, even if they are incorporated with *Eshu*. That is why *Eshu* is also called the Lord of the Unconsciousness (both of individual and collective). The *gira* of *Eshu* creates appropriate conditions for the release of the unconscious, when the inner darkness of an individual is exposed. There is no censorship in relation to this fruition that enables the individual to know the hidden parts of him or herself without the politeness acquired by the use of social masks. After the field of the medium's self is clean, he or she will be able to become a reflection of those who seek them, the consultants. Through the entity the consultant seeks to break the negative forces that prevent their contact with the divine. On the walk with man *Eshu* will go to "hell" if this is the individual's route. However its task is to bring man back from darkness to light. The performance of *Eshu* ceases when the route of consultant reaches the end.

Whether individuals like it or not, *Eshu* – according to its ways and methods – reveals what is hidden: the jealous and vengeful nature of men cemented by hate. Instigated by *Eshu*, men start to work, meaning that they are connecting with their inner darkness. The movement does not suggest retention; it suggests transformation. The most significant power of *Eshu* can be seen at the very moment when the first signs of transformation occur.

For the movement in the dancing body to be excellent, this driving force called *Eshu* must be considered. It is *Eshu* that feeds the plasticity by coordinating the concomitant action of protagonists and antagonists that deconstruct the crystallized forms and place the body in a process of continuous tension of opposites with leading edge dynamics.

8.3 In the *Gira* of *Pomba-Gira* – The dance of Maria Padilha

Who is *Pomba-Gira*? *Pomba-Gira* is a rose that was born among thorns.

In the middle of the crossroads of the four corners of the world, let the happy young lady dance. Not one, but hundreds of them, with long centuries of history. They are black, red, white, and scarlet. They are priestess, sorcerers, and ordinary women.

The legion of *Maria Padilha* is introduced under the badge of *Senhora Pomba-Gira*. Some aspects of her history were recorded in our research:[8]

> *They say Padilha has no homeland.*
> *This is not true.*
> *In every corner, in every beach,*
> *a garden,*
> *Padilha has her homeland, indeed.*
> *Where does this Padilha live?*
> *In a sand castle.*
> *Saravá gentlemen*
> *Hail the gypsy Padilha.*

If someone asks my name I say I am the daughter of a warrior woman. Êpa hei Iansã!

My name when I was alive? Dolores. That's how I was baptized; because I could not remember the name I was given. Dolores … I liked this name. Dolores comes from pain, comes from strong, warrior woman.

I do not really know where I came from, I know where I've been: many places, strange lands, witnessing both misery and wealth. I was a slave and I was a queen.

I found my roots' strength in Spain. My gypsy life does not mean that I was a nomad; I had to hide among them. I ran the four corners of the world. I experienced a lot in the East… Africa, Egypt. They say I was a Moroccan. Morocco is Africa.

> *My home has no walls,*
> *no window, it is roofless.*
> *Where does Maria Padilha live,*
> *But I do live at the crossroads.*

---

8   At the end of the research, when we had summarized the several experiences with Girasof Pomba Giras, we had the opportunity to interview Maria Padilha das Sete Encruzilhadas (Maria Padilha from the Seven Crossroads) incorporated in the pai-de-santo Carlos Alberto da Costa. Brasília (DF), 1995.

In a circle formed by *Ogans* and the drums under a fig tree, *Maria Padilha* danced over an open fire. *Maria Padilha* laughed and said:

> *Dance is like the wind, there is no defined track. It comes, goes, comes…But if you have the view that the "devil" has, you will see that life is a constant dance, and the greatest art of life is to dance without falling.*

> *Hê roda girê, roda girá ah…*
> *Hê roda girê, roda giráah …*
>
> *(Hey spin around…*
> *Hey spin around…)*

Where does *Maria Padilha* come from? She comes from the rocking of the waves, the storm and lightning, and the movement of the seven colors of the rainbow.

The moment indicates what the gypsy is supposed to dance. For *Maria Padilha*, there is no tomorrow, no yesterday; there is only now. The ritual will start to make room for its performance.

When I move my skirt, ask whatever you want, says *Maria Padilha*. She works: the skirts wrinkle, twist, strip, open like *sombreros*, spinning to the sound of the chants. *Padilha's* eyes look at the skirt and run all around our eyes. Now, *Padilha's* dance cleans the environment: the purifications are performed with the skirts that are spun by the body.

When the song begins, *Padilha* improvises. She assumes and sustains in her performance the feelings that are hidden among those that are present in the scenario, becoming her own sacrifice, expunging pain, bitterness, and hate. *Padilha* deeply dives into everybody's souls. Back to the surface, the entity assumes the place of a regular mortal:

> *My dance is like yours. If I am in peace with myself, I dance a bolero, a soft song. If I am experiencing an unrequited love, I desire to draw attention, so I dance a rumba. Therefore, the dance is like a veil, it depends on your mood, on letting it be. The "devil" is like this, it is carried away by the dance. But when I leave the matter, my movement becomes a new one, completely different; it is the movement of nature, I go with the waves and they bring me back.*

Does the dynamics promote alchemy or does the alchemy make the dynamics? In the *gira* of *Maria Padilha*, it is not possible to know, as both are her signs.

We are before a platform… no, it's not a platform, it's an earth, *terreiro*. At that moment, it does not matter, because sometimes time and space are concrete, sometimes they are abstract. Although hidden, time and space are alive in our imagination, as *Padilha* takes us into them. She stomps and strums the castanets. Her shoulders snake and she throws herself to the ground, trembling her entire electric, vigorous body. In a single impulse, *Padilha* stands up and enters a spiral of skirts, spinning with cadence and voluptuousness. The drums play the *Alujá*. *Alujá is the movement of ecstasy of the spirit, the fruition of a spiritual unity; it is a pleasure that goes beyond the body.* The beating of the drums is initiated by the movement of *Padilha*, which is decoded by *Ogan*.

The *conga* drums are played. The powerful sound resonates as if it were ancient. *Padilha* takes the shoes off. Her feet and the drums sound in unison, speaking that strange language kept by memory that takes us to the ancestors. The motion and the sound take the whole body of *Padilha* as well as the entire space. How to talk about *Padilha*'s dance in these times when the senses go beyond the form? The dance is like a windstorm and only *Padilha* can describe it:

> *Dance is the tune, the involvement between spirit, matter, and motion. The movement itself consists in the positive and negative energies that revolve around the spirit and the medium. In turn, the dance equalizes the chakras. It is as if you threw your chakras and my chakras inside a ball and they began to mix. Initially, they move in a disorderly manner, then they start to tune in until they are connected with each other forming a single chakra: that is when the perfect balance is synthesized in the movement. This is what dance represents to me: the energy synthesized between distinct beings.*

Padilha overjoys us by leading us to cross different landscapes-scenarios where moods change quickly. We glided for a while and then a succession of falls and suspensions began. *Padilha* ceases to move and becomes an image of helplessness before the world:

> *The dance is on the way out because, due to the violation of nature, it is not possible to coordinate anything anymore. The contours of nature's movements are being lost, and the human being follows this process. In your world, dancing became a disorderly thing; the pleasure of dance is lost, the spirit of dance is lost. Dance has never meant violence; it has always meant harmony.*

Pause, followed by silence. *Padilha* stays "on earth" for a long period of time. She explains in her speech: *I come in the sunlight, but I leave in the moonlight…*

The senses excite *Padilha*'s dance once again: she stomps and humps. *Sarambeque* in the *terreiro*. *Padilha* closes her eyes and smiles:

> *The dance itself is also dogmatic. You edify yourself through the dance because, through it, you can find answers that no one can give you.*

Padilha makes a sudden movement of trembling and makes a continuous hissing sound. Soon it was evident that *Padilha* had quickly gone, leaving at the same place the man who had received her in his body. He returns from a deep sleep, slowly, with an empty gaze. After all, there were many strokes in the stream where *Padilha* was gone.

What is reality and what is illusion in *Padilha*'s dance will depend on the eyes that see it, because she is a sly woman and witch:

On the move I seduce you. Have you heard that gypsies steal souls? I captivate souls, but I do not take them with me.

- Oh cigana linda,
leia a minha mão.
Diz-me um segredo
que eu te dou um tostão.
- Um tostão não quero,
eu não quero não.
Quero apenas um sorriso
dentro do seu coração.

(-Oh, beautiful gypsy,
read my palm.
Tell me a secret
and I'll give you a penny.
- I do not want a penny,
I do not want it.
I just want a smile
inside your heart.)

A gaze through the crack of the door expanded the spaces of our own body snuggling various life stories. The landscapes that began to circulate through our body impelled us to dance names bringing in themselves various transformations and hopes of freedom. We hope we can share these experiences.

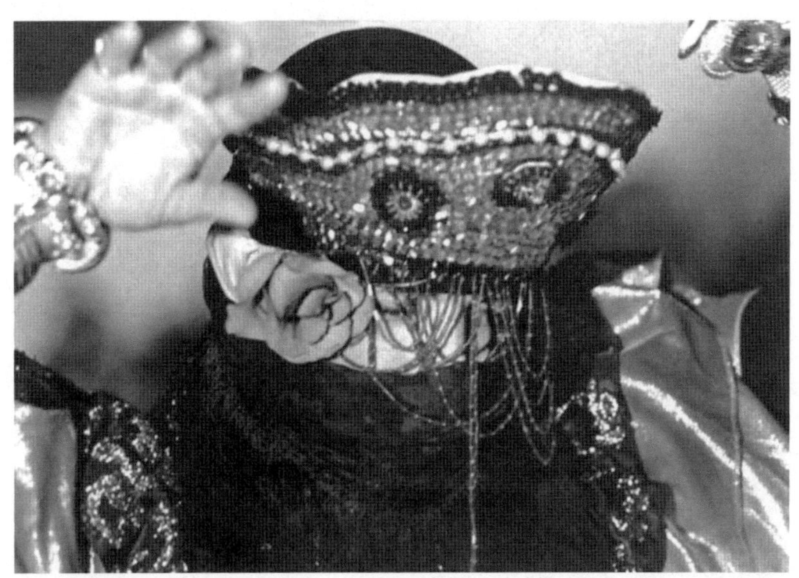

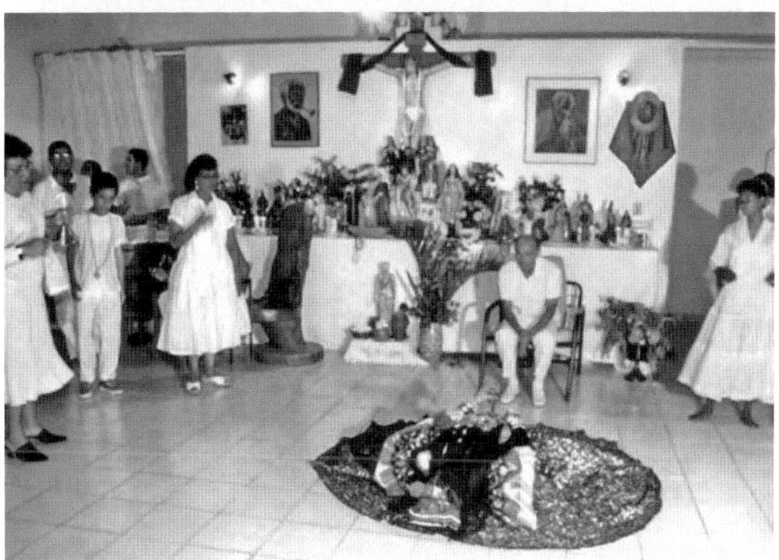

Pomba Gira Maria Padilha das sete encruzilhadas.
Brasília, DF - 1995
(Pomba Gira Maria Padilha of the seven crossroads)
Photos: Juan Pratginesto's

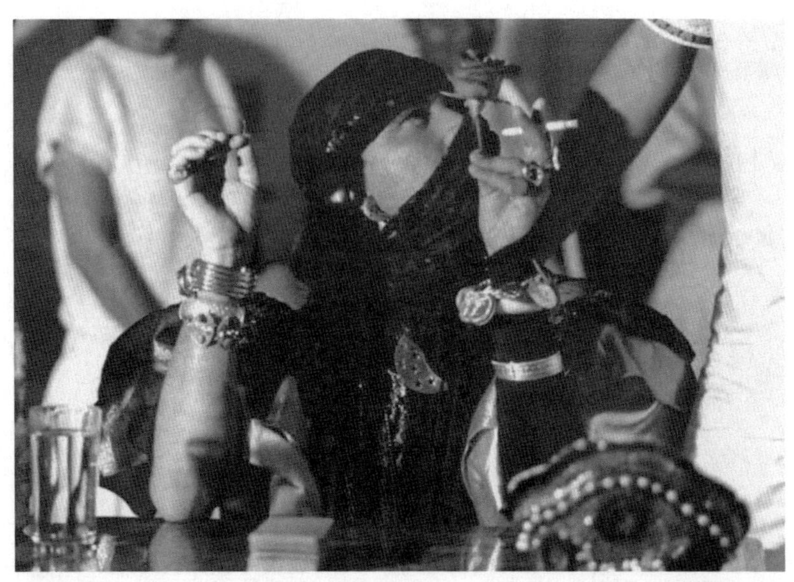

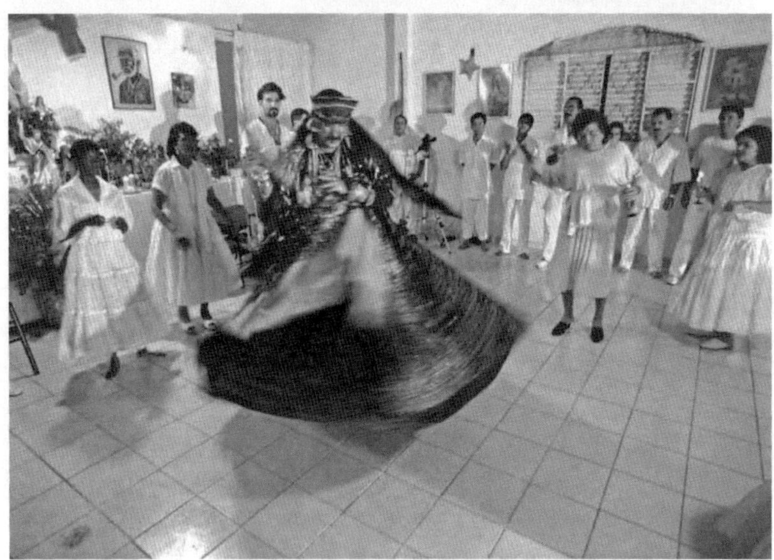

Pomba Gira Maria Padilha *das sete encruzilhadas.*
Brasília, DF - 1995
(Pomba Gira Maria Padilha of the seven crossroads)
Photos: Juan Pratginesto's

158

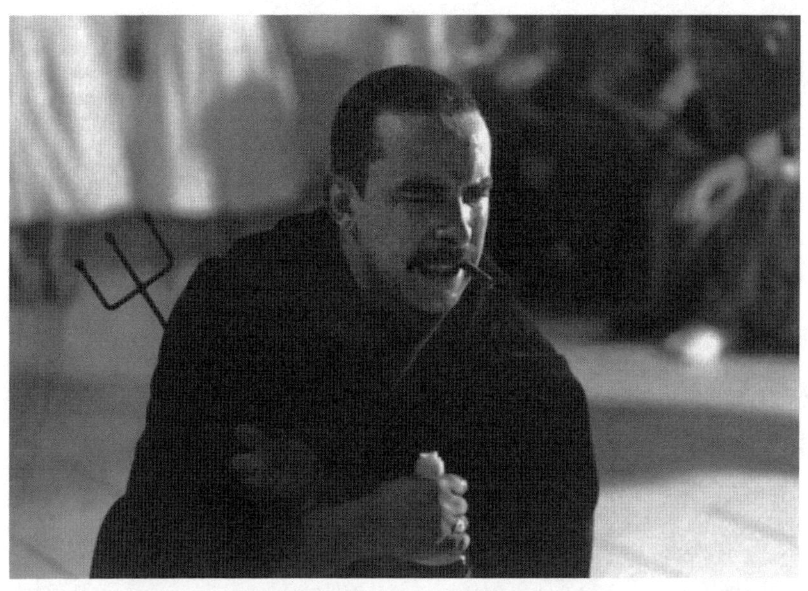

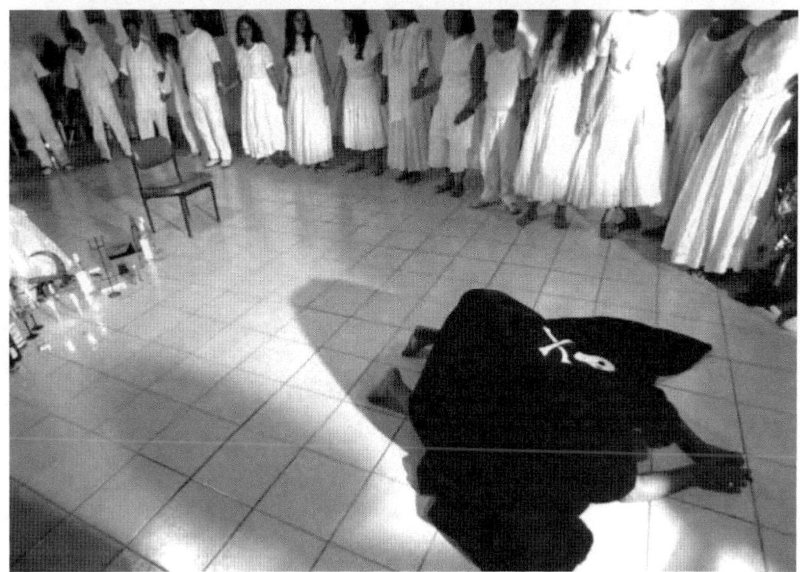

***Eshu,** incorporated in Carlos Alberto da Costa*
Brasília, DF - 1995
Photos: Juan Pratginesto's

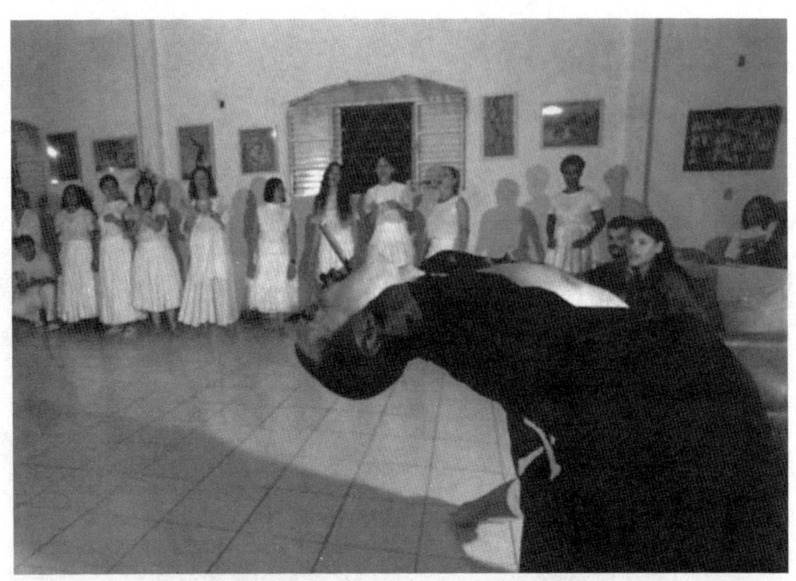

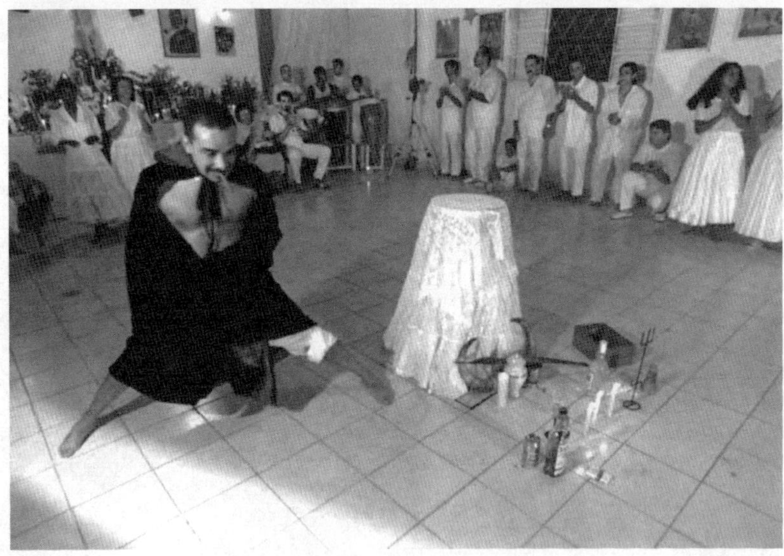

***Eshu,** incorporated in Carlos Alberto da Costa*
Brasília, DF - 1995
Photos: Juan Pratginesto's

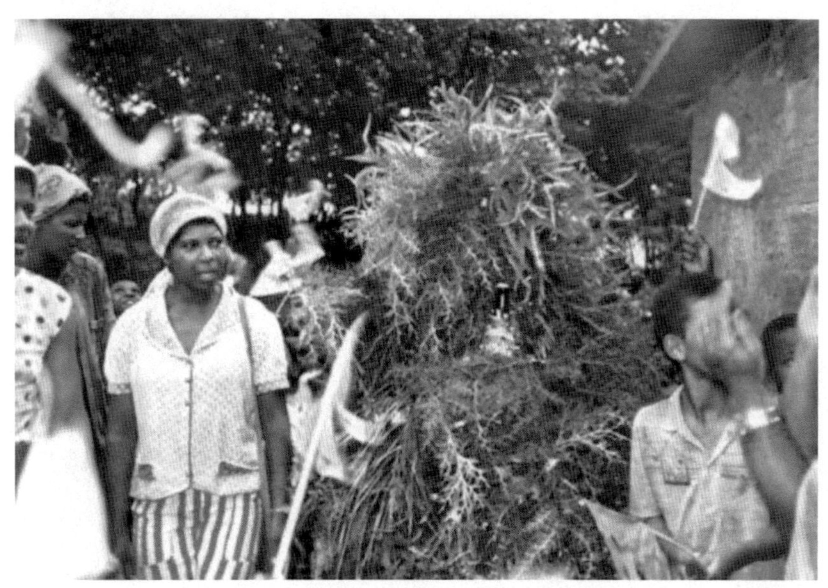

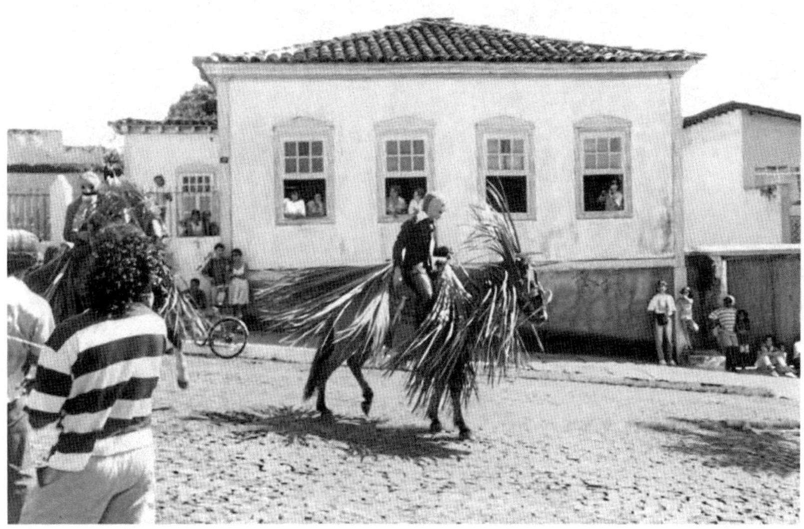

Above:
João do Mato
Arturos, Contagem MG – 1987
Author's archive

Below:
Mascarados,
Pirenópolis, GO - 1994
Author's archive

161

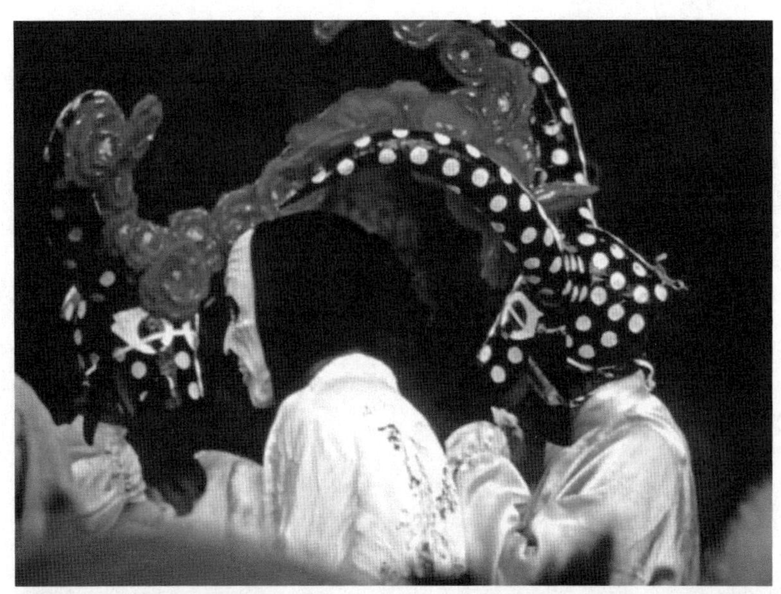

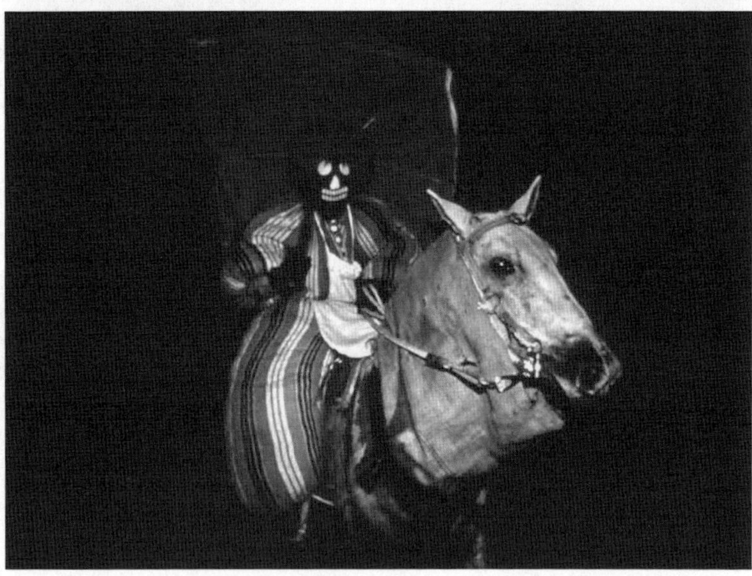

Mascarados,
Pirenópolis, GO - 1994
Photos: Arnaldo Lobato

162

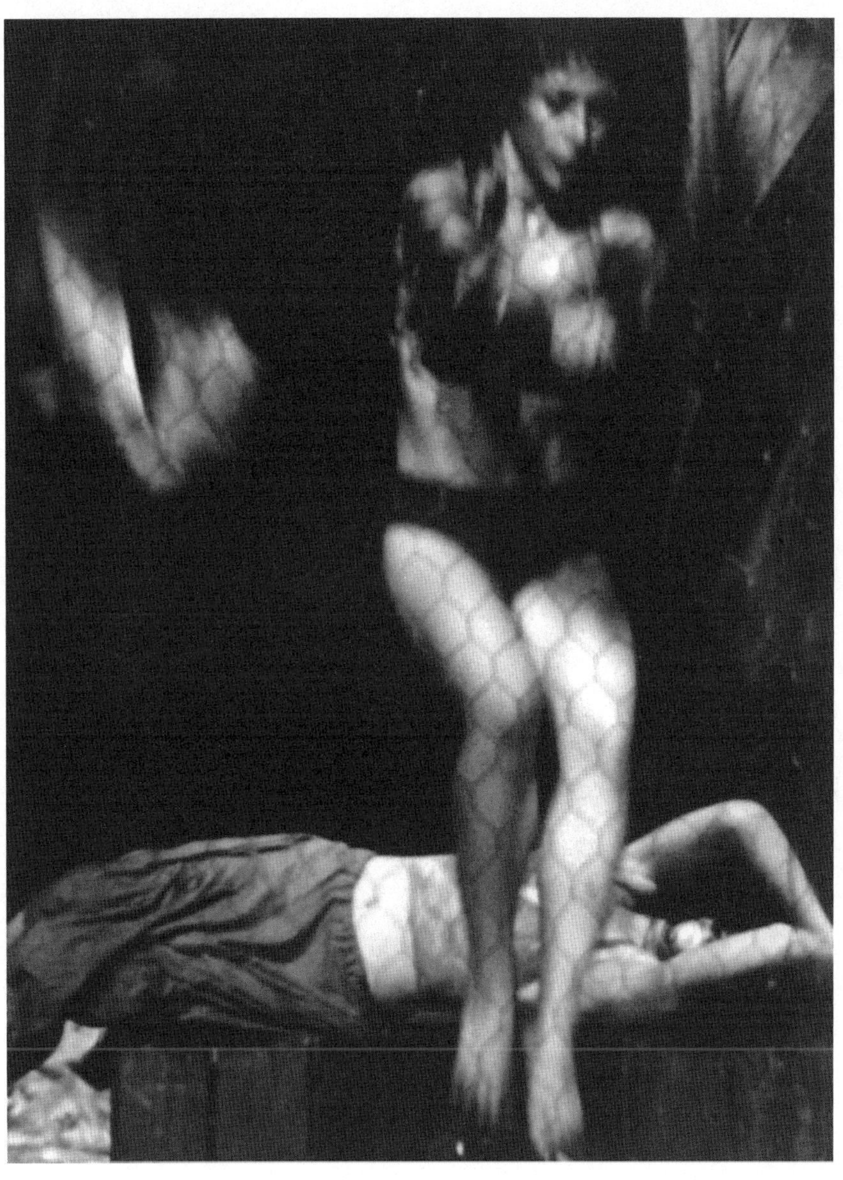

Larissa Turtelli and Daniela Kunh
Espetáculo Diante dos Olhos (Before the eyes performance)
Photo: André Favilha

163

9 The Learning Process of the Dancer-Researcher-Performer

The proposed line of work is focused on the learning process of the dancer-researcher-performer. The line of action of the process presents a view of the dancer as a researcher of him/herself in relation to certain realities that enable him/her to experience the roles emerging from these contacts. The fact that the process is connected to a national context that is the basis of various cultural manifestations does not mean that its main focus is a Brazilian aesthetics; in fact, it is focused on what this aesthetics offers: the development of artistic potentials in a direct relationship of the dancer with his or her surroundings.

From my own experience as a dancer-researcher-performer, I developed a "method" that was consolidated by applying it for a nine years period to some dancers who showed interest – many of them consisting of students of the Dance course at Unicamp. Projects were developed in the spaces of the dance lessons and research fields resulting in artistic creations that enabled the development of various stages of the "method". Its essence lies in the interrelation between different emotional records emerging from the experience in the field research with the affective memory of the performer.

Dance classes acquire the meaning of laboratory of sources: the dancer is the first subject to be researched by him/herself. Based on the principle of the "Physical Structure", the body-sense is systematically worked. The aim is to deeply reach the bones and muscles involved in each movement matrix. This association with inner images causes different sensations in each individual. The investigation of the themes from Brazilian cultural manifestations is conducted through the incorporation of their symbolic fields taking into account their specific dynamics. These Brazilian sources cause the dancer to be in conflict with him or herself and put to question his or her identity. These conflicts are seen as important elements in the dance forms as their movements are worked. The inner journey (emotional records and images) is developed in interaction with the outer movement aiming at a quality resulting from the reality of the subject-dancer.

The dancer is requested to create an inventory of his or her origins, cultural records, and his or her relationship with the land. As the dancer discovers his or her place (both in the world and in him or herself), and the integration of several aspects (seemingly fragmented at first) occurs. An imaginary space is constructed in order to enable the development of the Brazilian dance form in his or her body. In this space, they work their fear of committing mistakes, their prejudice, and the confrontation of their own weaknesses – while the dancer is in motion. Another question is what dance means in his or her body. The moment when the dancer begins to remove his or her armor is a precious moment in this phase. The dancer cannot move as before; he/she becomes fragile as if he/she could no longer dance. Then, conducting the movement from inside out with heightened senses, he/she begins to realize the unity of the body leading to a much more conscious response in the dance. The dancer's own movement and the movement of others are seen in a new perspective: free of labels.

In the field research, the dancer's body should be prepared for data collection. At least his/her feet are rooted into the ground. Therefore, his/her body is not so different from the bodies the dancer will research. The perception of the "gaze" exercised in dance classes is supposed to enable the dancer to read how the movement occurs in the field research with ability to detect the most obvious parts and the integrity of the dancing body.

The tracking stage is initiated by various references of the manifestation or social segment that will be the focus of the research. That is why the researcher must present empathy with it. The choice of the place and the group for the development of the research is determined, among other factors, by the quality of the movement; this may be restricted merely to a few people. The choice of the dancer-researcher-performer contains important, if at times unconscious references regarding the approach assumed in his/her subsequent work.

The preparation for the field requires certain centration, including all the attributes of what the axis means: posture, neutrality, and presence (= involvement with reality, devoid of preconceptions, related to dance). At the same time, an open body is necessary to receive the material of the research. Breath and patience are required to research "the dancing body" in its full context.

Integrated to the field, the researcher conquers his/her relationship with people on a step by step basis. Few questions are asked and nonverbal data is privileged. The stories are heard with special attention to the suggestions that they may be restricting. At the moment when the dancer-researcher-performer "loses" the reference of objective reason in order to be fully there, he/she crosses the limits of his/her world and penetrates the other's frame. This means that the dancer is co-inhabiting with the source. At this level, what was observed was the apprehension of key non-verbal elements that the body absorbed and stored in the unconscious in order to express them in the laboratory work. This content, received and expressed in the laboratory, also affects the artistic creative work.

In the field research, the guidance is provided taking into account the relationship between a researcher with his/her research site. In this sense, the dancer does not work with certainties; he/she works with complicity by both sides. Due to the emotional force contained in this research modality, the situations are constantly evaluated, always privileging the search for balance.

Usually, the laboratory stage comes after the field research, but these steps often intersect. The laboratories aim at the incorporation of the character. Field diaries and other records, such as audio and video, are important tools, but the work is in fact conducted by the body of the dancer-researcher-performer and what it expresses or not.

The laboratories are implemented through the creations of dynamics related to the contents and consequences of the forms stemmed from the researched sources. The responses of the dancer-researcher-performer to these dynamics guide the approach assumed in each day of the work. Initially, there is no fluidity of meanings expressed by the body. In this stage there are blockades in specific parts of the body and repetitions of certain movements that hinder the flow of the dynamics. The individual stops, despite the proposals encouraging him/her to go ahead. The dancer tends to hide, the movement becomes introspective. These situations reveal the need of opening a space for the individual in which he/she would be able to find out the contents that keep him/her from moving. The emotions that are opened must be developed, so that the dancer-researcher-performer may distinguish an elaborated emotion from an "emotionalism".[1] Thus, emotion must be the engine of a conscious movement, providing greater plasticity to the body.

Through the labs, the dancer experiences emptiness and chaos until the moment he/she reaches an orderly form. In the closed space of the room, the dancer-researcher-performer builds imaginary landscapes and acts within them. There are no concerns in relation to retaining what is being expressed, and the findings are not rationalized. The work is conducted, so that the landscapes may merge and undergo transformations. Naturally, there are repeated landscapes, as some of them are interwoven with "someone" circulating or inhabiting them. The dancer is continuously requested to externalize these inner images in the landscapes-scenarios, so that they may return, modeling some parts of the body in motion. In this stage, the data from our research sources (field's and performer's) is integrated and the movement form is merged. The movement-synthesis occurs when a key image (a sum of multiple images) gains contour and place. Through the movement the dancer sees inside him/herself, some characteristics of the charac-

---

1   "Emotionalism" - repressed emotion. unknown, which acts in a represented form and does not circulate through the body of the person, remaining visible in his or her facial expressions.

ter in its original space are revealed. Then the dancer "incorporates" it and all his/her work begins to be developed through this character.

After the character is "installed", the body acquires the dynamo. The parameters of ugly or beautiful no longer exist. The performer's body locks are released with the help of the character. Various aspects of the field research are represented in the character; its basis is associated with the content already known by the dancer-researcher-performer.

The materials extracted from the labs are determined, as the dancer-researcher-performer improves the incorporation of the character. Therefore, this is the axis of the scenic work building process. The direction begins to set boundaries conducting the contents that were open to be designed and synthesized. The outline of some scenes is made during the practice of development of the character until the indicative stage of creation of a structure: the script.

The script frames a large volume of representations primarily aiming at fluidity in the body of the dancer-researcher-performer. In this case, there is a concern regarding the clarity of what is desired to be expressed, diminishing the interference of the script that, in relation to the perspective of the performance, remains as a background. This means that there are no strategies to cover up the limits of the performer and no formal construction that is not integrated in him/her.

During the process, scenographic spaces, objects and costumes are elaborated with the direct participation of the dancer-researcher-performer in their production. The Physical Structure originating from the Brazilian cultural manifestations is a reference of technical work, and it is opened to other references that may contribute to the elaboration process of each body that will be exposed. The emotions moving the script are elaborated until the moment when they can be conducted consciously.

The whole process is worked in the threshold of the requirements for each dancer-researcher-performer. However, the individual is more important than the artistic product as the aesthetic quality depends on his/her integrity.

The structure of the performance is fragile, requiring the dancer-researcher-performer to give life to each fragment that composes it. The capacity to transform the structure of the performance results from the achievement of the performer when he/she learns how to share it with the audience, even in the face of rejection. In this deeply experienced stage, the dancer acknowledges the burden concerning his/her own development, when the applause is not the most expected form of recognition of what is done.

Given the nature of this process, it is crucial for the individual to choose it in order to develop him/herself. The direction is responsible for managing the research sources to individualize the process. There are no forms of repetition in relation to the dynamics used in the various stages, as each group (even each person) presents characteristics that mobilize different forms of conduction. In certain circumstances, each stage has to be well-designed; in others, the stages intersect with one another. The length of time in the work of the dancer-researcher-performer is also related to the situations faced by him/her.

Like a big puzzle, different pieces fall into place. In this game there is no space for casualties, only for interactions, revealing the coherence of the path that was built.

By following this path, the dancer-researcher-performer has the process in his/her hands, in his/her perception, in the whole body. However, the body has to follow its own path waiting for the proper time of decantation of what it experienced and what it is willing to work on.

It was observed that a description of the process, although highly detailed, can always raise misconceptions in its interpretation as all the stages are related to our own experience. Regarding the results obtained in the form of performances, we limit ourselves to conduct a generalized approach; however, the existence of particularities in the development of each one of them is recognized. We will now introduce some data related to the already explained content in order to contribute to a better understanding of the learning process of the dancer-researcher-performer.

9.1 The speech of dancers concerning the process

The moments when the foundations of the process are built were established. They consisted of periods prior to the deepening of field research and the creation of performances. Some topics of the development of learning process are highlighted here through the reports of the dancers. The most representative reports on the relationship of the students with the learning process procedures applied by the dancer-researcher-performer were chosen.

Dance classes acquire the meaning of a laboratory of sources: the dancer is the first subject to be researched by him/herself:

Lately, I've been learning to control anxiety in relation to what my body produces; without accepting it at all, but without declaring war against time.

For me, this is like diving in your own image. It's like diving into the water and feeling the whole body involved. Everything is on the edge, the body is aware of all reactions.

I gradually felt my feet were like roots looking for the ground to penetrate it more and more. I realized that the body generates the intention of the movement to be performed, and not the form of such intention.

I feel that now I can take advantage of an aspect that I see as important at work: the respect for individuality of each person. I spend more time alone, experiencing, and allowing myself to feel. So I think that I believe for the first time that I have some potential.

The inner journey (images and emotional records) is developed in interaction with the outer movement, always seeking an expression that stems from the reality of the subject-dancer:

I could not let the images emerge – what kind of image is that? (I thought). It was so far away that not even the landscape would appear to me. I even tried to imagine something that I liked, but it was fake and it soon disappeared. Things started to make sense to me during an exercise in which you (Graziela), starting from a pulse, asked me to intensify it and allow it to take over the body. Then you asked me to diminish the pulse so it could remain within the body, just as a sensation. This was the day when I managed to see a landscape; it just appeared. You also asked us to leave the "feet on the tracks". Along with this landscape, I also moved around without asking for my body. It was as if my body had developed its own intelligence. From this day on, the images began to emerge.

I had the possibility to avoid getting restrained by the acquisition of steps or sequences; instead, I could try to establish an association between intention, action, and reaction.

The major concern with the base (feet), the contour of the ground, and the "tail" enabled a good technical development with freedom to feel the movement and perform it from my body. At first, it scared me, but actually it made me good because I could do what I was feeling and not what I had to copy. The images help me a lot.

I could not make any movement in front of the altar. It seemed to be a heresy. As they told me when I was a child, you cannot dance in the church, or in the cemetery, or on Ash Wednesday, Holy Saturday, or even in the Day of the Dead. It was worthless to think rationally that all those things were so silly. I was muscularly paralyzed by these memories.

There was a moment of insecurity, desiring protection – "the character" entered the caravel and left.

The dancer is requested to create an inventory of his or her origins, cultural records, and his or her relationship with the land:

My grandmother pulled and danced Cana Verde (Green cane) in front of me, in her kitchen. I did not understand what it was.

In the universe of "my backyard" I had a healer grandmother, a grandfather who made promises, and my mom that was devoted to popular religiosity. I discriminated all of these things; I'd rather be different, by building a false identity. I now realize that there is a much

An imaginary space is built to allow the development of the form of the Brazilian dance in the dancer's body.

It's like returning to a road that, although known, has not been used in a long time. On this route, many memories came up.

An amazing personal immersion. Strange, dirty road. One day of search. An image that moves a form.

My movement is acquiring density, balance. I have lost the anguish of the feet.

I would like to get to the procession, but I never can.

My body is full of sensations, with no definite shape, or history, or it is not a body, it is only a sensation. Maybe it is like raw clay, shapeless. The ground is sensitive to my movements, or maybe I am sensitive to the ground. In the next step, I can fall into nothingness. This is fear. The body lives this reality; it assumes the movement, reacts, and lives – a dense, full body.

I see a large circle with dark dirt soil and gravel. The place is surrounded by old houses with closed doors and windows because it is raining. A person is alone in the middle of the circle. This person is struck by a lightning; he/she is the lightning itself. A canoe in the river… Someone is standing in the canoe and the movement of the waters plays with his/her axis. The body has no memory; it is young, it is a girl, it is old. The body feels a sharp pain, trembling as if it would fall apart, but it can stand them. The body is wet, the tight clothing reveals a strong woman's body. I am sure she was protecting everyone, she is a lightning rod. The sinuous body picked up something with its hands and brought it to her stomach. I got stiffened, I became the image. I'm in a litter; people see me from the bottom and sing to me. I am taken by a canoe that leaves. It shakes and shakes… This time the work was different, the movement brought the memories.

In the inventory of this dancer we found data pertaining to her family, related to processions in canoes made in devotion to Divine and to Our Lady.

That is how she described her first experiences during the field research:

The field research enabled me to know a very different world. First of all, we are people. And that's how I was treated. There were no interviews, but only conversations.

We traveled paths with the "folia" for about twelve hours. Our involvement with the group was quite deep; at the end of the day, it seemed as if we were together for many days.

10 Conclusion

Characterizing the meaning of the Brazilian dance implies a series of issues. Popular sources were considered as one of the aspects that should become part of the discussions led by official institutions due to its importance in the organization of the Brazilian cultural structure. Therefore, regardless of the method or line of approach assumed in the works in dance, it is crucial that the dancer and/or choreographer "mark their feet with mud", that they have a direct contact – body to body – with the universe of popular culture. Otherwise, mistakes will continue to occur in the representations that, being distant from sources, use them to create a "Brazilian movement". In this case, the *made in Brazil* bodies reinforce the stereotypes of a dance based on an ethnocentric view of those who only see popular culture as an exotic object.

The proposed method may not be perfectly appropriate to a large number of talents. However, it was found to be appropriate to many who are dissatisfied with the exclusively formal results in the dance. Therefore, it is believed that new talents may arise as a result of the development of dancer-researcher-performer learning process. Although apparently simple, the results obtained so far represent an abundant, quality collection. This is corroborated by observing a small group of young dance-researcher-performers that are aware of their condition, believing in their potentialities and facing the exercise of discipline, as they know that freedom to dance must be redeemed on a daily basis. In this line of work, the dance does not result from any spontaneous mechanism; it reveals to be a dance constructed with strictness. Once more we recall that the body must be flexible, individualized, and open to new achievements.

As the present work resulted from a life experience linked to our training as dancers, it is not specifically intended at discussing the research concepts or the phenomenon of dance from the perspective of pre-established methodologies. Recording the learning process of the dancer-researcher-performer has become a commitment to the new dancers, as many of them have provided us with answers through the work carried out, based on our line of research and creation.

Therefore, this work primarily aimed at sharing the embryo of a proposal of life and dance expecting that further steps may be taken by those who are willing to fully act, with courage, dignity, and balance, during every moment of their own development as a person and as a dancer.

In the following years, many steps have been taken. Artists from various places, including foreigners, felt identified with the method. These artists consolidated outside the academic environment, experienced the BPI (Dancer-Researcher-Performer) method and found it as an effective way to re-connect with their own selves, getting in contact with their originality. The preparation of directors in the BPI method is continuous, thus enabling a more consolidated training. Today, the teaching artists, graduate students, and undergraduates are part of the group "Dancer-Researcher-Performer (BPI) and Dance from Brazil", recognized by the National Council for Scientific and Technological Development (CNPq).

This book is kept alive thanks to the confidence of the people who confirm the BPI in their bodies, acquiring new expressions by adding their deepest characteristics to the researched sources.

11 Addendum

Synopsis of Performances Related to the Learning Process of the Dancer-Researcher-Performer

1. GRAÇA BAILARINA DE JESUS ou 7 *Linhas de Umbanda, Salvem o Brasil*
   (Grace, Ballerina of Jesus or 7 Lines of Umbanda, Hail Brazil) - **1980**

by Graziela Rodrigues, João Antônio and Celso Araújo.
Dancer-researcher-performer: *Graziela Rodrigues.*
Direction: *João Antônio de Lima Esteves.*
Final text: *Celso Araújo.*
Scenography: *Ademar Dornelles.*
Costume: *Iolanda Silva.*
Production: *Ensaio, Teatro e Dança.*
Executive production: *José Pereira da Silva.*
Presentations:
   Teatro Santo Antônio – Salvador (BA), 1980.
   Tenda Xangô Ayrá do Caboclo Itajaci (Casa de Candomblé) – Brasília (DF), 1980.
   Teatro Dulcina – Rio de Janeiro (RJ), 1980.
   Teatro Dulcina – Brasília (DF), 1980.
   Teatro Goiânia – Goiânia (GO), 1980.
   Teatro Ruth Escobar – São Paulo (SP), 1980.

2. CAMINHADAS (Walking) - 1983

by Ilo Krugli, Graziela Rodrigues and Tião de Carvalho.
Dancer-researcher-performer: *Graziela Rodrigues.*
Actor and dancer: *Tião de Carvalho.*
Direction: *Ilo Krugli.*
Direction assistant: *Pedro Della Paschoa.*
Special participation: *Group "16 meninos da Treze de Maio", Penha Pietras.*
Musical direction: *Marcus Vinicius.*
Musicians: *Cássio Roberto Picollo, Fernando Getti, Isa Uehara, Pedrão do Maranhão. Scenario and costume: Ilo Krugli and Osvaldo Gabrieli.*
Light: *Roberto Mello.*
Production: *VENTO FORTE.*
Presentations:
   Teatro Martins Pena - São Paulo (SP), 1983.
   Teatro Artur de Azevedo - São Paulo (SP), 1983.

Teatro Vento Forte - São Paulo (SP), 1983.

Teatro Maria Della Costa - São Paulo (SP), 1983.

Praça da Sé - Projeto Dançando na Praça - Secretaria de Cultura do Estado de São Paulo - São Paulo, 1983.

Teatro Cacilda Becker - Rio de Janeiro (RJ), 1984.

Teatro Municipal- Campinas (SP), 1984.

3. PORTAR BANDEIRAS (Carrying Flags) - 1984

by Graziela Rodrigues and Pedro Della Paschoa.

Dancer-researcher-performer: *Graziela Rodrigues.*

Dancers: *Adriana Bontetti, Adriana Schor, Adriana Zanittini, Ana Christina Certa in, Cláudia Rodrigues, Elena Costa, Inês Guaneiro, Kátia Brito, Luchia Neves, Márcia Cabral, Maurício Freire, Olavo Rodante, Thelma Bonavita.*

Special participation: *Grupo Popular do Ferreira (Marlene e Mario)* and *Borba, composer from Pérola Negra School of Samba.*

General direction: *Graziela Rodrigues.*

Scenography and executive production: *Pedro Della Paschoa.*

Costume: *Adão Pinheiro and Maria Conte.*

Soundtrack: *Sérgio Avellar.*

Presentations:

Circo Escola Picadeiro - São Paulo (SP), 1984.

4. CORAÇÃO VERMELHO I (Red Heart I) - 1985

by Graziela Rodrigues and Maria Conte.

Dancer-researcher-performer: *Graziela Rodrigues.*

Direction: *Toninho do Valle.*

Music (composition and execution): *Edgar Lippo.*

Choreographic assistant: *Adernar Dornelles.*

Costume and scenography: *Márcio Tadeu.*

Light: *Abel Kopanski.*

Executive production: *Maria Conte.*

Graphic arts and photograph: *Ricardo Tillkiam.*

Vocal technique: *Krystyna Kasperowicz.*

Circus technique: *Alice Medeiros and Marilena Silva.*

Presentations:

Teatro Vento Forte - São Paulo (SP), 1985.

Teatro Procópio Ferreira - São Paulo (SP), 1985.

5. CORAÇÃO VERMELHO II (Red Heart II) - 1986

by Graziela Rodrigues.
Dancer-researcher-performer: *Graziela Rodrigues.*
Direction: *Toninho do Valle and João Antônio de Lima Esteves.*
Scenario and costume: *Márcio Tadeu.*
Choreographic assistant: *Ademar Dornelles.*
Vocal technique: *Krystyna Kasperowicz.*
Musical direction: *Edgar Lippo.*
Musicians: *Carrapa, Cláudio, Nonato.*
Light: *Sérgio Viana.*
Production: *CRC - Produções Ltda.*
Presentations:
> *Teatro Aluísio Magalhães - Brasília (DF), 1986.*
> *Teatro Municipal - São João Del Rey (MG), 1986.*
> *Teatro Goiânia - Goiânia (GO), 1986.*
> *Pátio do Quartel - Goiás Velho (GO), 1986.*
> *Teatro Municipal - Anápolis (GO), 1986.*

6. BAILARINAS DE TERREIRO (Terreiro Ballerinas) – 1990

Direction: *Graziela Rodrigues.*
Dancers-researchers-performers: *Grácia Navarro, Renata Bittencourt, Rosana Baptistela.*
Percussion: *Mestre Antônio.*
Assistance in scenography and costume designer: *Márcio Tadeu.*
Seamstress: *Dalvina R. da Silva.*
Photograph: *Ricardo Oliveira.*
Production: *Departamento de Artes Corporais, Instituto de Artes - Unicamp.*
Presentations:
> *Departamento de Artes Corporais da Unicamp-Campinas (SP), 1990.*
> *Espaço Cultural Tulha (II Festival Internacional de Teatro)-Campinas (SP), 1991.*
> *Teatro Vento Forte - São Paulo (SP), 1991.*

7. ESTRELA BOIEIRA (Ox Star) – 1991

Direction: *Graziela Rodrigues.*
Dancers-researchers-performers: *Diane Ichimaru, Eloisa Domenici.*
Direction assistant: *Rosana Baptistela.*
Production: *Departamento de Artes Corporais, Instituto de Artes - Unicamp.*

Presentations:

Auditório do Instituto de Artes da Unicamp - Campinas (SP), 1991.

Museu Campos Sales (Projeto Renascer) - Campinas (SP), 1991.

Largo da Catedral de Campinas (I Festival de Teatro de Rua) - Campinas (SP), 1991.

Teatro Vento Forte - São Paulo (SP), 1997.

Teatro Lona Azul (Projeto "Oque fazer no verão") - Campinas (SP), 1992. Estação São Bento do Metrô (Abertura do Projeto Arte Universidade) - São Paulo (SP), 1992.

Largo da Catedral de Campinas (I Encontro Nacional de Teatro de Rua) - Campinas (SP), 1992.

Teatro Evolução (Semana de Dança Contemporânea) - Campinas (SP), 1992. SESC - Campinas (SP), 1992.

8. O SEGREDO DA FLOR (The Secret of the Flower) - 1992

Artistic guidance: *Graziela Rodrigues.*
Dancer-researcher-performer: *Patrícia Sene.*
Production: *Departamento de Artes Corporais do Instituto de Artes - Unicamp.*
Presentations:

Auditório do Instituto de Artes da Unicamp-Campinas (SP), 1992.

SESC Carmo - São Paulo (SP), 1993.

Projeto Vira a Cidade - Prefeitura de Ribeirão Preto (SP), 1993.

II Encontro Brasileiro de Teatro de Grupo - Ribeirão Preto (SP), 1993.

Semana do Teatro - Ribeirão Preto (SP), 1993.

Mercado da Ribeira - Recife (PE), 1993.

Praça da Preguiça - Olinda (PE), 1993.

IV Congresso Afro Brasileiro - Fundação Joaquim Nabuco - Recife (PE), 1994.

9. INTERIORES (Interiors) – 1994

Direction: *Graziela Rodrigues.*
Dancers-researchers-performers: *Ana Carolina Melchert, Claudia Soares, Clermont Phiten, Lara Rodrigues, Paula Caruso* and *Paula Salles.*
Musical direction, arrangements and compositions: *Divanir A. Gattamorta.*
Participation in composition and musical execution: *Tião de Carvalho*
Participation in musical execution: *Mestre Antônio.*
Costume and scenography: *Márcio Tadeu.*
Seamstress: *Dalvina R. da Silva.*
Assistance in props and make-up: *Heloísa Villaboin.*
Photo: *Roberto de Angelo.*
Production: *Departamento de Artes Corporais, Instituto de Artes - Unicamp*

Presentations:

Auditório do Instituto de Artes da Unicamp-Campinas (SP), 1994.

Estação do Metrô São Bento (Projeto Arte Universidade) - São Paulo (SP), 1995. Departamento de Artes Cênicas da Unicamp - Campinas (SP), 1995.

Telebrás - Campinas (SP), 1995.

Instituto de Estudos da Linguagem da Unicamp - Campinas (SP), 1995.

Escola Federal de Engenharia - Itajubá (MG), 1995.

Estação do Metrô São Bento (Projeto Arte Universidade) - São Paulo (SP), 1995.

Praça Largo das Andorinhas - S. M. de Cultura - Campinas (SP), 1995.

Mostra de Dança do Mercosul - Centro de Convivência - Campinas (SP) and Memorial da América Latina - São Paulo (SP), 1995.

Presídio Ataliba Nogueira - Campinas (SP), 1995.

Fundação Cultural Carlos Drumond de Andrade - Itabira (MG), 1995. Simpósio Latino Americano de Ciências de Alimentos - Campinas (SP), 1995.

Cine Teatro Atibaia - S. M. de Cultura - Atibaia (SP), 1995.

Estação do Metrô São Bento (Projeto Arte Universidade) - São Paulo (SP), 1995.

Praças de Pirenópolis - S. M. de Cultura - Pirenópolis (GO), 1995.

Centro Cultural de Paulínia - Paulínia (SP), 1996.

Estação do Metrô de São Bento (Projeto Arte Universidade) - São Paulo (SP), 1996. Festival do Folclore - S. M. de Turismo - Paulínia (SP), 1996.

Encontro FAPESP/CAPS - Águas de Lindóia (SP), 1996.

Confraria da Dança - Campinas (SP), 1996.

10. DIANTE DOS OLHOS (Before the Eyes) - 1996

Direction: *Graziela Rodrigues.*

Dancers-researchers-performers: *Daniela Kuhn* and *Larissa Turtelli.*

Direction assistant: *Ana Carolina Melchert.*

Sound and recording: *Denise Garcia.*

Scenography and costume designer: *Márcio Tadeu.*

Light: *Amaran.*

Technical support: *Paula Caruso.*

Production: *Departamento de Artes Corporais, Instituto de Artes - Unicamp.*

Presentations:

Departamento de Artes Corporais Unicamp - Campinas (SP), 1996.

Confraria da Dança - Campinas (SP), 1996.

11. Viandeiras (Spinnerets) - (1999)

Dance Performance.

Production: Departamento de Artes Corporais da Unicamp.

Participates as Director, Choreographer and Writer.

Presentations:

Departamento de Artes Corporais Unicamp Campinas SP – 1999.

12. Valsa do Desassossego (Unrestness Waltz) (2004–2006)

Dance Performance.

Production: Independent production funded by Caravana Paulista de Teatro (Secretaria do Estado da Cultura de São Paulo and Cooperativa Paulista de Teatro).

Participates as Director and Writer.

Presentations:

SESC Pinheiros - Praça de Eventos. São Paulo, SP - August 12th and 13th, 2006.

Praça Jorge Tibiriçá – Caravana Paulista de Teatro – Coop. Paulista de Teatro, Secretaria de Estado da Cultura e Governo do Estado de São Paulo – Ibitinga, SP – June 23rd and 24th, 2006.

Praça Maria Aparecida Resitano – Caravana Paulista de Teatro – Coop. Paulista de Teatro, Secretaria de Estado da Cultura e Governo do Estado de São Paulo – São Carlos, SP – June 10th, 2006.

Instituto Pombas Urbanas – Caravana Paulista de Teatro – Coop. Paulista de Teatro, Secretaria de Estado da Cultura e Governo do Estado de São Paulo – São Paulo, SP – June 3rd, 2006.

Praça Coração de Jesus – Caravana Paulista de Teatro – Coop. Paulista de Teatro, Secretaria de Estado da Cultura and Governo do Estado de São Paulo – Paulínia, SP – May 7th, 2006.

Paço Municipal de Campinas – Dia Nacional de Conscientização da Esclerose Múltipla – GEMC Grupo de Esclerose Múltipla de Campinas – August 30th, 2005.

Parque Cidade de São Bernardo – Projeto de Apoio às Artes Cênicas – Prefeitura de São Bernardo do Campo, SP – July 10th, 2005.

POUPA TEMPO SÉ – Sesc Carmo – São Paulo, SP – June 2nd and 3rd, 2005.

Centro Coreográfico da Cidade do Rio de Janeiro – Evento "São Paulo Em Cena" – Rio de Janeiro, RJ – September 18th and 19th, 2004.

UPA – Universidade de Portas Abertas – Campinas, SP – Parking lot of the Departamento de Artes Corporais da UNICAMP – September 3rd and 4th, 2004.

Parking lot of the Departamento de Artes Corporais da Unicamp – Campinas, SP – August 17th, 18th, 19th, 20th and 24th, 25th, 26th, 2004.

Oficina Cultural Oswald De Andrade – Premiere in the program "A Arte do Espetáculo fora do Teatro" – São Paulo, SP – June, 15th, 2004.

13 A Flor do Café (Coffee's Flower) (2008–2011)

Dance Performance.

Production: Departamento de Artes Corporais da Unicamp.

Participates as Artistic Director, Choreographer, Scenographer, Costume Designer and Soundtrack Composer.

Presentations:

Parque Ecológico Emílio José Salim - Campinas - SP - 2008.

I Mostra de Teatro e Dança - Cunha, MG - 2009.

I Simpósio Internacional de Imagem Corporal e I Congresso Brasileiro de Imagem Corporal - Unicamp - Campinas - SP - 2010.

V Encontro da Mulher - Cabo Verde, MG – 2011.

14. Nascedouro (Hatcher) - (2008–2010)

Dance Performance.

Production: Departamento de Artes Corporais da Unicamp.

Participates as Artistic Director, Choreographer, Scenographer, Costume Designer and Soundtrack Composer.

Presentations:

Parque Ecológico Emílio José Salim - Campinas - 2008
Tour in 3 XAVANTES tribe at Reserva Indígena Pimentel Barbosa - MT - 2009
I Simpósio Internacional de Imagem Corporal e I Congresso Brasileiro de Imagem Corporal - Unicamp - Campinas - SP - 2010

15. Fina Flor, Divino Amor - Iyabá Legba Hey! (Refined flower, Divine Love) - (2011–2014)

Dance Performance.

Production: Funding – ProAC (Secretaria de Estado da Cultura de São Paulo), FAEPEX (Fundo de Apoio ao Ensino à Pesquisa e Extensão - UNICAMP) and FAPESP (Fundação de Amparo à Pesquisa do Estado de São Paulo).

Participates as Director, Author of the Conception, and as Writer.

Presentations:

Pavilhão de Artes Cênicas do Pólo Cinematográfico - Paulínia, SP - 2011.
Auditório Municipal - Valinhos, SP - 2011.
Centro Cultural - Mogi Mirim, SP - 2011.
Conferência Internacional Corpos (Im)Perfeitos - Almada, Portugal - 2012.
XVII Festival Internacional de Dança do Recife - Recife - 2012.
1º International Journal of Arts - Natal - 2012.
Ocupação Funarte Brasília - Artes Cênicas Pesquisa e Diversidade - Brasília - 2013.
Aldeia SESC – Mostra de Artes Cênicas do SESC Alagoas - Maceió - 2013.
Instituto Cultural Sete Porteiras do Brasil (Umbanda temple) – São Paulo – 2013.
VI Seminário de Pesquisa em Dança - UFPA - Belém - 2013.

*Trilhas e Trânsitos: 20 Vinte Anos do GIPE-CIT -Teatro do Movimento (UFBA) –
Salvador – 2013.*

Projeto Dança e Pesquisa: Interseções Artístico-Acadêmicas. Usina do Gasômetro. Porto Alegre – 2014.

Núcleo de Ensino e Criação em Dança - Departamento de Arte Corporal of Escola de Educação Física e Desportos, UFRJ - Rio de Janeiro – 2014.

Departamento de Artes Corporais of Instituto de Artes, Unicamp - Campinas – 2014.

16. Soibare: Corpo de um Brasil Xavante (The Body of a Xavante Brazil) (2011–2013)

Dance Performance.

Production: Departamento de Artes Corporais da Unicamp.

Participates as Director.

Presentations:

Tribute to Aracy Lopes da Silva - Departamento de Antropologia da USP - São Paulo - 2011.

Arte em Foco 2012 - Belo Horizonte - 2012.

Aldeia SESC – Mostra de Artes Cênicas do SESC Alagoas - Maceió – 2013.

17. Coraci Mironga (2012–2013)

Dance Performance.

Production: Departamento de Artes Corporais da Unicamp.

Participates as Director.

Presentations:

Departamento de Artes Corporais of UNICAMP - Campinas - 2012

Escola de Samba "Nenê de Vila Matilde" (Samba school) - São Paulo - 2012

VI Mostra Lugar Nômade de Dança - São Paulo - 2013

Das Theater Im Hof Der Naunynritze - Berlin, Germany – 2013.

Graça, Bailarina de Jesus (Grace, Ballerina of Jesus)

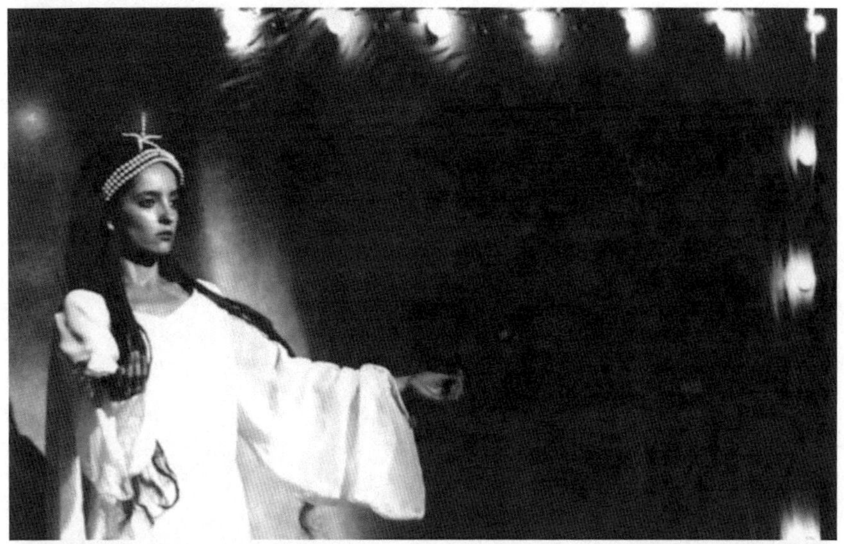

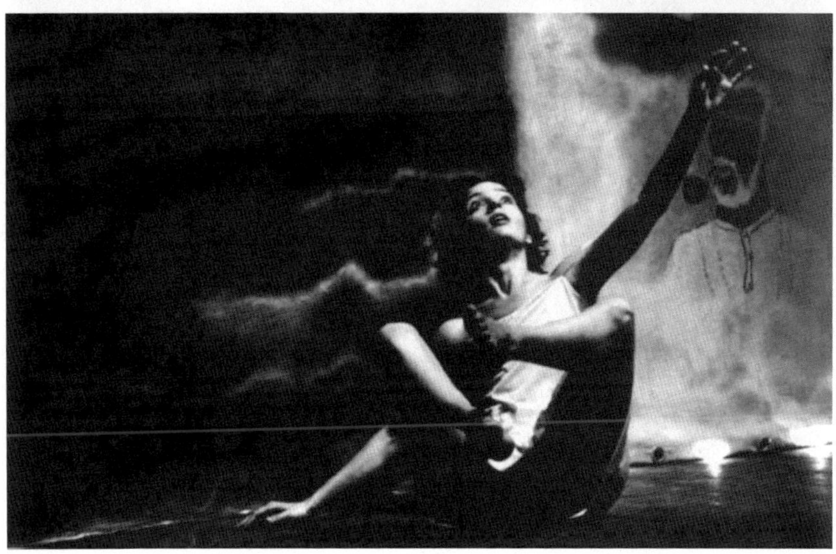

Graziela Rodrigues
Photos: publicity

183

Graça, Bailarina de Jesus (Grace, Ballerina of Jesus)

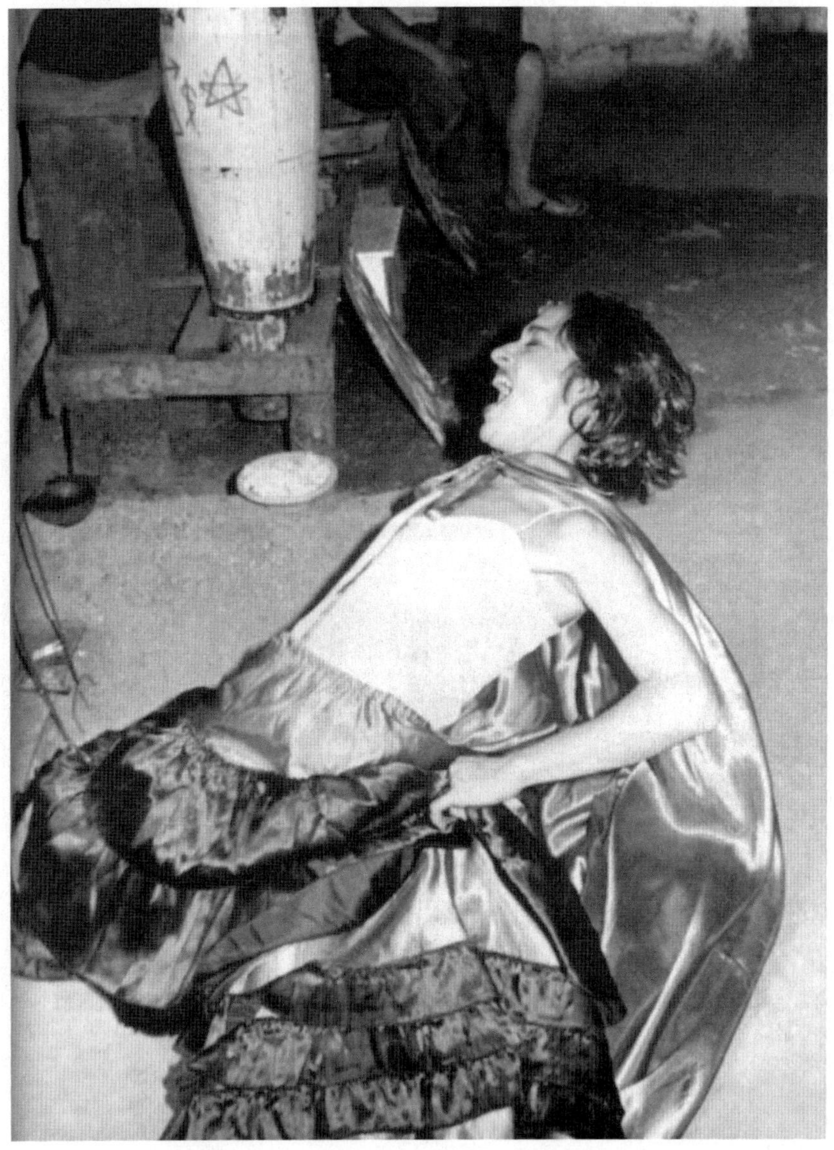

Graziela Rodrigues
Photo: publicity

184

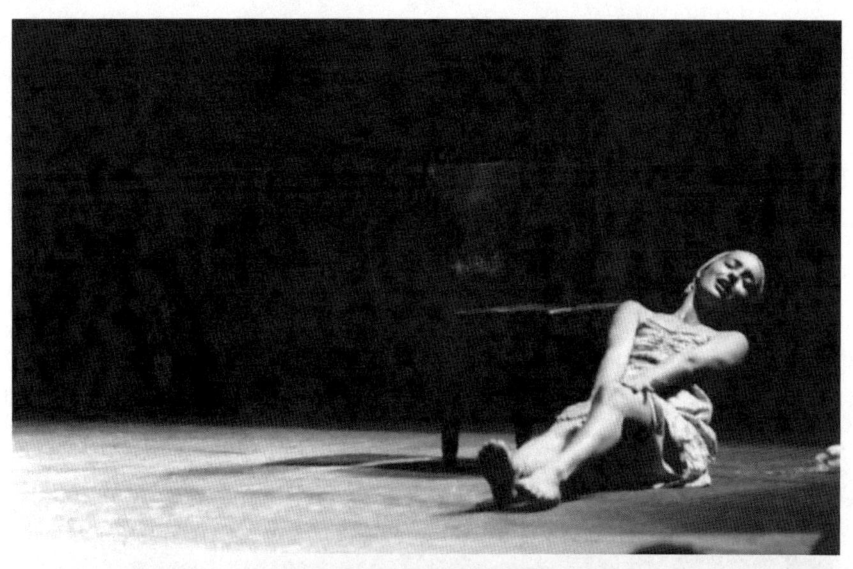

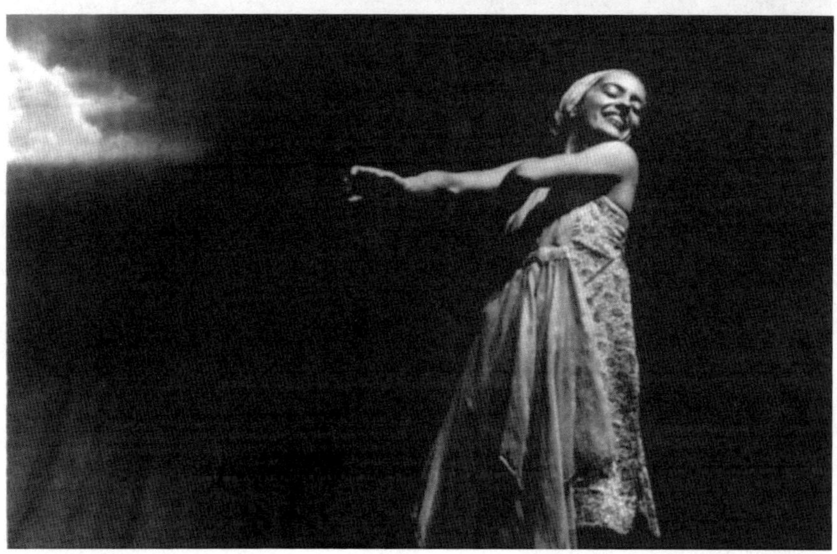

185

Graça, Bailarina de Jesus (Grace, Ballerina of Jesus)

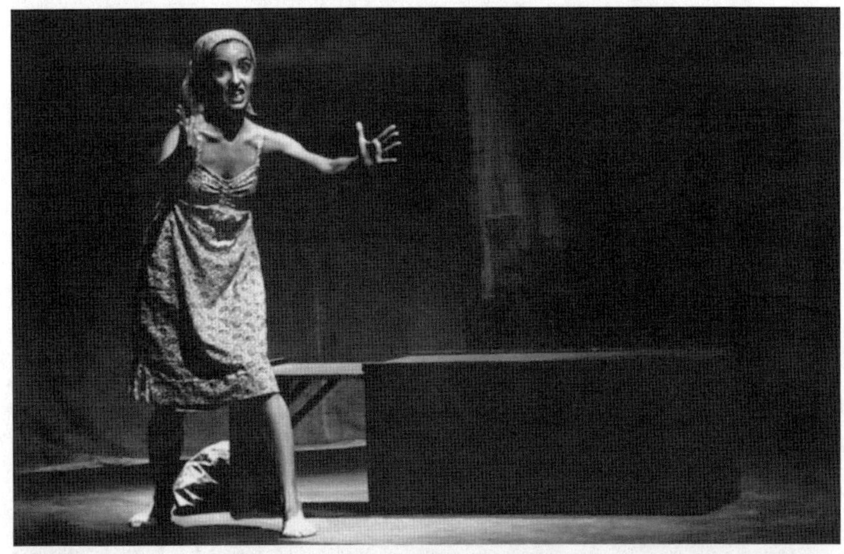

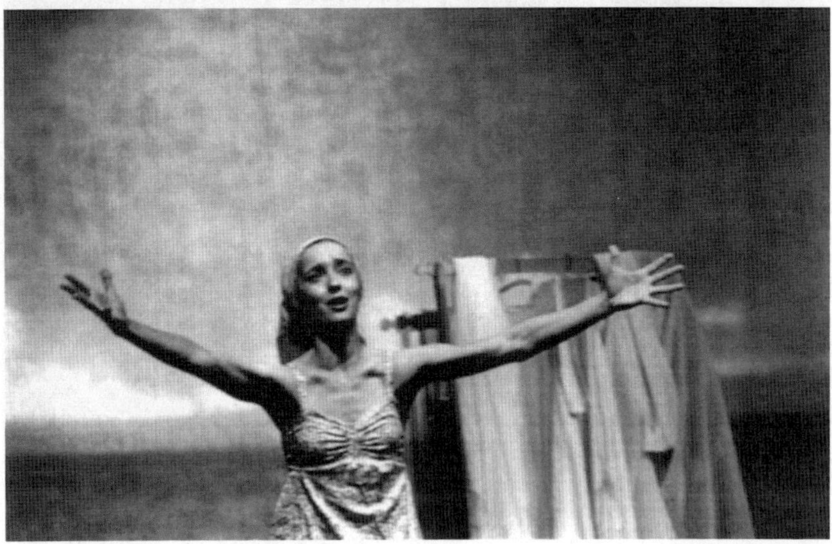

Caminhadas (Walkings)

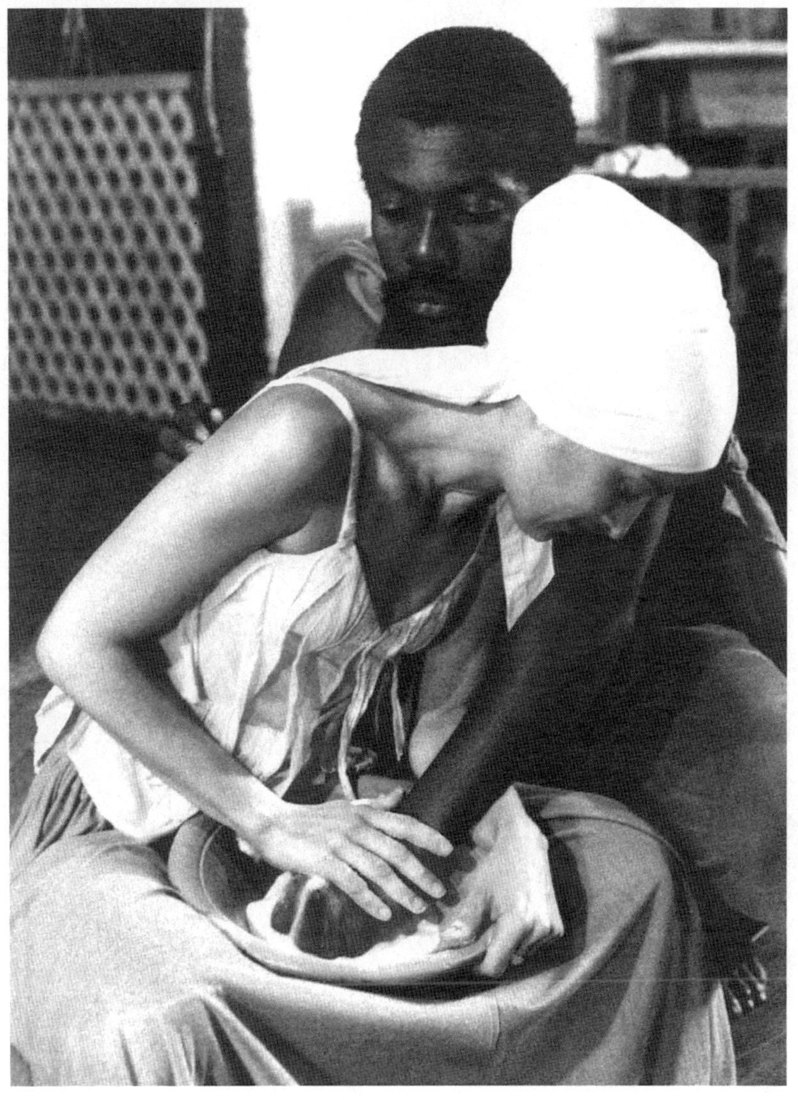

Graziela Rodrigues and Tião de Carvalho
Photo: Author's archive

Graziela Rodrigues and Tião de Carvalho
Photo: Pedro Della Paschoa

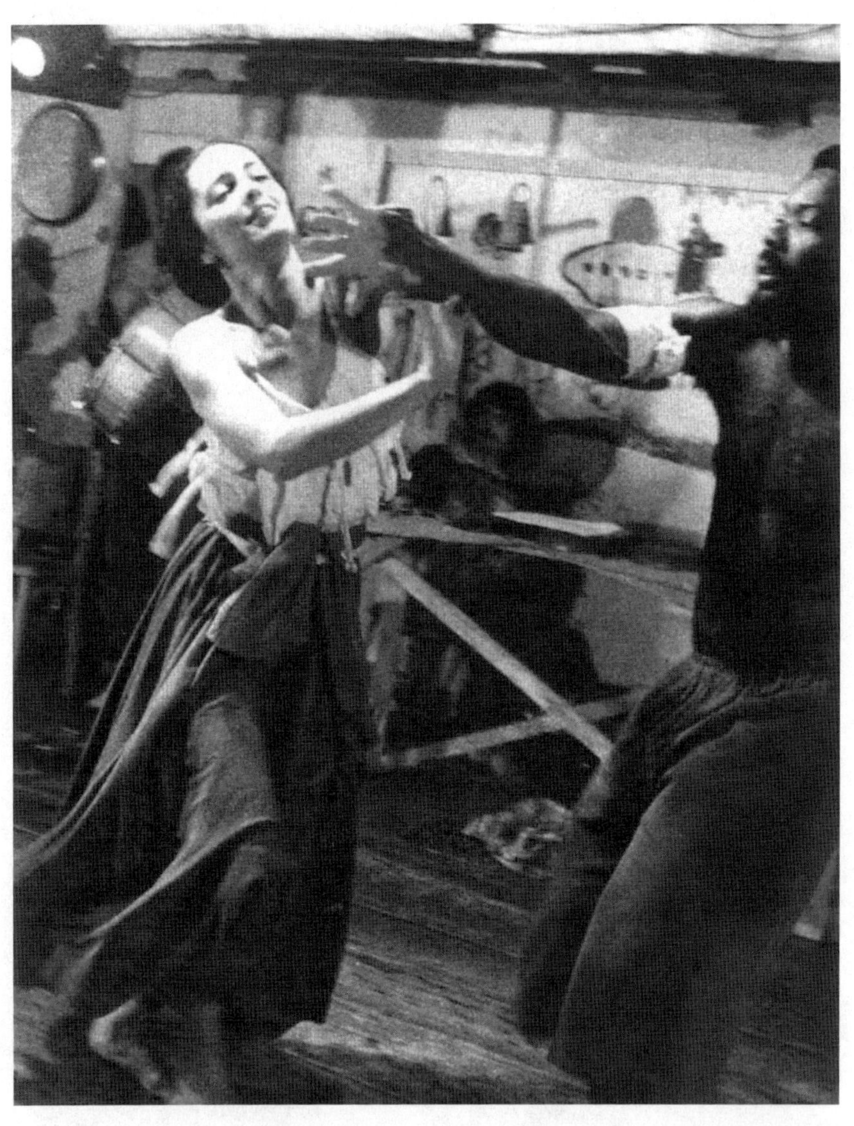

188

Caminhadas (Walkings)

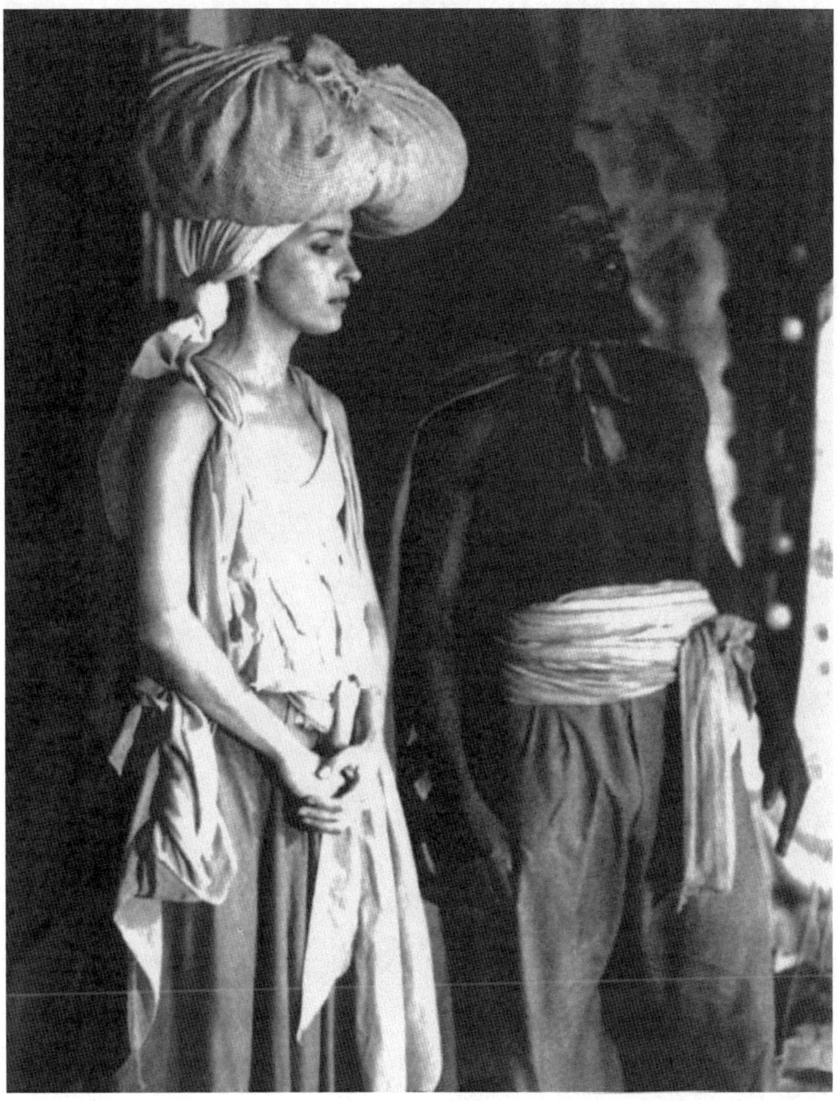

Graziela Rodrigues and Tião de Carvalho
Photo: Author's archive

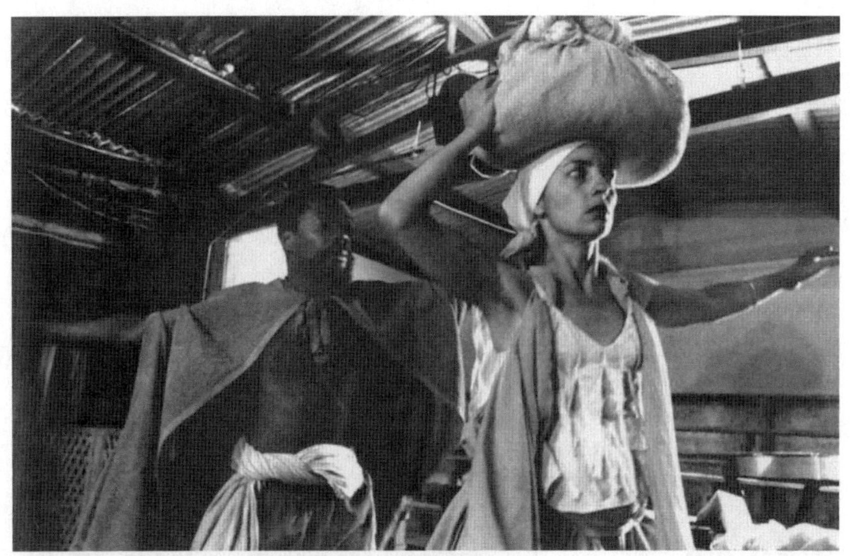

Graziela Rodrigues and
Tião de Carvalho
Photo: Author's archive

Graziela Rodrigues
Photo: Author's archive

190

Coração Vermelho (Red Heart)

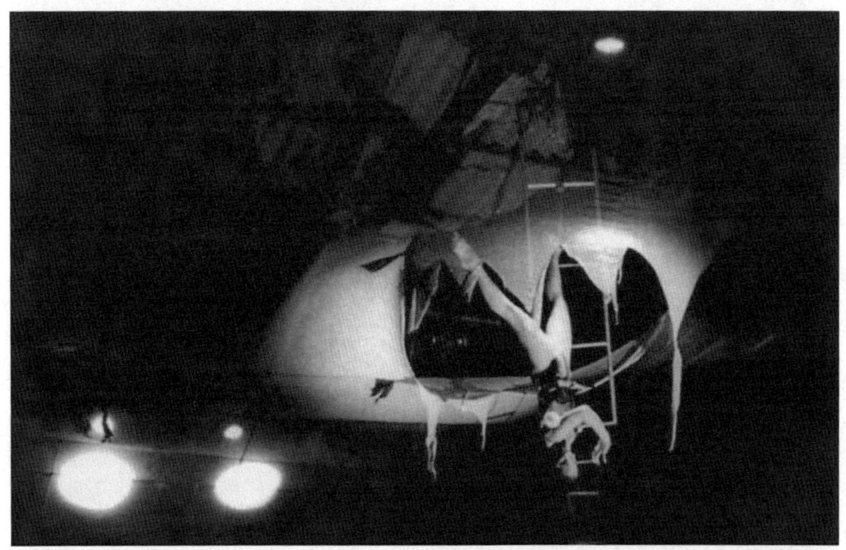

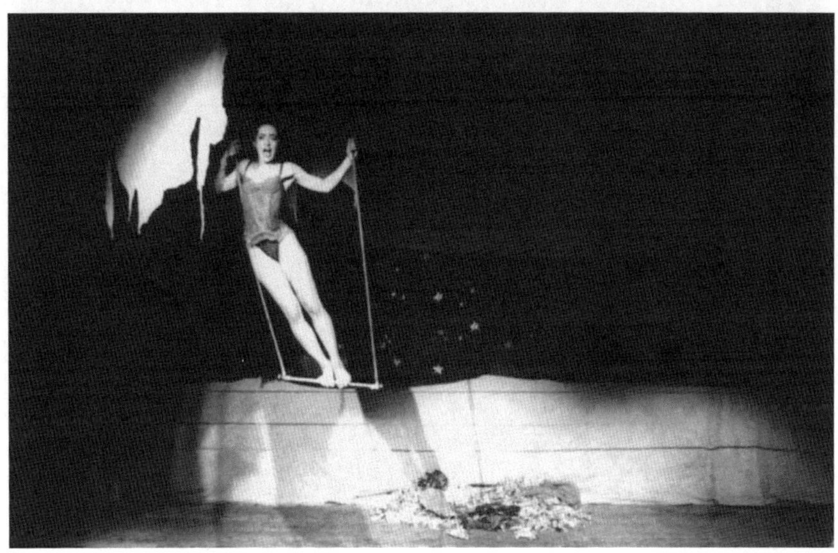

Graziela Rodrigues
Photos: Author's archive

Graziela Rodrigues
Arquivos Multimeios/Divisão de Pesquisas - IDART
Photo: João Cabral

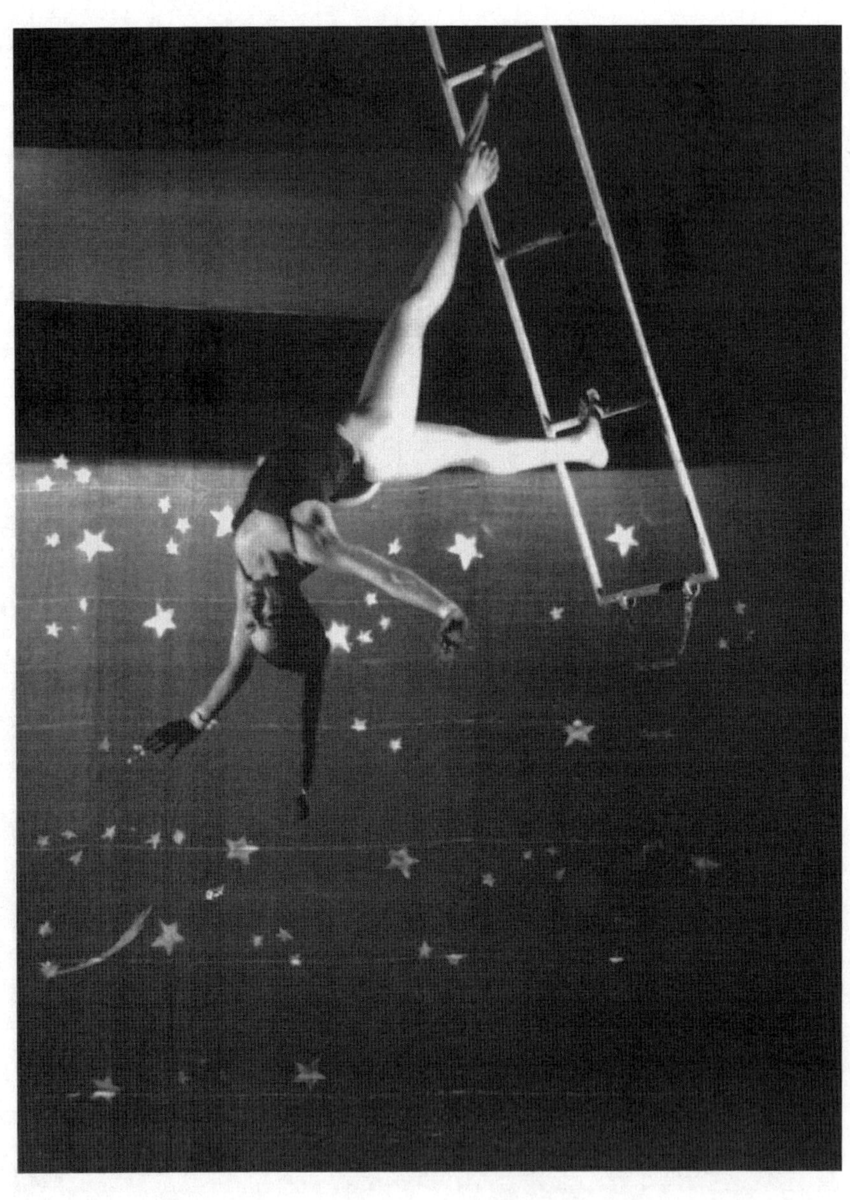

192

Coração Vermelho (Red Heart)

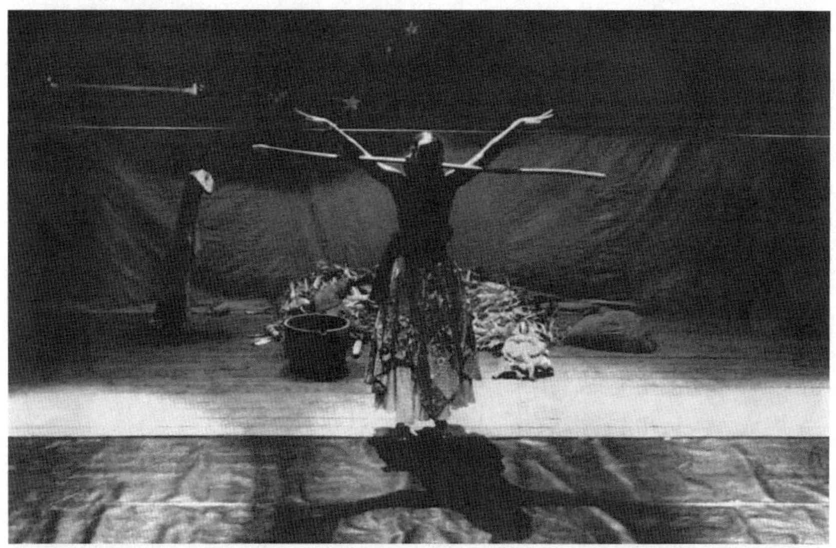

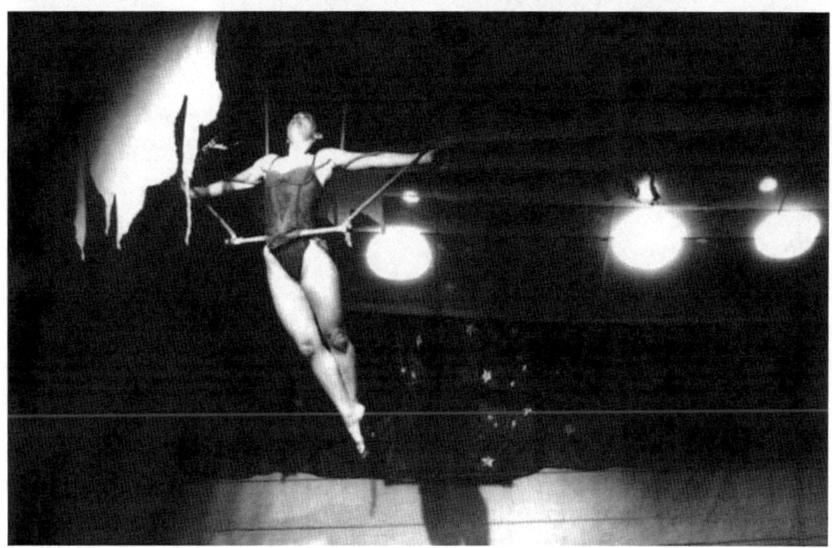

Graziela Rodrigues
Photos: Author's archive

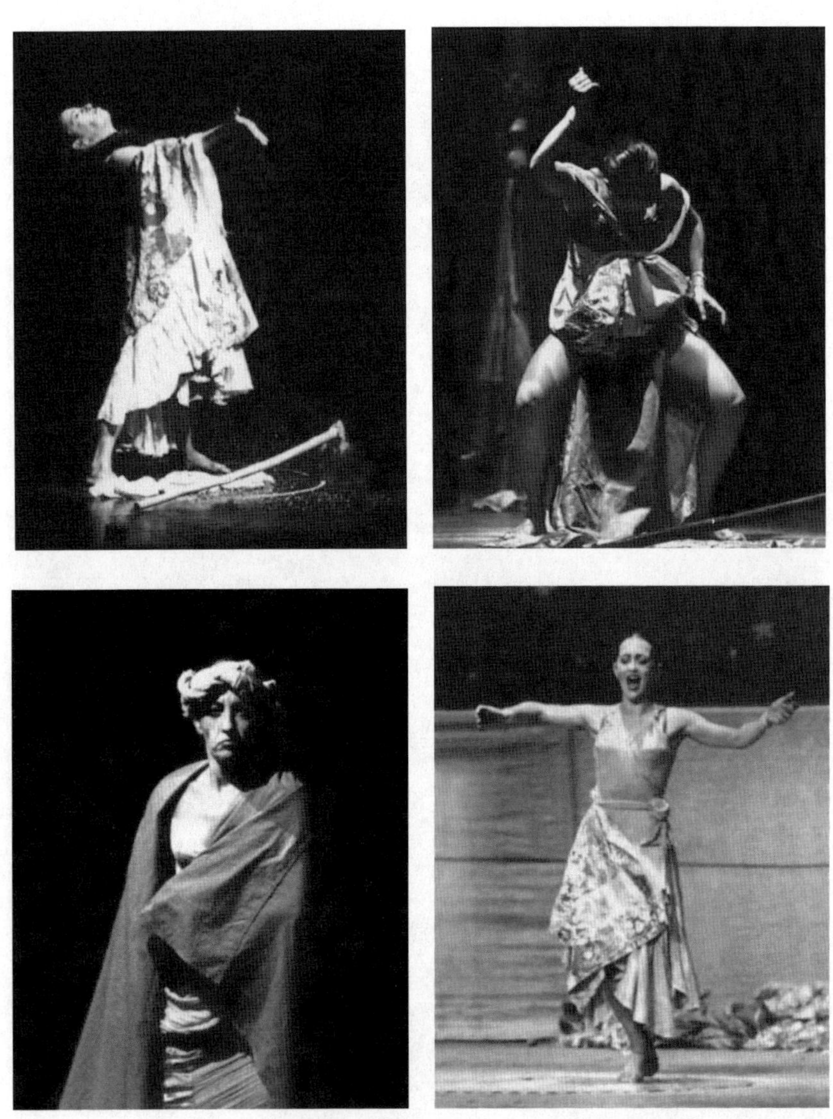

194

Bailarinas de Terreiro (Terreiro Ballerinas)

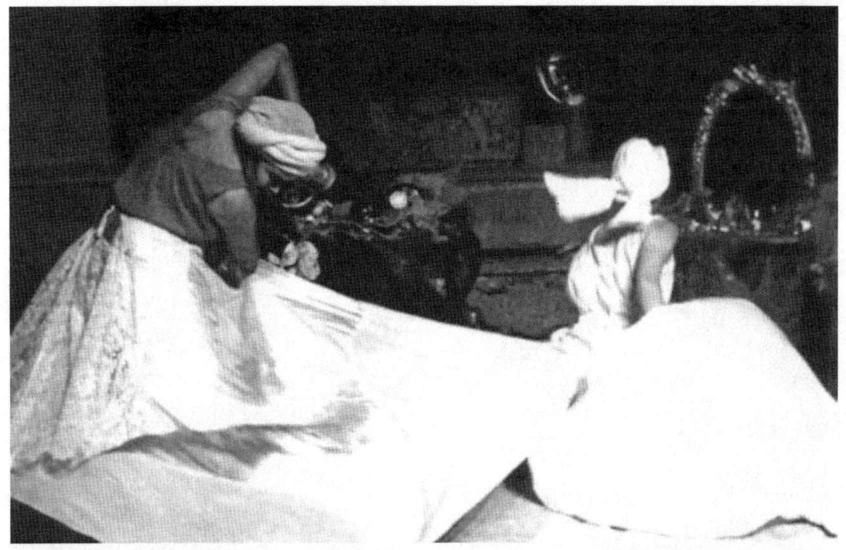

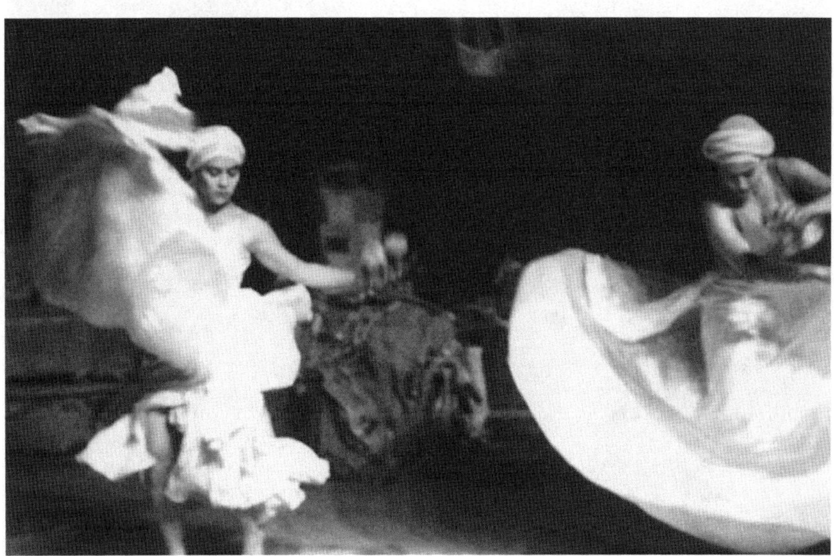

Rosana Baptistela and Gracia Navarro
Photos: publicity

Bailarinas de Terreiro (Terreiro Ballerinas)

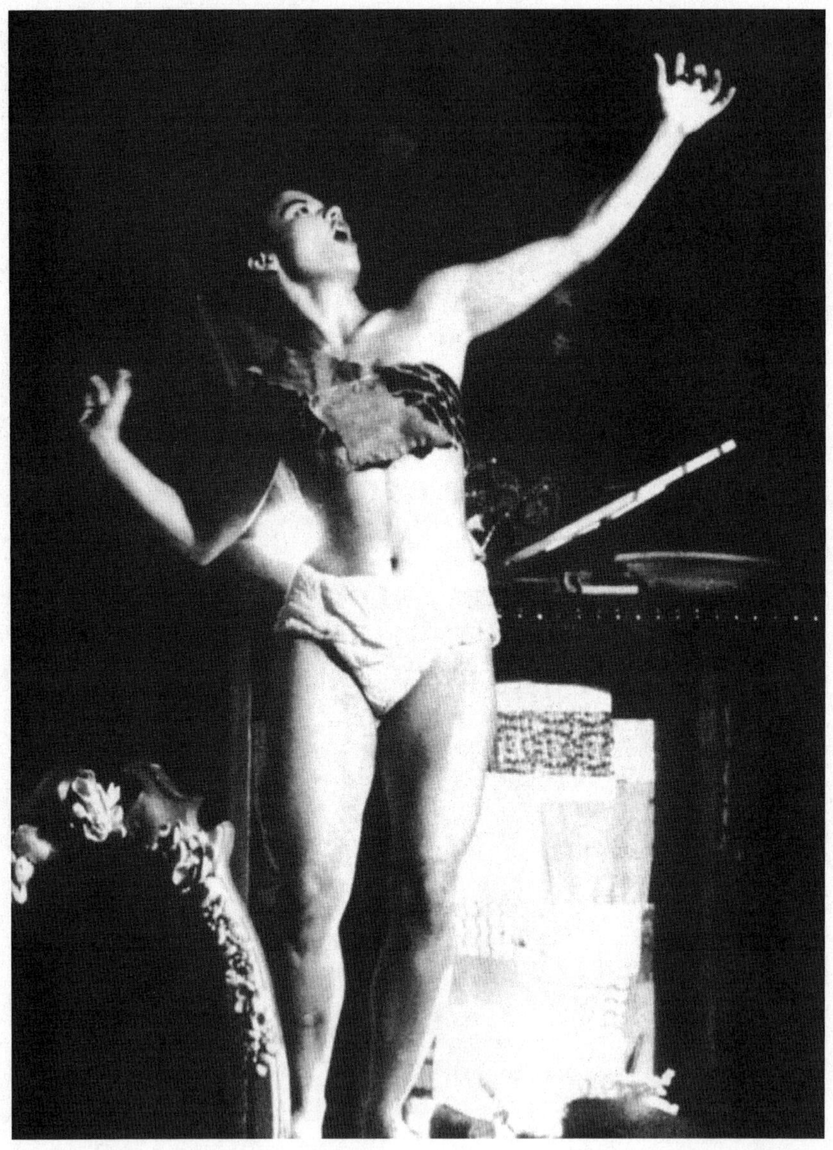

Rosana Baptistela
Photo: Martinho Caires

196

Estrela Boieira (Ox Star)

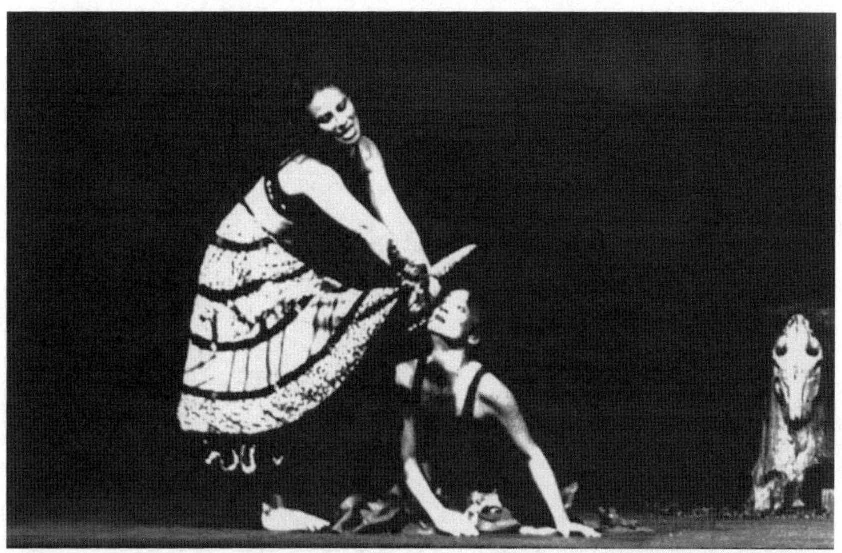

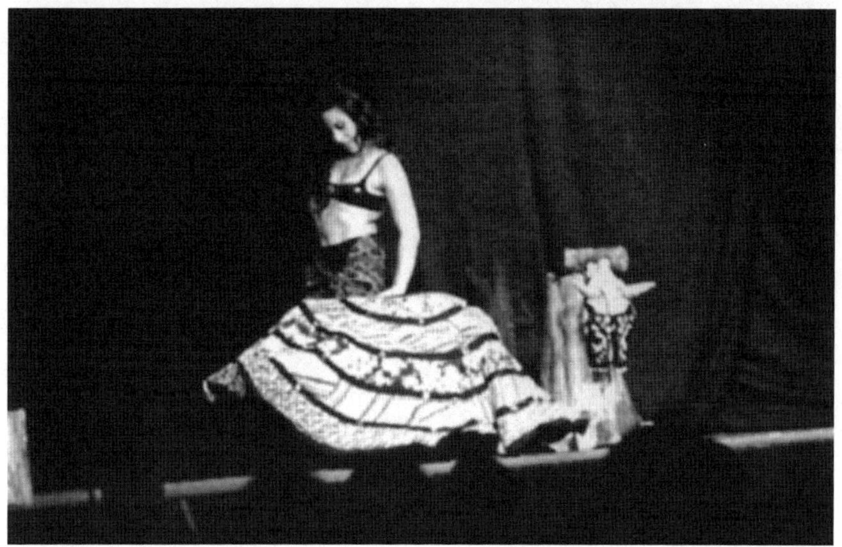

Diane Ichimaru and Heloisa Domenici
Photos: publicity

197

Estrela Boieira (Ox Star)

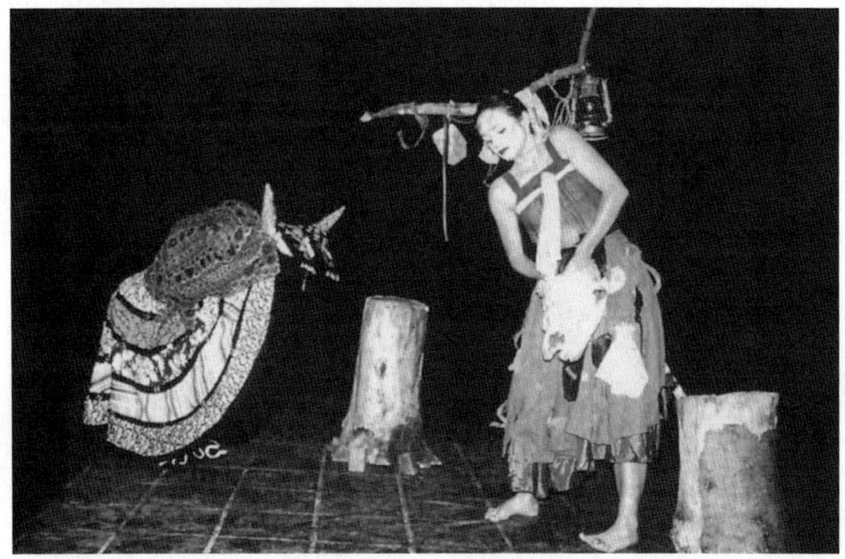

Diane Ichimaru and Heloisa Domenici
Photo: publicity

Interiores (Interiors)

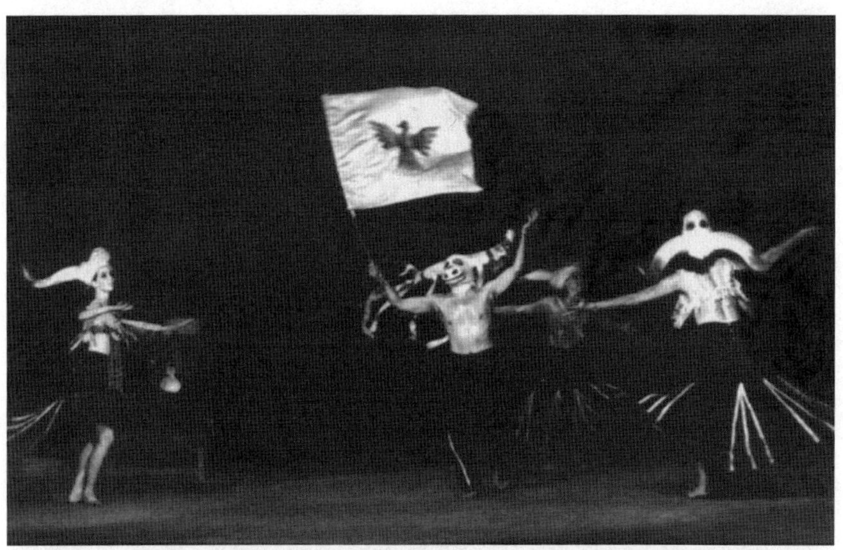

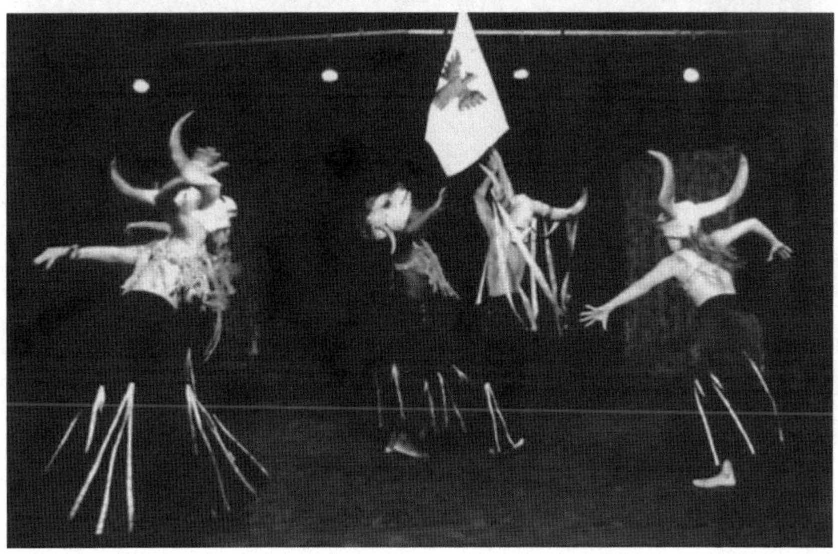

Photos: Roberto de Ângelo

Interiores (Interiors)

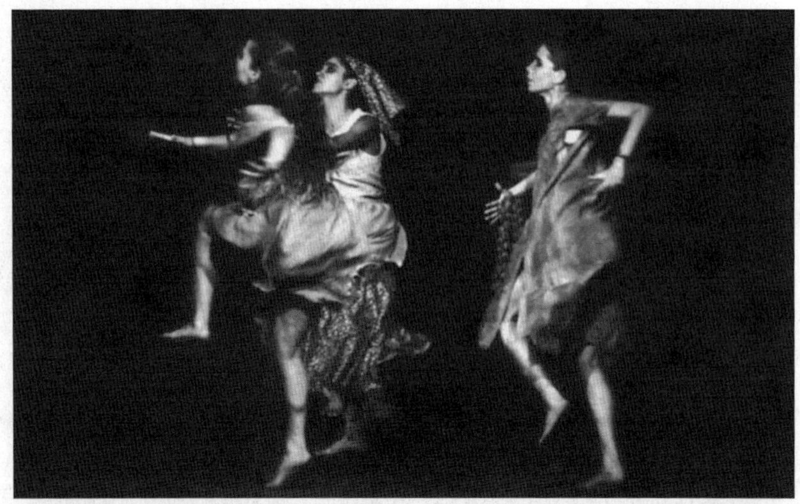

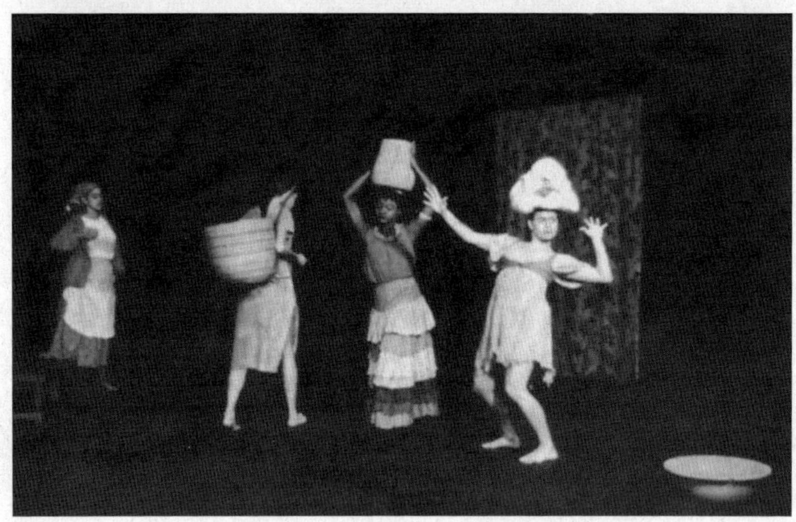

Above:
Lara Rodrigues; Paula Caruso; Ana Carolina Melchert

Below:
Paula Caruso; Ana Carolina Melchert; Paula Salles; Lara Rodrigues
Photos: Roberto de Ângelo

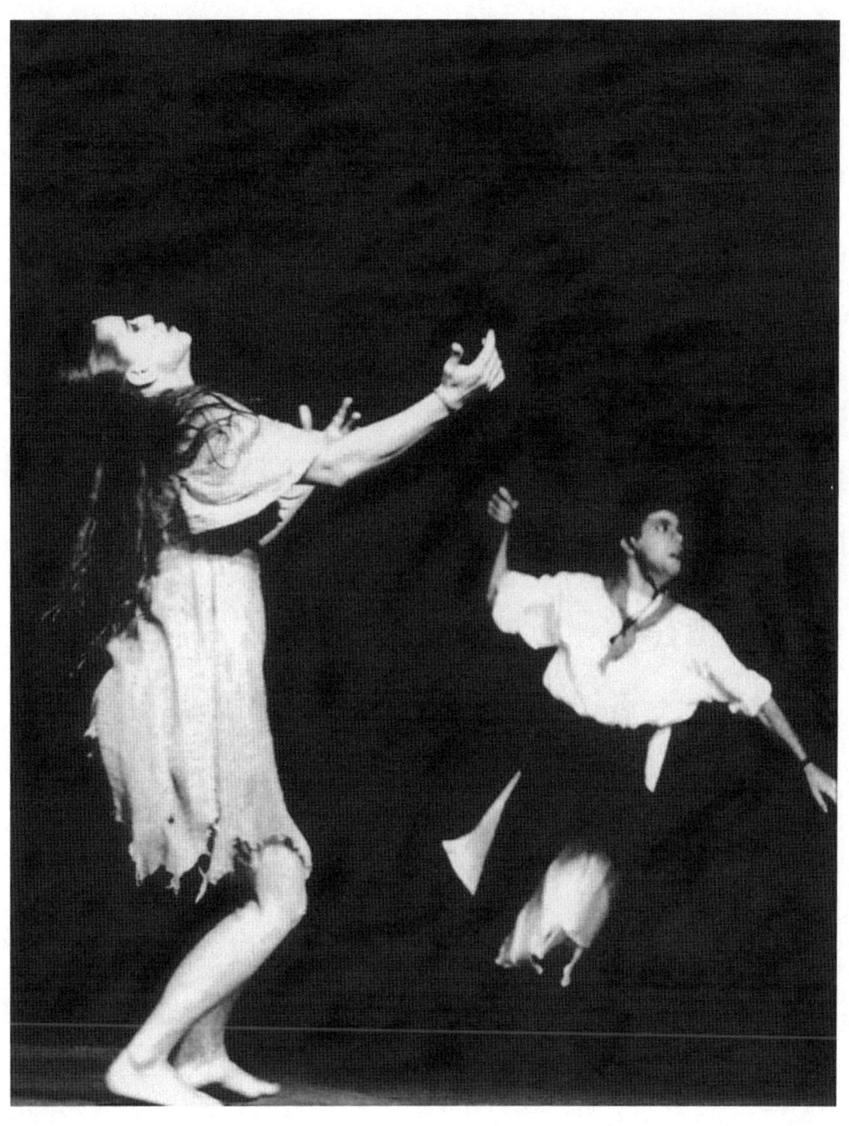

Lara Rodrigues and Clermont Phitan
Photo: Roberto de Ângelo

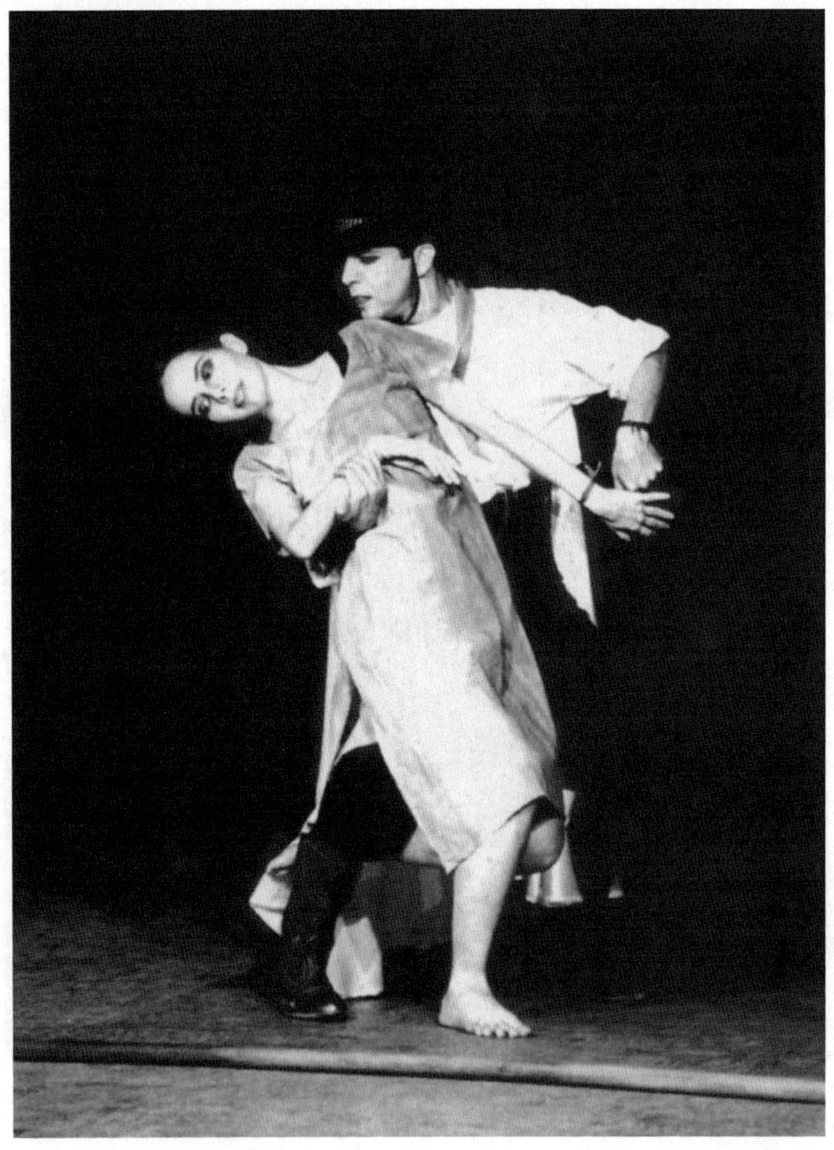

Ana Carolina Melchert and Clermont Phitan
Photo: Roberto de Ângelo

Diante dos Olhos (Before the Eyes)

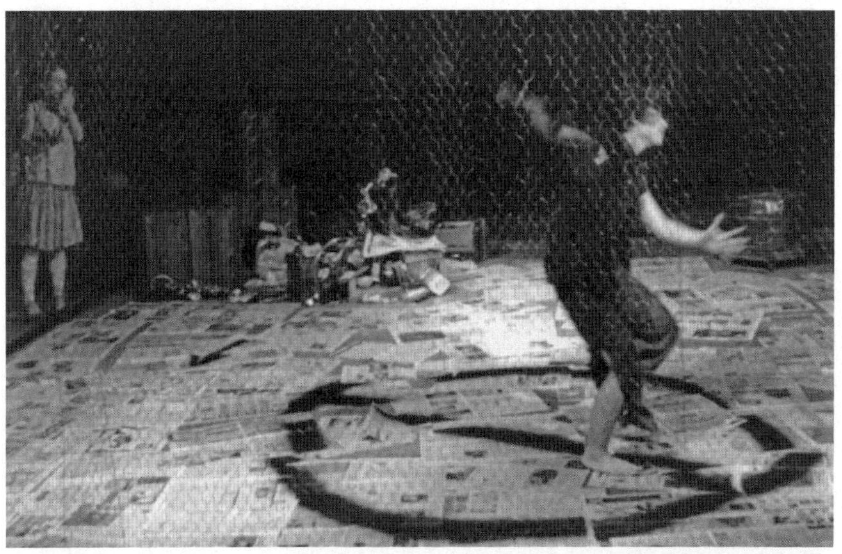

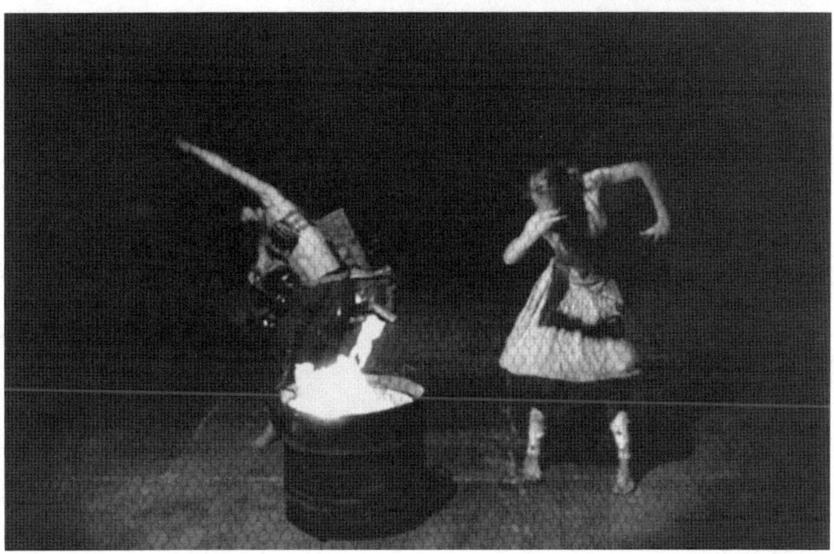

Larissa Turtelli and Daniela Kunh
Photos: André Favilla

203

Diante dos Olhos (Before the Eyes)

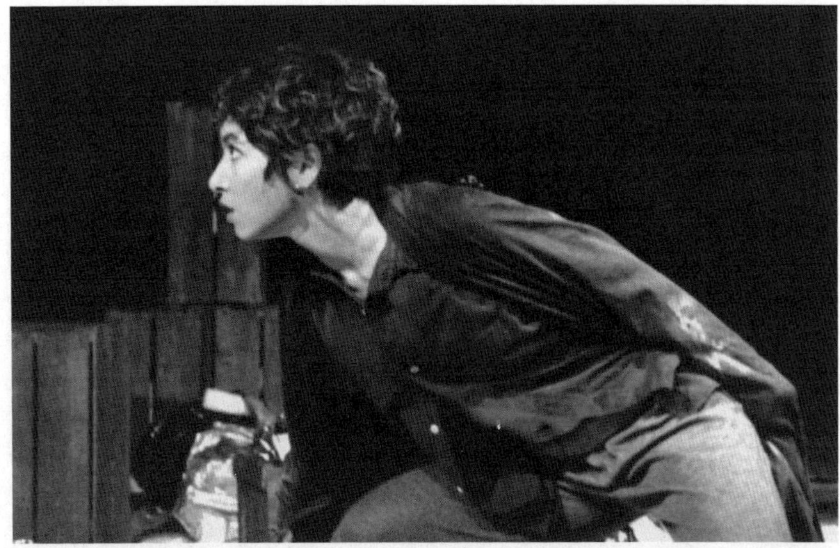

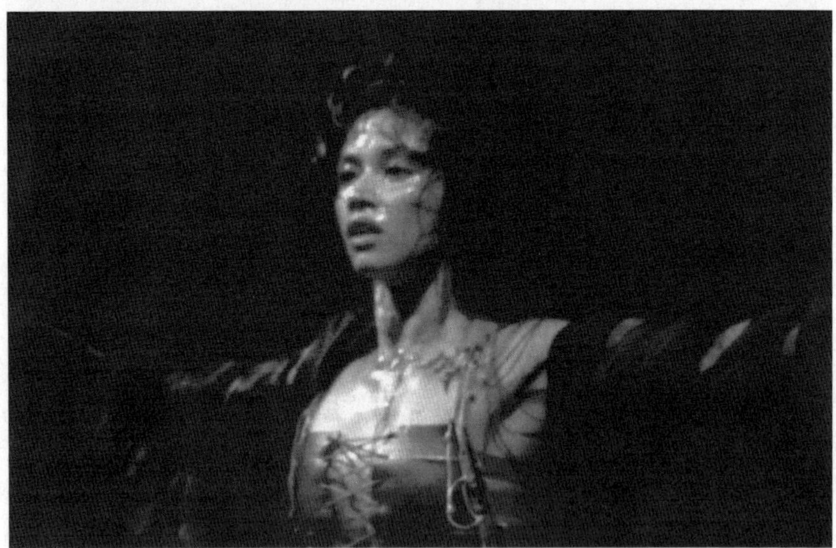

Above:
Larissa Turtelli
Photo: André Favilla

Below:
Larissa Turtelli
Photo: Daniela Pamplona

204

Viandeiras (Spinnerets)

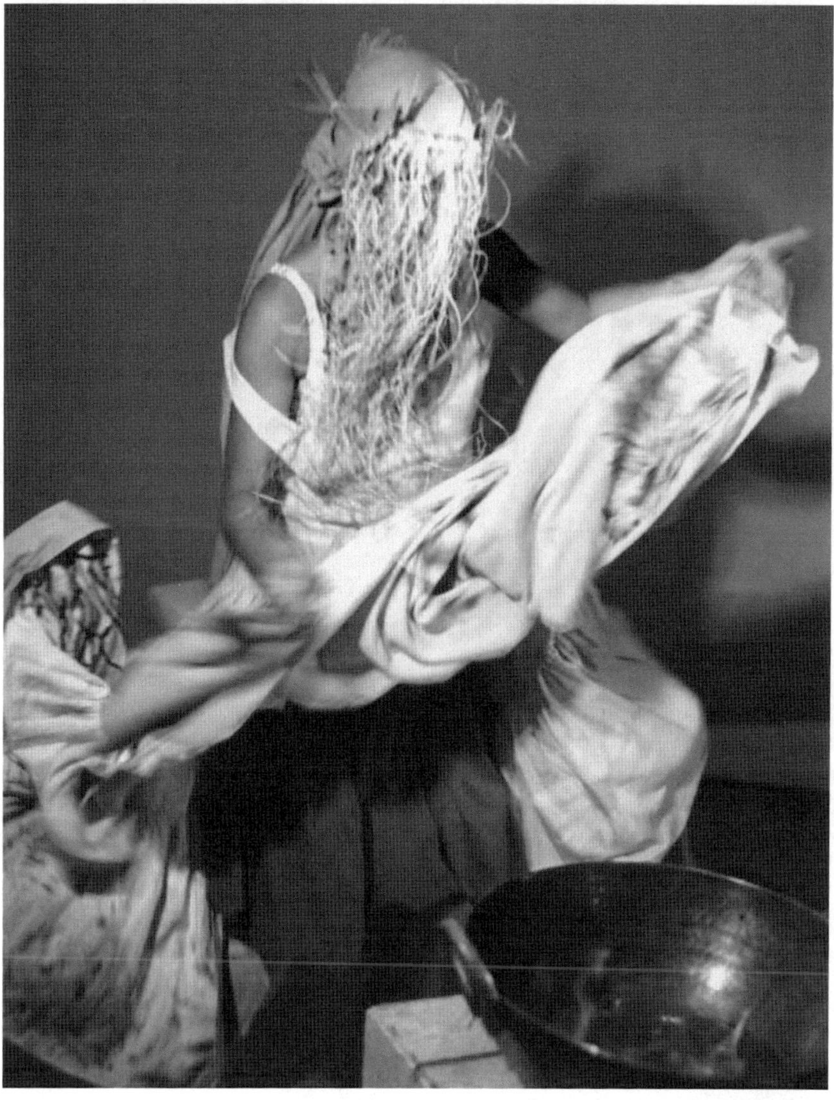

Letícia Doretto
Photo: João Maria

Viandeiras (Spinnerets)

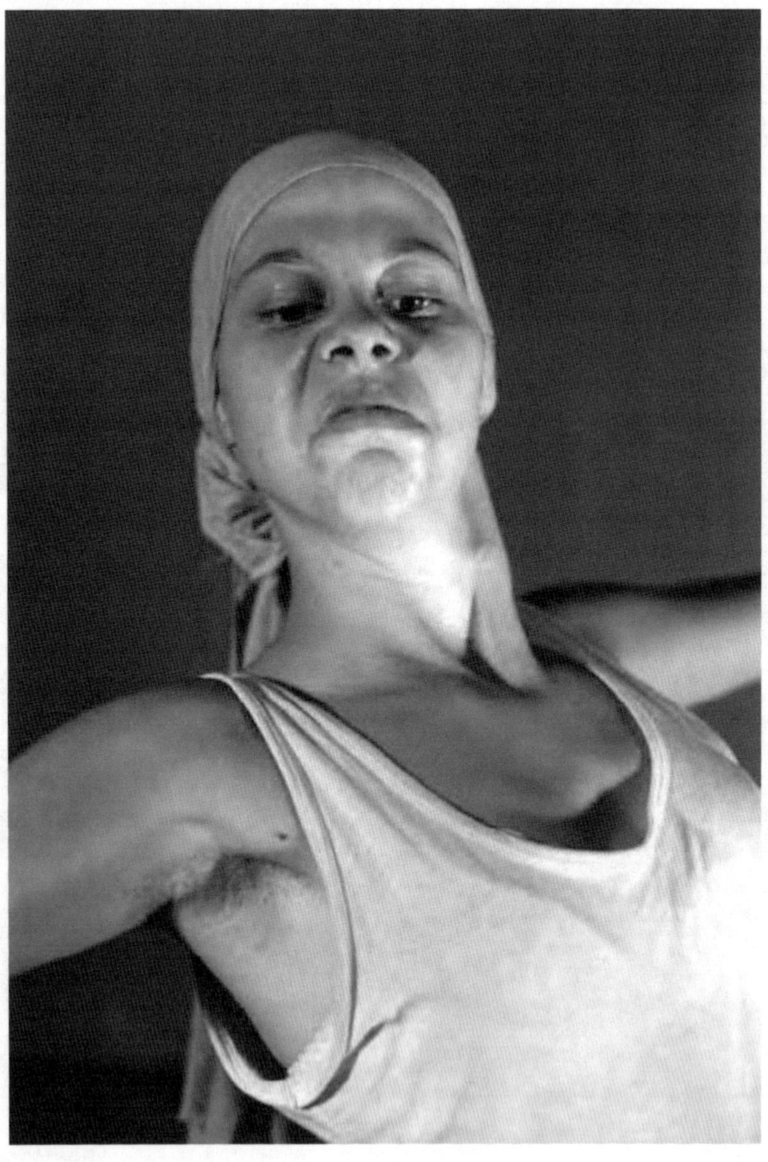

Letícia Doretto
Photo: João Maria

Viandeiras (Spinnerets)

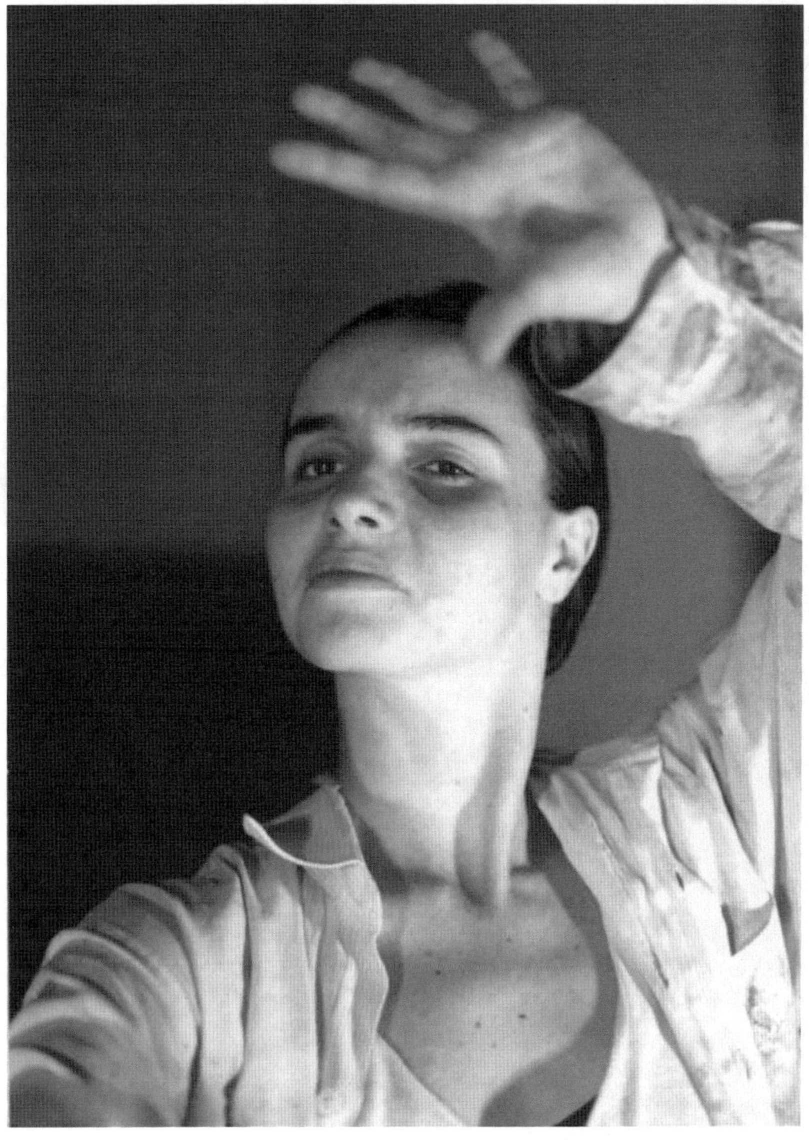

207

Valsa do Desassossego (Unrestness Waltz)

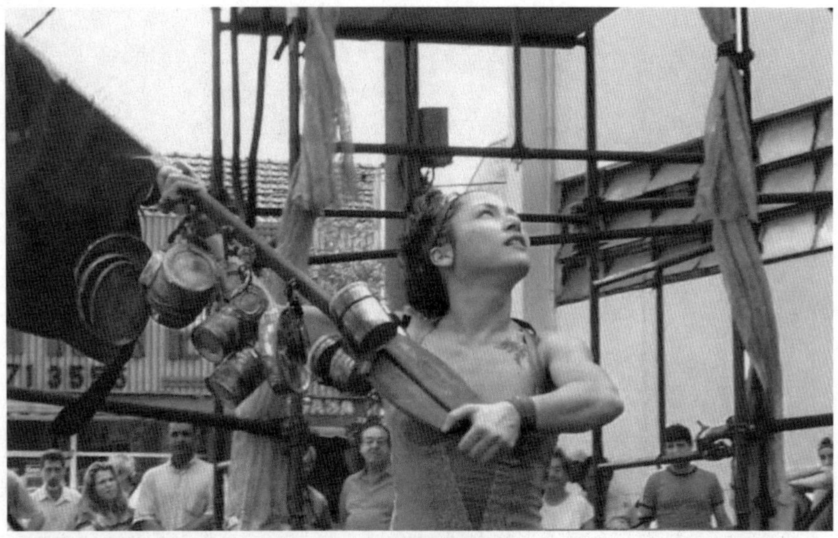

Larissa Turtelli
Photo: Isabella Franceschi

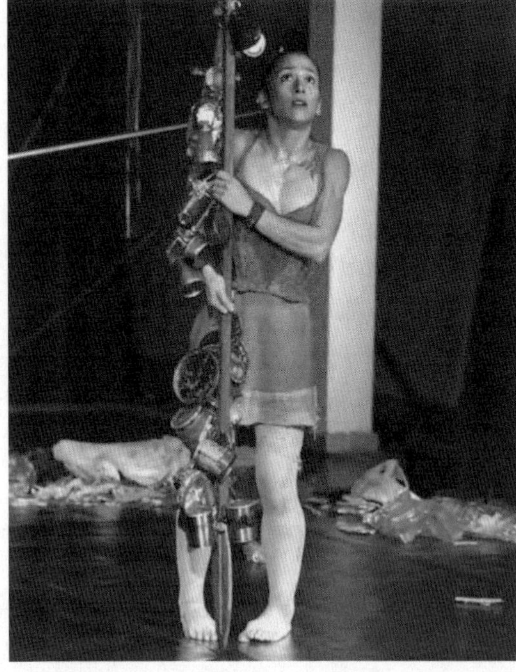

Larissa Turtelli
Photo: Frank Jeske

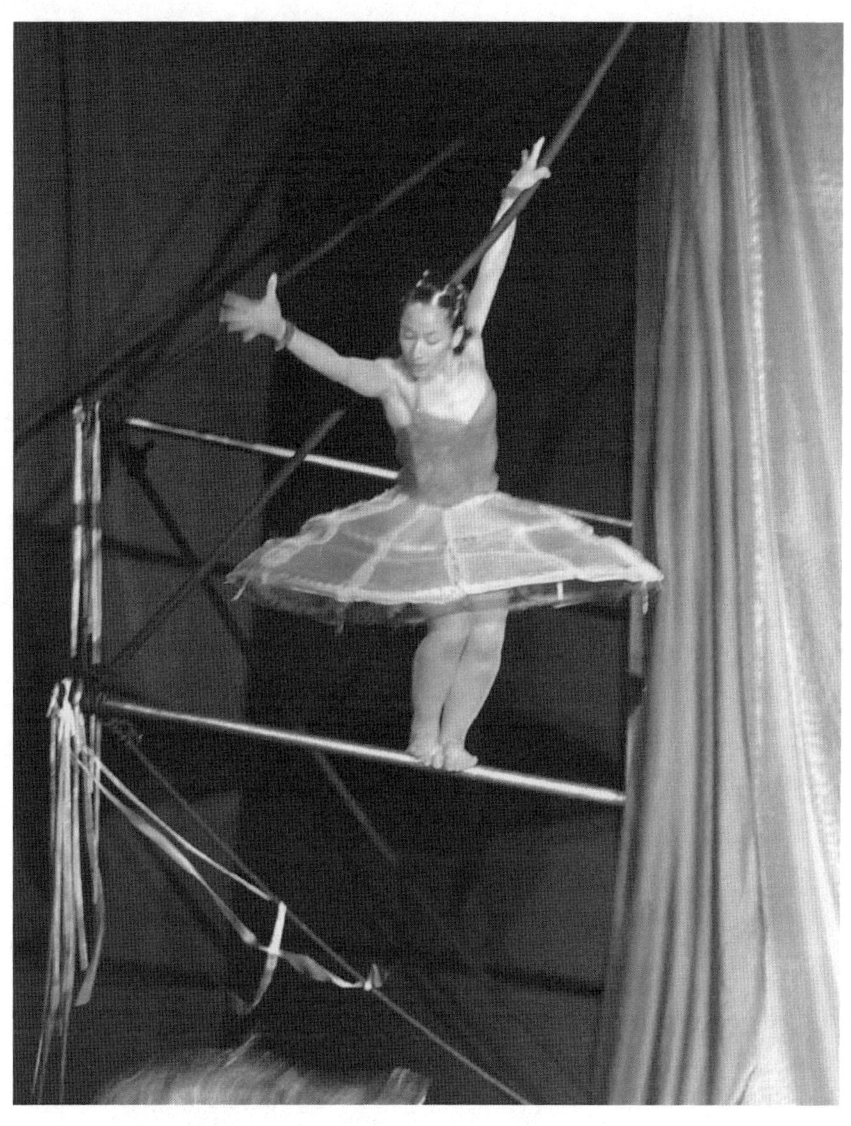

Larissa Turtelli
Photo: Frank Jeske

209

Valsa do Desassossego (Unrestness Waltz)

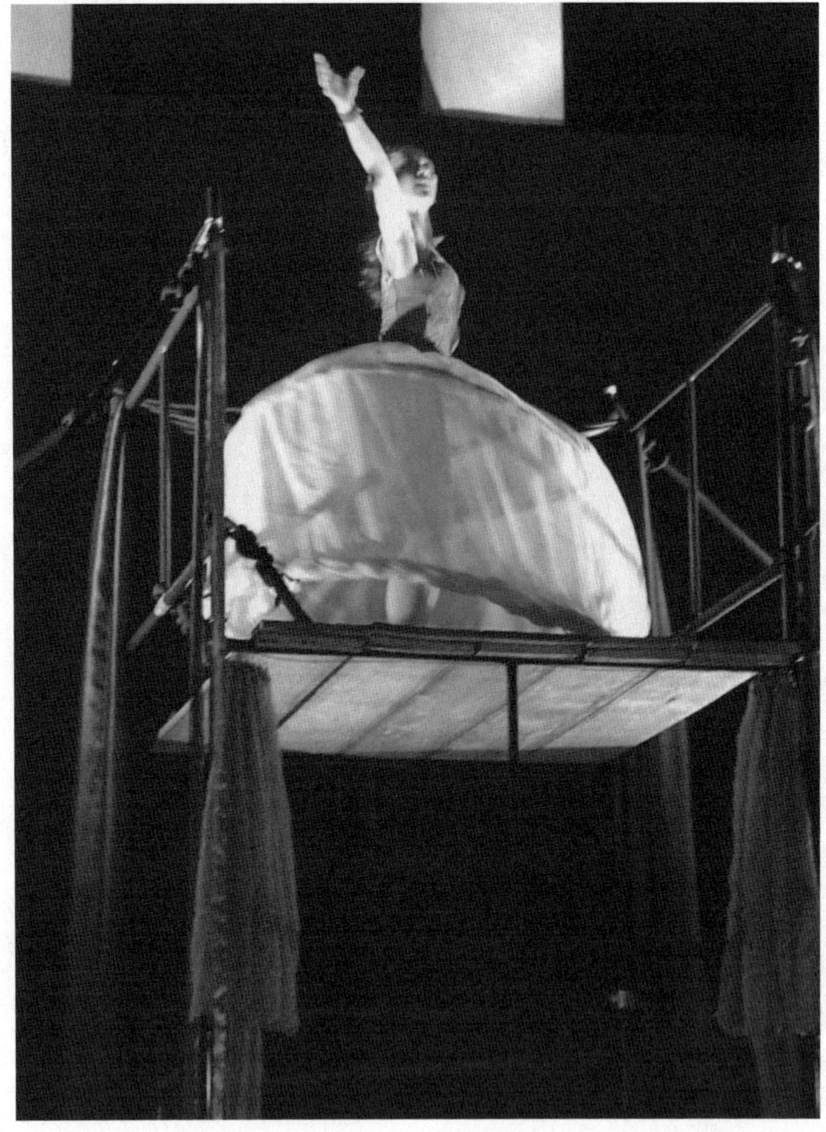

Larissa Turtelli
Photo: Frank Jeske

A Flor do Café (Coffee's Flower)

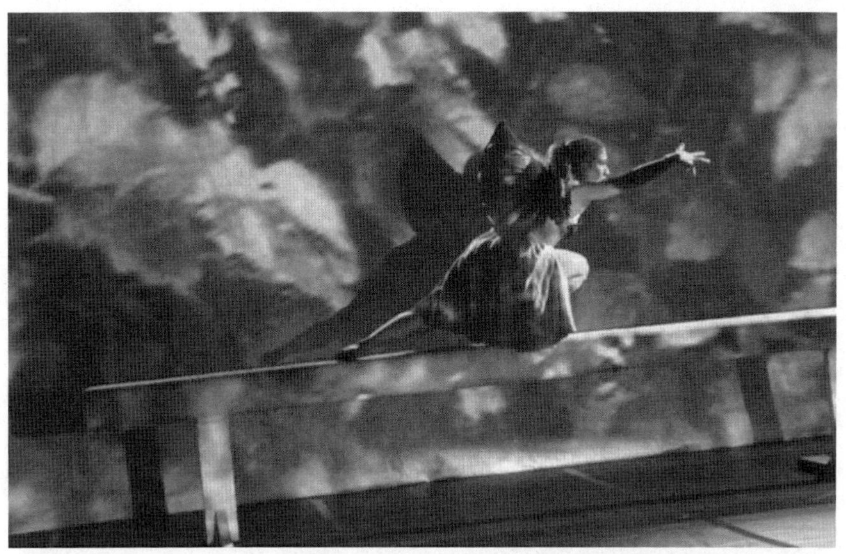

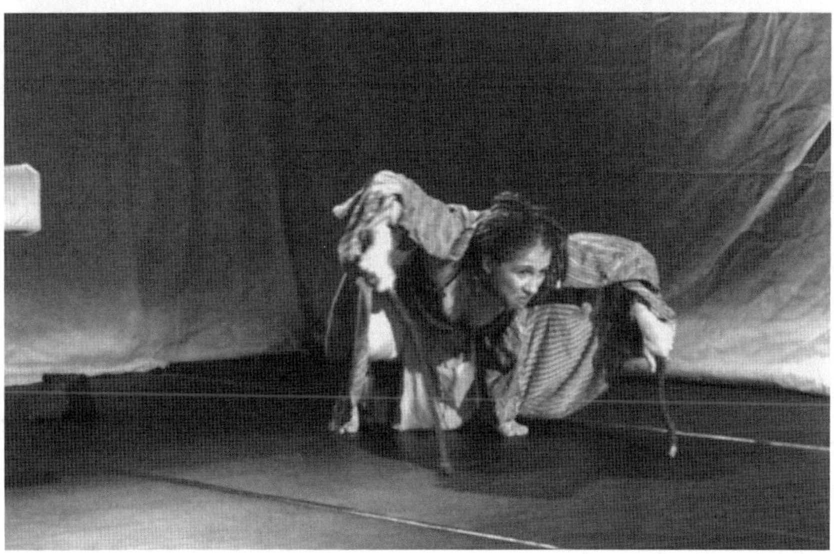

Nara de Moraes Cálipo Dilly
Photos: Beeroth de Souza

A Flor do Café (Coffee's Flower)

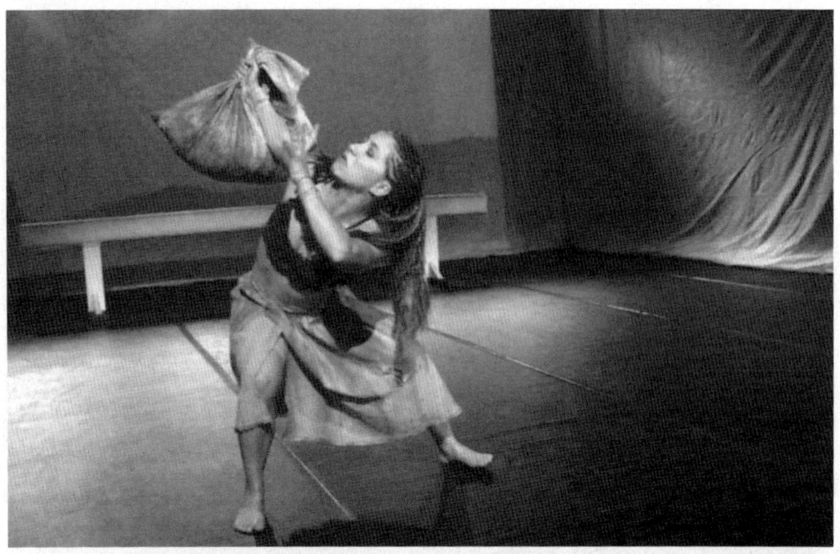

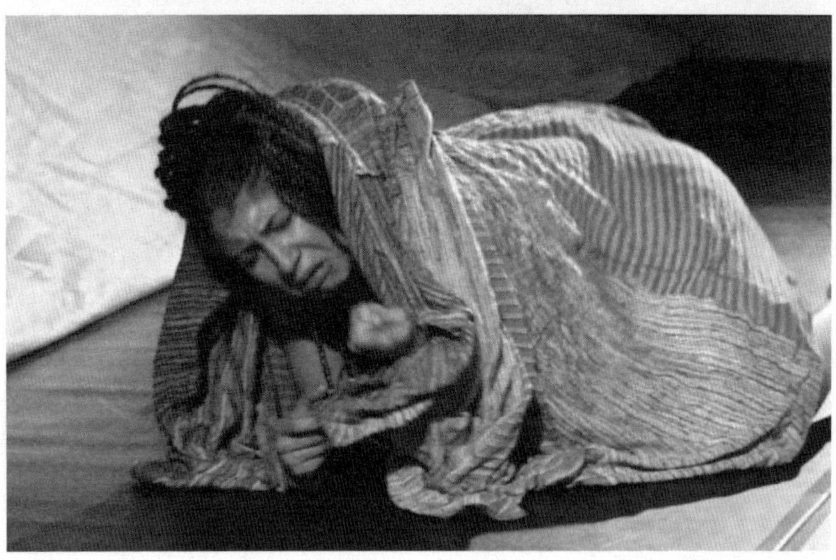

Nara de Moraes Cálipo Dilly
Photos: Beeroth de Souza

Nascedouro (Hatcher)

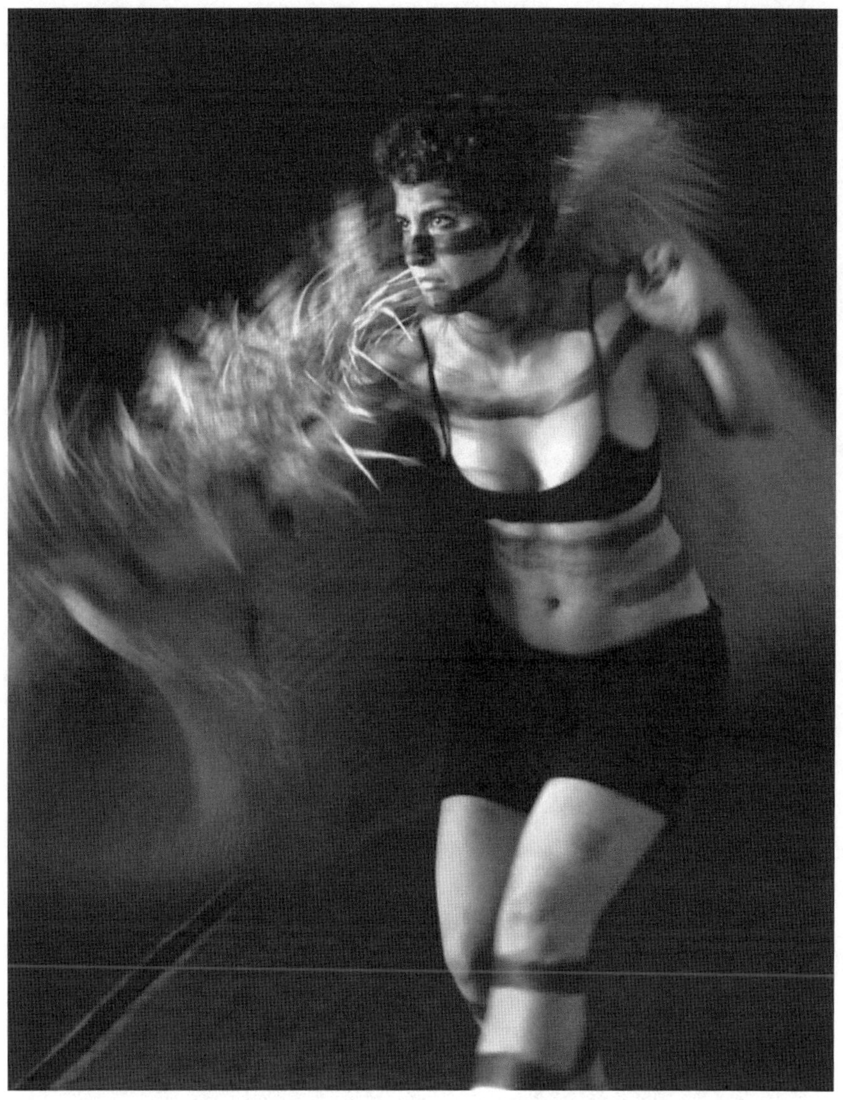

Elisa Massariolli da Costa
Photo: Isabella Pereira

213

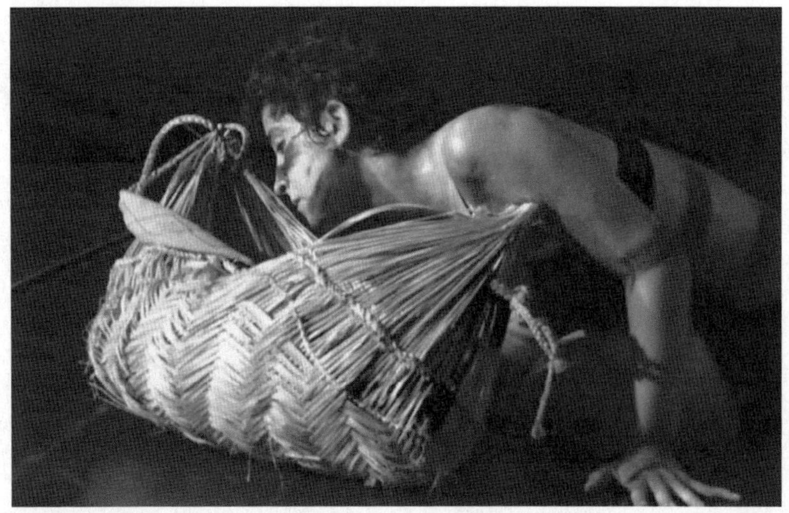

Elisa Massariolli da Costa
Photo: Isabella Pereira

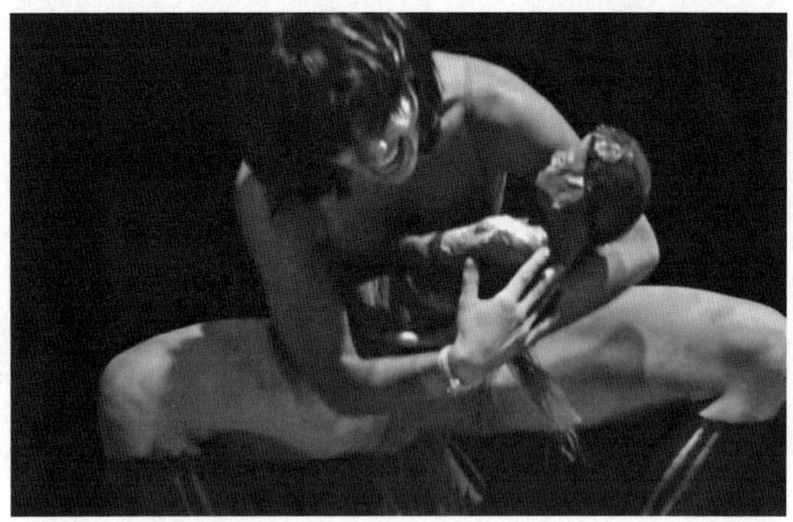

Elisa Massariolli da Costa
Photo: Andressa Coutinho

Fina Flor, Divino Amor - Iyabá Legba Hey! (Refined flower, Divine Love)

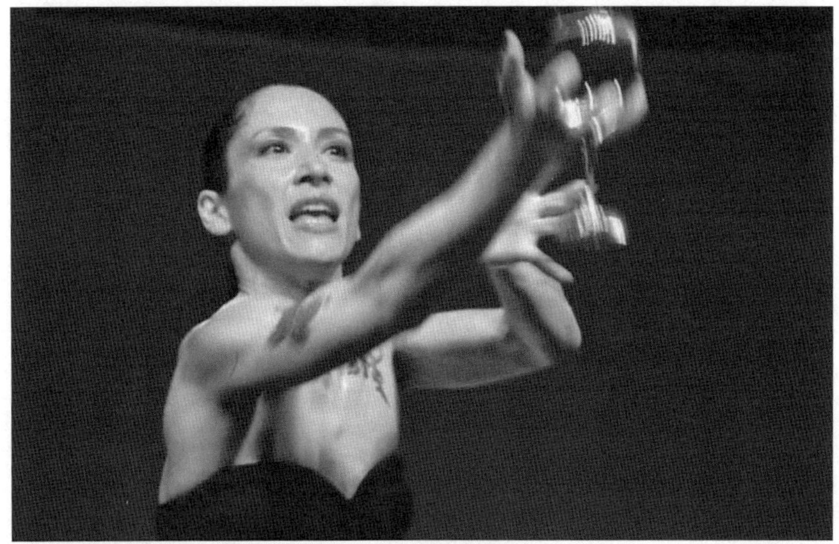

Larissa Turtelli
Photo: Andressa Coutinho

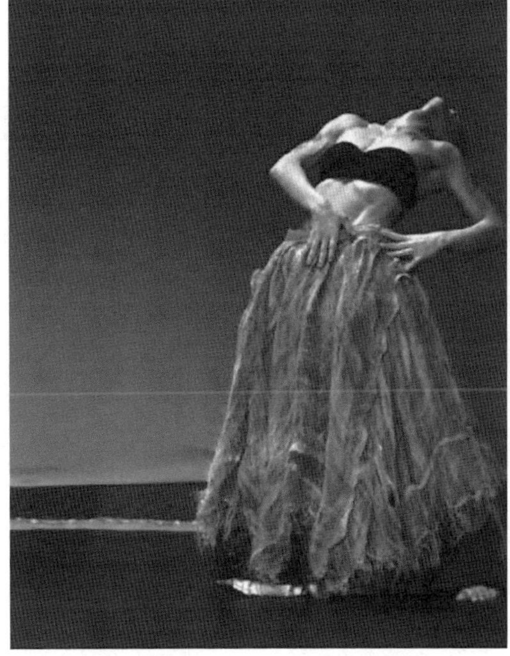

Larissa Turtelli
Photo: Débora Branco

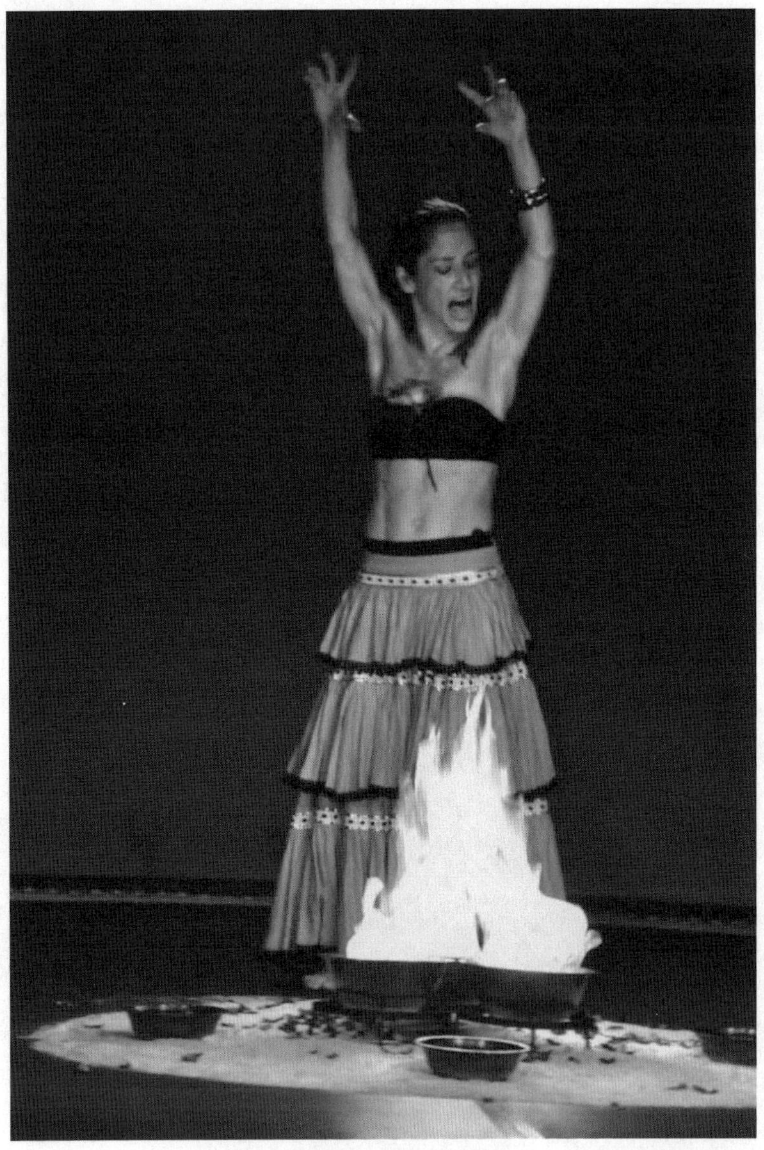

Larissa Turtelli
Photo: Andressa Coutinho

216

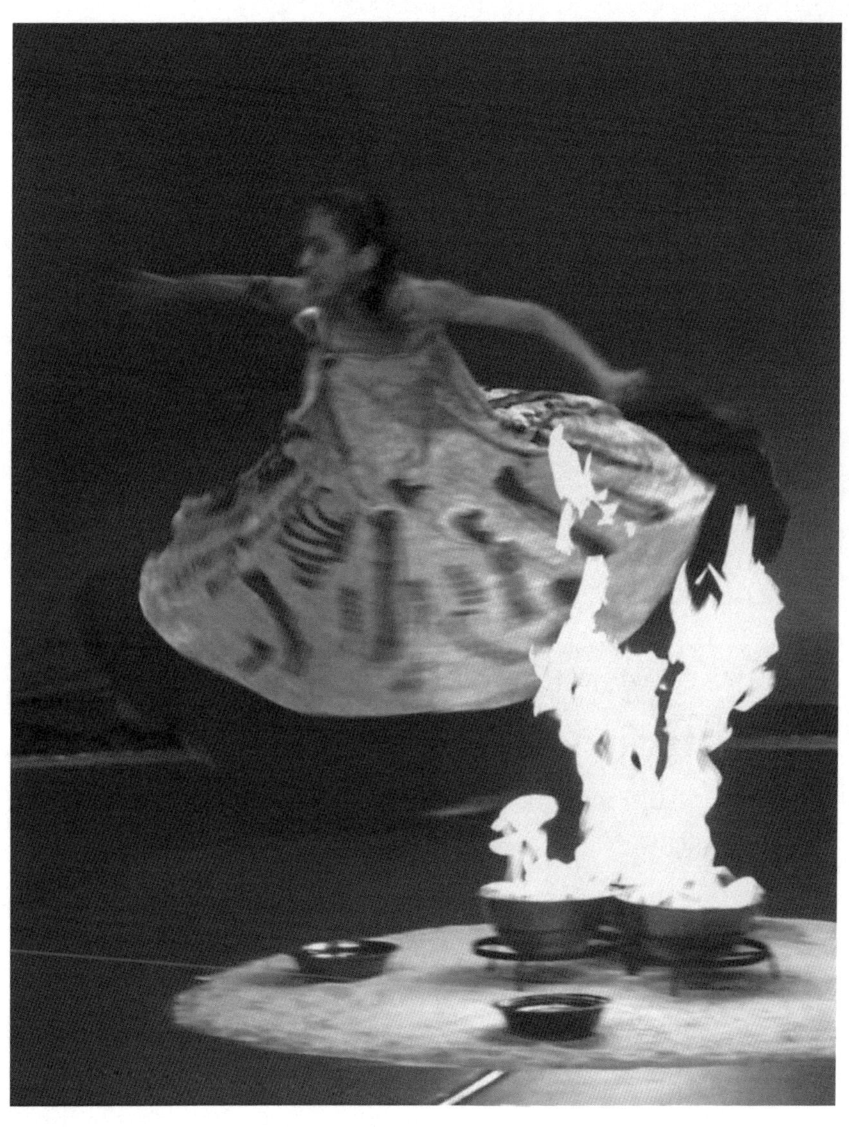

Larissa Turtelli
Photo: Débora Branco

Soibare: Corpo de um Brasil Xavante (The Body of a Xavante Brazil)

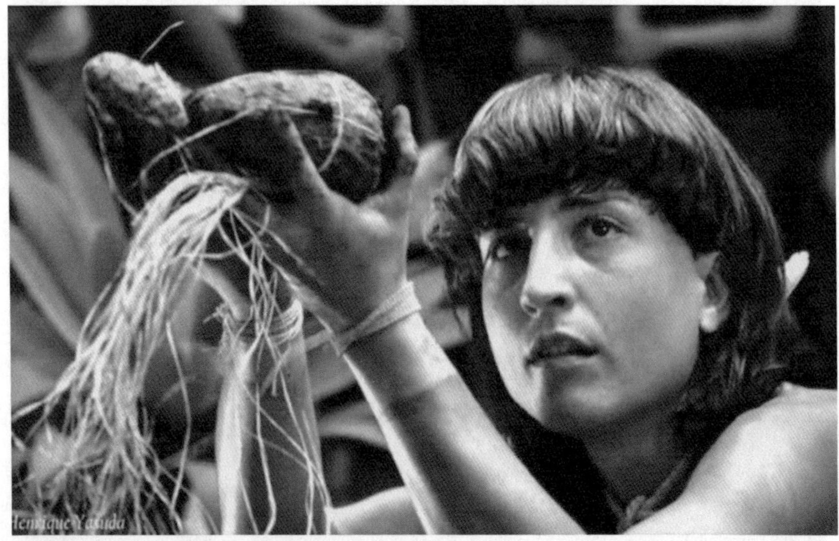

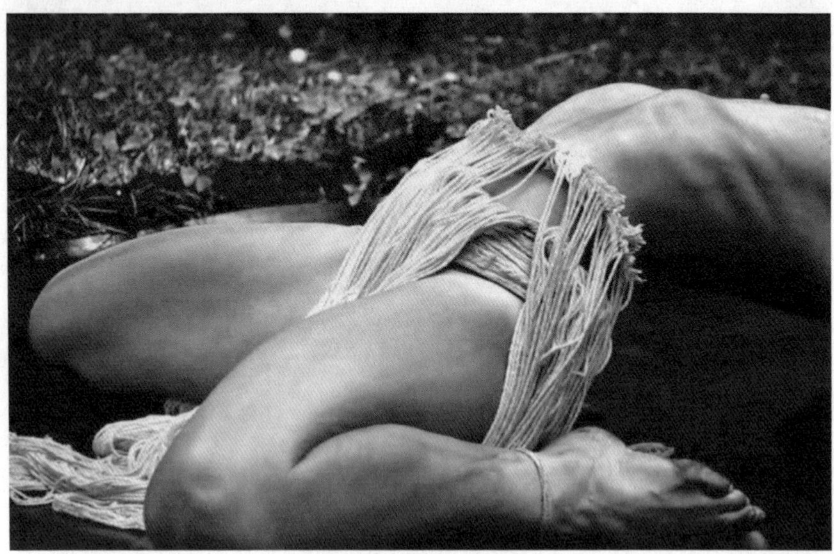

Elisa Massariolli da Costa
Photos: Henrique Yasuda

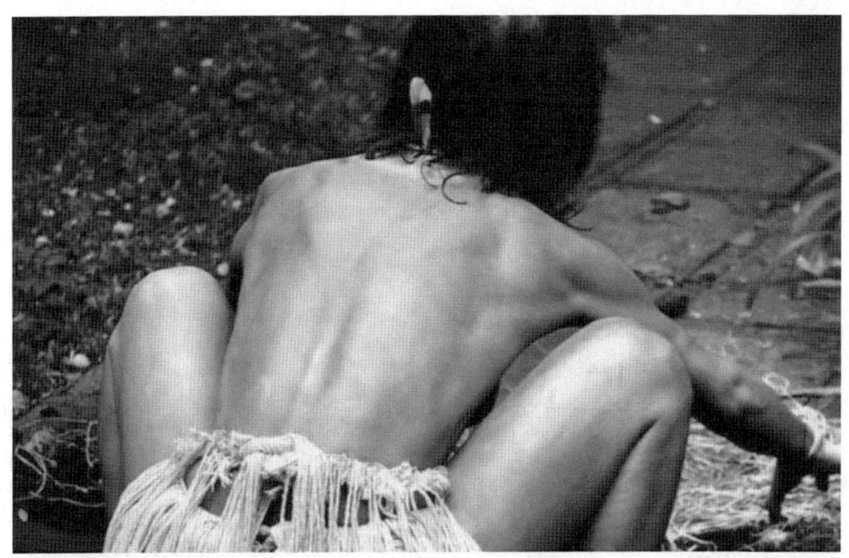
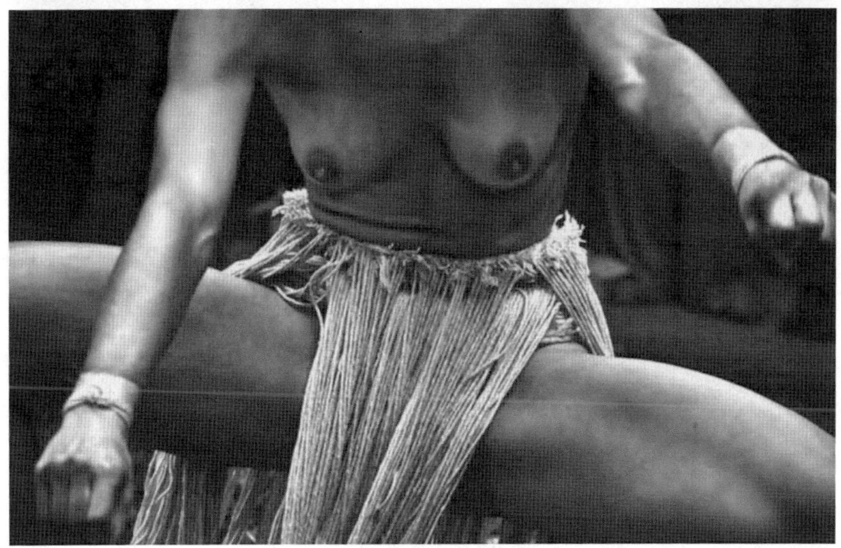

Elisa Massariolli da Costa
Photos: Henrique Yasuda

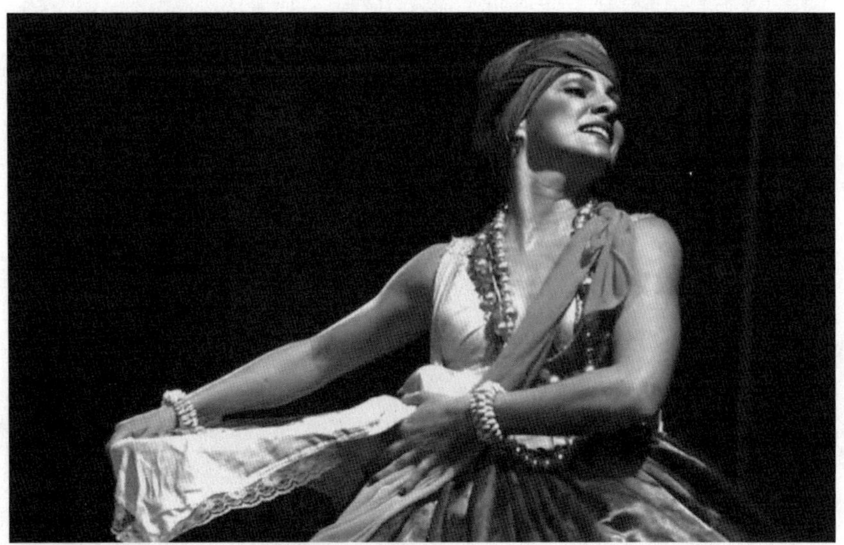

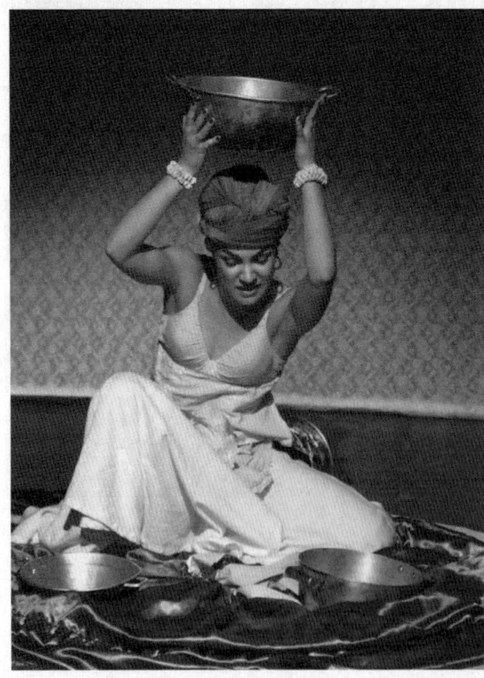

Mariana Jorge
Photos: Débora Branco

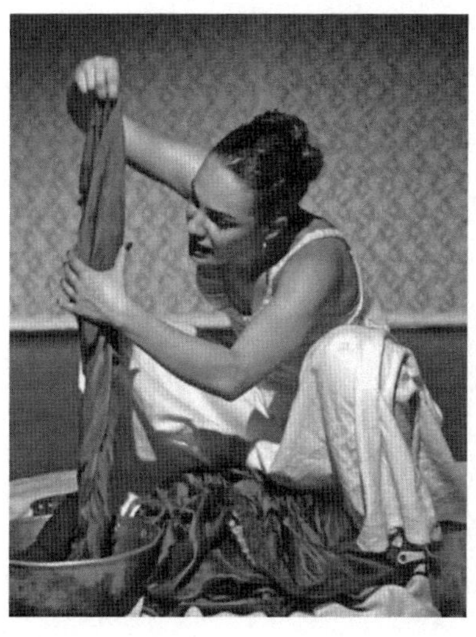

Mariana Jorge
Photo: Débora Branco

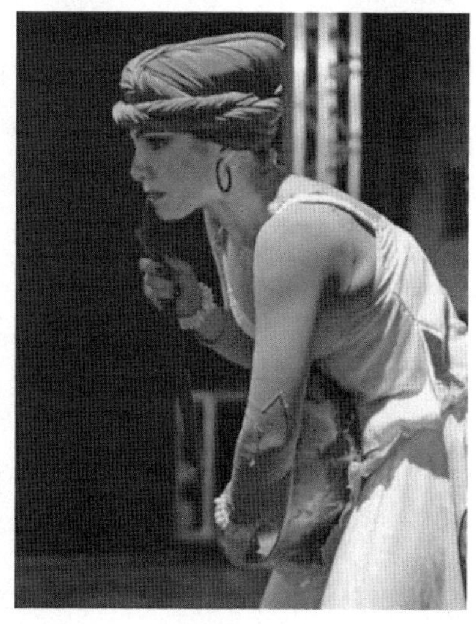

Mariana Jorge
Photo: Secretaria de Cultura de Amparo

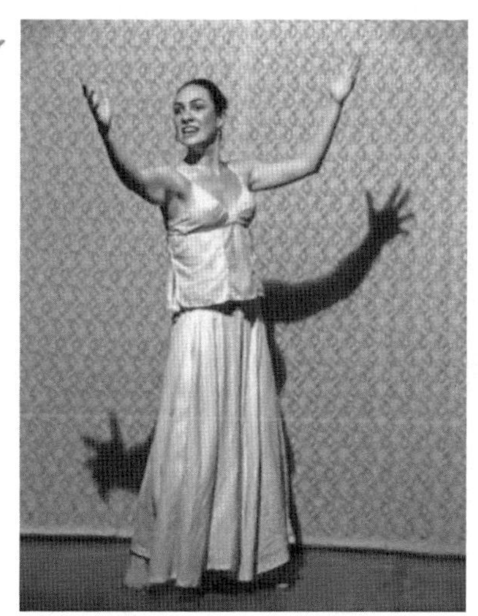

Mariana Jorge
Photo: Débora Branco

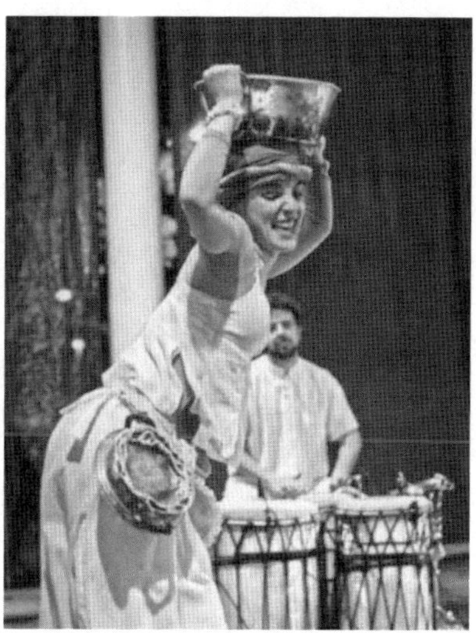

Mariana Jorge and Chico Santana
Photo: Secretaria de Cultura de Amparo

12 Bibliographical Reference

Barbieri, Cesar: "Um jeito brasileiro de aprender a ser". DEFER Centro de Informação e Documentação sobre a capoeira (CIDOCA/DF): Brasília 1993, p. 196.

Campos, Hélio: "Mestre Xaréu". Gráfica Presscolor: Salvador 1990.

Cox, Harvey: "A Festa dos foliões. Um ensaio teológico sobre festividade e fantasia". Editora Vozes: Petrópolis 1974, p. 183.

Gomes, Núbia / Pereira, Edmilson: "Negras raízes mineiras. Os Arturos". Ministério da Cultura/EDUFJF: Juiz de Fora 1988, p. 631.

Merleau-Ponty, Maurice. Moura, Carlos Alberto Ribeiro de (transl.): "Fenomenologia da percepção". Editora Martins Fontes (coleção Tópicos): São Paulo 1994, p. 662.

Mester, Carlos: "Por trás das palavras". Editora Vozes: Petrópolis 1984.

Meyer, Marlyse: "Caminhos do imaginário no Brasil". Editora da Universidade de São Paulo: São Paulo 1993, p. 229.

Meyer, Marlyse: "Maria Padilha e toda a sua quadrilha: de amante de um rei de Castela à Pomba-Gira de Umbanda". Editora Duas Cidades: São Paulo 1993, p. 171.

Oliveira, Valdemar de: "Frevo, capoeira e 'Passo'". Companhia Editora de Pernambuco: Recife 1977.

Moura, Carlos Eugênio Marcondes de (ed.): "Olôórisá: escritos sobre a religião dos orixás". Agora: São Paulo 1987.

Souza, José Cavalcante de, et al. (transl.): Os pensadores/Enciclopédia (encyclopedia); São Paulo: Abril Cultural 1972.

Pereira, Edmilson de Almeida: "Árvore dos Arturos". Edições D'Lira: Juiz de Fora 1988.

Pereira, Edmilson de Almeida: "Rebojo". Edições D'Lira: Juiz de Fora 1995.

Rego, Waldeloir: "Capoeira de Angola. Ensaio sócio-etnográfico". Editora Itapuã: Salvador 1968, p. 416.

Umbanda: Uma religião brasileira/Revista (magazine). Editora Escala: São Paulo, ano I, n. 1, n. 2, n. 3. 1994.

Verger, Pierre Fatumbi. Nóbrega, Maria Aparecida da (transl.): "Orixás. Deuses Iorubás na África e no Novo Mundo". Editora Corrupio: São Paulo 1981, p. 295.

Interdisciplinary Studies in Performance

Edited by Mirosław Kocur

The series aims at presenting innovative cross disciplinary and intercultural research in performance practice and theory. Its mission is to expand and enrich performance studies with new research in theatre, film, dance, ritual, and art, as well as in queer and gender studies, anthropology, linguistics, archaeology, ethnography, sociology, history, media and political sciences, and even medicine and biology. The series focuses on promoting groundbreaking methodologies and new directions in studying performative culture by scrutinizing its transformative and transgressive aspects.

The series Interdisciplinary Studies in Performance publishes in English and German monographs and thematic collections of papers by scholars from Poland and from abroad.

Vol.	1	Paul Martin Langner / Agata Mirecka (Hrsg.): Tendenzen der zeitgenössischen Dramatik. 2015.

Vol.	2	Veronika Darian / Micha Braun / Jeanne Bindernagel / Mirosław Kocur (Hrsg.): Die Praxis der/ des Echo. Zum Theater des Widerhalls. 2015.

Vol.	3	Magdalena Barbaruk: The Long Shadow of Don Quixote. Translated by Patrycja Poniatowska. 2015.

Vol.	4	Mirosław Kocur: On the Origins of Theater. Translated by David Malcolm. 2016.

Vol.	5	Matteo Bonfitto: The Kinetics of the Invisible. Acting Processes in Peter Brook's Theatre. 2016.

Vol.	6	Graziela Rodrigues: Dancer – Researcher – Performer: A Learning Process. 2016.

www.peterlang.com